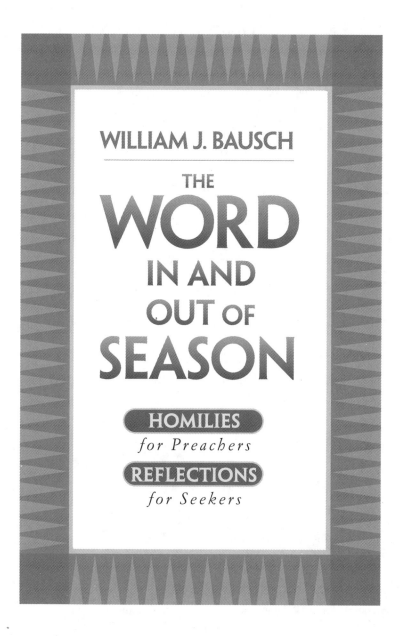

WILLIAM J. BAUSCH

THE

WORD

IN AND
OUT OF

SEASON

HOMILIES
for Preachers

REFLECTIONS
for Seekers

TWENTY-THIRD PUBLICATIONS
BAYARD Mystic, CT 06355

Dedication

To the people of
St. Denis Church in Manasquan, New Jersey
who first heard these homilies and
publicly offered encouragement and praise.
(What their private thoughts were,
I don't know—and I'm not asking!)

Twenty-Third Publications/Bayard
185 Willow Street
P.O. Box 180
Mystic, CT 06355
(860) 536-2611
(800) 321-0411

ISBN:1-58595-003-3
Library of Congress Catalog Card Number: 99-75663
Printed in the U.S.A.

CONTENTS

Feasts & Celebrations

The Parables

Lessons of Scripture

INTRODUCTION

"A word spoken in due season, how good it is!" says Proverbs 23. This bit of biblical wisdom shapes the idea behind this book. Like spring to summer to fall to winter, the mysteries of our redemption take on the colorings of the great autumn patriarchs, the wintery prophets, the spring of promise, and the summer of fulfillment. And in each due season the saving word must be expounded and proclaimed so that all may experience "how good it is." This match of word and season has inspired the outline of this book. It moves from Advent and Christmas to Lent, Easter, and Pentecost, on to feasts and celebrations, then to the parables, and finally, to the overall lessons of Scripture.

These homilies, such seasonal words spoken in the course of the liturgical year, have two audiences in mind. The first is preachers. The sixty homilies herein are presented as aids, thought-starters, or outright models to be copied with whatever modifications are necessary to make them contemporary or local. I myself rely on other homilists for inspiration, especially notables such as Fr. Walter Burghardt, Leonard Sweet, or William Willimon, to mention a few (pay attention to the credits and notes at the end). In the same way, I hope that this collection will inspire you as you prepare your homilies. You may find yourself taking a notion or idea from this book, perhaps even the very words, to use as a springboard into the development of a homily. This is what we all do and must do: receive from others and pass on to others in order to keep the cycle going, a cycle that can never exhaust the word of God.

It is important, of course, to remember that these homilies were spoken, delivered, and proclaimed. Therefore, what you have here is an edited version for the printed page. This may take some of the power out of the preached word (especially when passion and empathy are present) but makes it more accessible for the reader. After all, as every preacher knows, the written word—even the best translation of Homer, for example—is no match for the original telling. Voice, inflection, gesture, emphasis, laughter, tears, and all the rest can raise a mediocre homily to something worth listening to. These same techniques used poorly can reduce a great homily to mediocrity.

The second audience for this book is the general public who walk through the seasons seeking sustenance for their spiritual lives as the great mysteries unfold. Hence the subtitle, "Reflections for Seekers." Many people have told me directly or written to me saying that they use my homily books for spiritual reading. I suspect that's because the homilies are short, encapsulate a message, and are easy pick-up or bedtime reading.

So whether you are a preacher, a spiritual seeker, or an interested reader, may this book provide a source of reflection and inspiration for you, throughout the seasons and throughout the years.

ADVENT *and* CHRISTMAS

1

MEMORY, MYSTERY & MAJESTY

Advent is the season of the coming of Jesus. In fact, we Christians celebrate three such comings: Jesus has come in memory, does come in mystery, and will come in majesty. Memory, mystery, majesty: let's take a look at each.

Go back with me in history. Early on the morning of September 23 in the year 63 BC, a boy was born in the city of Rome. A messenger stood ready in the home of the boy. Immediately upon hearing the words, "It's a boy!" the messenger raced to the Senate building and breathlessly announced to the waiting assembly: "The ruler of the world is born." And he was right.

The baby was named Octavius. At age twenty, he ruled the Roman Empire, along with Lepidus and Marc Antony, following the assassination of Julius Caesar. By the age of forty, Octavius had maneuvered both Lepidus and Marc Antony out of their ruling positions; he was now, indeed, the ruler of the world.

Octavius was roundly declared by the Roman Senate to be not just Octavius but "Caesar Augustus," the "supreme ruler." At his bidding, ships of war sailed; at his word, legions marched, his enemies falling as grain before the scythe. He was in many ways the greatest Caesar of them all. More than any other member of his family, Octavius made

"Caesar" not simply a name but a title, a title which is echoed in our time in the German "kaiser" and the Russian "czar." He was even immortalized in the Julian calendar, with August, the eighth month, bearing his royal name.

When Octavius was about sixty-six years old, he still stood astride the world like a colossus, one foot on the land, one foot in the sea. And in that sixty-sixth year of his life, in a remote village of no consequence located within his vast empire, another announcement of a birth went out: "To you is born this day in the city of David a Savior, who is the Messiah, the Lord."

In the quiet story of this second birth, Octavius is mentioned merely as an instrument of God, a functionary in the divine plan whose decree had brought Mary and Joseph to Bethlehem. "In those days a decree went out from Emperor Augustus that all the world should be registered," we read in the gospel of Luke. Caesar Augustus, the emperor of the world, was an unwitting player in the fulfillment of the ancient prophecy:

> And you, Bethlehem, in the land of Judah, are by no means least among the rulers of Judah, for from you shall come a ruler who is to shepherd my people Israel.

And so, on a night we now take for granted, the whole of history was turned upside down. A unique person entered our world. Not an angel; not another prophet. This was God's own son. He entered our world as we enter it, born of a woman's body. He entered our world with the same human makeup as us: our minds and our marrow, our genes and our glands. He entered our world in a forgotten corner of the earth, laid in a feeding trough for animals, with only one man and one woman to witness his birth. He entered our world as powerless as we, what someone has referred to as "omnipotence in bonds." I suspect he cried and felt cold until Mary gathered him in her arms. Most likely, he didn't quite know what to make of the shepherds; he may hardly have heard the choir of angels singing, "Glory to God."

But this baby—fragile, vulnerable, subject to disease, cold and heat—this baby, the very image of powerlessness, achieved more than Octavius ever dreamed. True, by the age of thirty-three he was dead; but by his death he conquered death—and with it, the world. On his way to the cross it was said of him: "Look, the whole world has gone after him!"

Since that time our world has not been the same. Oh, on the surface much seems the same. Hate, alas, still hounds us and war still wounds us. Children still starve and the elderly are often forgotten. Cancers riddle our flesh and death never takes a holiday. But in Christ Jesus, men and women need no longer be slaves to sin and Satan; evil has been shown to be less powerful than good. Each one of us can be one with God and one with each other, now and forever.

As the early church writers declared, "God became human to make us divine," to give us a share in God's own life and to make us children of God, brother and sister to Christ, redeemed by his blood and filled with his Spirit.

So now, as we Advent Christians prepare for Christmas, we are asked to remember not only what God has done in becoming one of us, but to remember who we are, our enormous dignity as children of God. So that we can remember, both Bethlehem and Calvary demand that we change our lives, change the way we live.

Advent is Christ coming in such memories.

Jesus also comes in mystery, the mystery of "now." If memory is to take on flesh today, it must take on my flesh. If Jesus is to take on flesh today, he must take on my flesh. So many people take Christ for granted, give him less time than we give to shaving or doing our nails. We do the basics: worship on weekends, resist gross temptations, walk a thin line between good and evil. But Advent is the time to cut compromise out of our lives, to stop being half-hearted about church and religion, about morality and love. It is the time to remove the obstacles that keep us from being enthusiastic in our faith, joyful in our hope, and generous in our love.

The mystery of Advent is expressed in the time of now, the time for virtue now, for affirmation now, for what really matters now, for nobility now. Christ comes in mystery now, not later. This poem captures what I'm trying to say:

I looked at you and smiled the other day;
I thought you'd see me, but you didn't.
I said "I love you" and waited for what you would say;
I thought you'd hear me, but you didn't.
I asked you to come outside and play ball with me;
I thought you'd follow me, but you didn't.
I drew a picture just for you to see;

I thought you'd save it, but you didn't.
I made a fort for us back in the woods;
I thought you'd camp with me, but you didn't.
I found some worms 'n' such for fishing, if we could;
I thought you'd want to go, but you didn't.
I needed you just to talk to, my thoughts to share;
I thought you'd want to, but you didn't.
I told you about the game hoping you'd be there
I thought you'd surely come, but you didn't.
I asked you to share my youth with me;
I thought you'd want to, but you couldn't.
My country called me to war;
you asked me to come home safely,
but I didn't.

Christ comes in mystery now. As Abraham Joshua Heschel reminds us, the question of religion is not what we do with our solitude, but what we do with the presence of God among us. Christ came in the day of Octavius, and he comes in our day, too. And so these are the questions to ask ourselves during Advent: how do I acknowledge the presence of Christ? What am I doing to honor his presence? Where are the areas of my life in which Christ does not yet abide?

Finally, we have majesty. The burden of the Advent Scripture readings is that Christ will come again. At that time, there will be fearful signs in the sky...people will die of anticipation...the powers of heaven will be shaken...be on guard...the great day will close on you like a trap...pray constantly for strength. These are the symbols of the endtime.

All this imagery speaks one truth: time will run out. Judgment will be meted out. Christ will come on the clouds of heaven, tenderly seeking his friends, seeing only them. Why? Because his enemies, those who hate him, the unfaithful, his lukewarm friends—all of these have hidden themselves from his eyes, from his call, from his mercy, from his longing. This is why Advent has a penitential tone to it; it tells us to cast aside the barriers, come out from hiding, declare yourself a Christian, show yourself a disciple. Be moral and decent before that great day arrives when Christ will come in majesty.

The season of Advent is once again upon us. As we journey through this rich and glorious season, let us remember these three words: memory, mystery, and majesty. Christ has come in memory, comes now in mystery, and will come again in majesty.

2

GOD THE THIEF

MATTHEW 24:37–44

"If the owner of the house had known in what part of the night the thief was coming, he would have stayed awake and would not have let his house be broken into. Therefore you also must be ready, for the Son of Man is coming at an unexpected hour."

In his letter to the Thessalonians, St. Paul warns, "The day of the Lord will come like a thief in the night." Twice in the Book of Revelation it is written, "I will come like a thief." We pause at this rude biblical figure of speech. God as the Good Shepherd, as the mother hen who gathers her chicks, as the way, the truth, and the life: yes, we can grasp these images. But God as a thief? We hate thieves. If you have ever had your house broken into, you know the sense of violation. The safe, secure sanctuary you call home never feels quite so safe anymore. An intruder has had the gall to finger your most intimate possessions. Is that what God is like? God a thief in the night?

But there it is in Scripture, and we must come to terms with this image. So how is God like a thief? I would suggest that this is so in three ways. First, like any thief worth his salt, God will circumvent our elaborate security systems. He will break through our false illusions. And one of these illusions is that we and our possessions are immutable, that our house and our money and our clothes and our car will last forever.

Another illusion is that the conditions of harmony and peace lie entirely in the use (or non-use) of force, and not in the human heart. Yet another illusion is that we are the center of the universe. The greatest spiritual truth is that our lives are not our own—yet we act as if they are.

Some of us indulge ourselves and eat to excess, then spend thousands of dollars on diet aids, exercise equipment, and personal trainers. All the while, there are people in the Sudan and other Third World countries who are being starved into oblivion. We continually upgrade our stock portfolios and follow extravagant lifestyles, as if the market will never crash or our current way of living come to an end. We live comfortably in a peaceful nation in a largely prosperous time. Yet secure behind locked doors, linked by FAXes, pagers, and cellular phones, connected by e-mail, people have never felt more scared or alone.

We act as if our money and our possessions are our lifelines, but like all lifelines there are two ends. However tightly we may grasp one end of this lifeline, if the other end is not secure, we will falter. God, the thief, steals our sense of security by showing us that the other end of our materialistic lifeline is straw. The stock market falls, our health wanes, our good looks fade, or we drop as we shop. The one-dimensional items, which we have made into the linchpins of our lives, are snatched away; we feel violated at the theft.

But this theft, like all tragedies, should leave us pondering what really matters, like people whose homes and possessions are snatched away by the thievery of natural disasters. These people, stripped of all illusions, will often exclaim with newfound insight: "At least we are still alive; at least we still have one another." God the thief steals our false sense of security so that we may anchor ourselves in the one thing necessary: love of God and love of neighbor.

Secondly, like all thieves, God comes unannounced. A friend of mine just returned from the funeral of her niece in Ohio. This niece, a delightful person, was twenty-four years old. She woke up one morning, dressed for work, sat down for a cup of coffee, and fell over dead from an aneurysm. Her peers, looking down at the coffin, at this life snatched away so early, are wondering: what really matters?

Thirdly—no surprise—God is out to steal. God is out to steal our hearts, to offer us real joy and lasting happiness. Not comfort, mind you, or a life free of hurt; but joy and inner peace that no one can take from you. A sense of the sacred in the world, a horror of violating the planet, the need to be your brother's keeper, to lose your life in order to save it: this is the security God offers.

God as thief is a powerful image. To illustrate this concept in another way, I want to share a story about a little boy who, like God the thief, stole a teacher's heart.

Teddy Stallard certainly qualified as "one of the least": disinterested in school; musty, wrinkled clothes; hair never combed; one of those kids with a deadpan face; an expressionless, glassy, unfocused stare. When Miss Thompson spoke to Teddy, he always answered in monosyllables.

Now Miss Thompson was a teacher with ambitions to someday become a vice-principal, a principal, and even superintendent of schools. So she played her cards carefully. For example, even though Miss Thompson said out loud that she loved all in her class the same, deep down inside she wasn't being completely truthful. She made an exception for Teddy Stallard.

Oh, she didn't outwardly disdain him. She was too savvy for that; it wouldn't look good on her evaluation. But, truth to tell, she didn't like the boy. Whenever she marked Teddy's papers, she got a certain perverse pleasure out of putting Xs next to the wrong answers, and when she put the Fs at the top of the papers, she always did it with a flair. She should have known better; she had Teddy's records and she knew more about him than she wanted to admit. The records read:

First grade: Teddy shows promise with his work and attitude, but poor home situation.

Second grade: Teddy could do better. Mother is seriously ill. He receives little help at home.

Third grade: Teddy is a good boy but too serious. He is a slow learner. His mother died this year.

Fourth grade: Teddy is very slow, but well-behaved. His father shows no interest.

Christmas came, and the boys and girls in Miss Thompson's class brought her Christmas presents. They piled their presents on her desk and crowded around to watch her open them. Among the presents there was one from Teddy Stallard. She was surprised that he had brought her a gift, but he had. Teddy's gift was wrapped in brown paper and was held together with Scotch tape. On the paper were written these simple words: "For Miss Thompson from Teddy."

When she opened Teddy's present, out fell a gaudy, rhinestone bracelet with half the stones missing, and a bottle of cheap perfume. The other boys and girls began to giggle and smirk over Teddy's gifts, but Miss Thompson at least had enough sense to silence them by immediately putting on the bracelet and putting some of the perfume on her wrist. Holding her wrist up for the other children to smell, she said, "Doesn't it smell lovely?" And the children, taking their cues from the teacher, readily agreed with "oohs" and "aahs."

At the end of the day, when school was over and the other children had left, Teddy lingered behind. He slowly came over to her desk and said softly, "Miss Thompson...Miss Thompson, you smell just like my mother...and her bracelet looks real pretty on you, too. I'm glad you liked my presents." When Teddy left, Miss Thompson got down on her knees and asked God to forgive her.

The next day when the children came to school, they were welcomed by a new teacher. Miss Thompson had become a different person. She was no longer just a teacher; she had become an agent of God. She was now a person committed to loving her children and doing things for them that would live on after her. She helped all the children but especially the slow ones, and especially Teddy Stallard. By the end of that school year Teddy showed dramatic improvement. He had caught up with most of the students and was even ahead of some.

She didn't hear from Teddy for a long time. Then one day, she received a note that read:

Dear Miss Thompson,

I wanted you to be the first to know: I will be graduating second in my class.

Love, Teddy Stallard.

Four years later, another note came:

Dear Miss Thompson,

They just told me I will be graduating first in my class. I wanted you to be the first to know. The university has not been easy, but I liked it.

Love, Teddy Stallard.

And four years later:

Dear Miss Thompson,

As of today, I am Theodore Stallard, M.D. How about that? I wanted you to be the first to know I am getting married next month, the 27th to be exact. I want you to come and sit where my mother would sit if she were alive. You are the only family I have now: Dad died last year.

Love, Teddy Stallard.

Miss Thompson went to that wedding and sat where Teddy's mother would have sat. She deserved to sit there; she had done something for Teddy that he could never forget.

Let me tell you this: Miss Thompson, who is still a much-beloved teacher, went to that wedding and sat where Teddy's mother would have sat. She thought to herself, "This is better than being a superintendent." Her blind ambition and drive for success had been snatched away. Her subtle dishonesty and disdain were stolen by a child she disliked. Her superficial dreams were violated by charity. You know what? Miss Thompson was a victim of God the thief.

3

NO ROOM

LUKE 3:1–6

"In the fifteenth year of the reign of Emperor Tiberius, when Pontius Pilate was governor of Judea, and Herod was ruler of Galilee, and his brother Philip ruler of the region of Ituraea and Trachonitis, and Lysanias ruler of Abilene, during the high priesthood of Annas and Caiaphas, the word of God came to John, son of Zechariah in the wilderness."

With these words from Luke's gospel, we are majestically introduced to a fearful prophet, John the Baptist, son of Zechariah and Elizabeth. We are told in this gospel that he went about proclaiming a baptism of repentance. Not a popular subject, that. And John was not a popular prophet, with his ascetic lifestyle, his odd camel's hair clothing, his diet of locusts, and his habit of calling certain groups of people a "brood of vipers."

John the Baptist was not exactly Kris Kringle; you don't get sweetness and light from him. His mien was more like fire and brimstone. And yet, like a root canal, we need John the Baptist. Without him we would fester and die. We must hear his right and righteous preaching which calls us back to the basics.

Yet we preachers are still reluctant to turn to John in the context of our jolly, pre-Christmas shopping time. But it is Advent, and so here

John is and here he will be for the next few Sundays. And so I have no choice but to don his mantle and, like John, disturb and offend you. Let me begin by reminding you that when Christmas finally arrives in a few weeks, we will all be thrilled to once more hear the ancient, well-known, and endlessly told tale of the birth of Christ. Once more we will be fascinated by the circumstances of his birth, especially the part where we read, "there was no place for them in the inn." No room in the inn: after almost two thousand years of Christianity that theme still has something to say to us.

Listen to this story, told by Marvin A. McMickee:

Many years ago, I went to Santa Fe, New Mexico to give a workshop. I arrived at the airport in Albuquerque and rented a car for the drive to Santa Fe. By the time I left the airport it was evening, so I could not see any of the landscape around me.

When I made the return trip to Albuquerque a few days later, it was early on a clear Saturday afternoon. Now the beauty of God's creation was wondrously apparent to me. Great expanses of land dotted with sagebrush and cactus stretched out in all directions, as far as the eye could see. The scene was breathtakingly beautiful.

All along the way from Santa Fe to Albuquerque I found myself humming bits and pieces of the hymn "How Great Thou Art." Something else caught my attention, however, during that drive through the countryside of New Mexico. All along the way were highway signs announcing nearby Indian reservations, and far off in the distance you could see the communities in which Native Americans were now living.

Of course! I was driving through land which was once the home solely of the Apache, the Hopi, and the Navajo. As the United States made its way West under the claims of Manifest Destiny, however, it was determined that there was no room for the Apache, the Hopi, and the Navajo. And so these native people were removed from their ancestral homelands in order to make room for white settlers.

Most of them were killed by diseases from which they had no immunity, or by regiments of the U.S. Army from whom they received little mercy. Those who remained alive were forced onto windswept and desolate tracts of land called reservations, where unemployment, alcoholism, and depression soon ran rampant. And thus today, an Indian reservation is a living, breathing testimony to the fact that for the last 200 years this country has had a "no room" policy toward Native American people.

Of course, Native Americans are not the only victims of "no room" policies. African Americans have endured slavery, segregation, Jim Crow laws, and unspeakable acts of terror because of this same attitude toward them. A minister friend who is black told me this story: in 1952, when the minister was a four-year-old child, he took a train with his family from Chicago to Washington, DC. He was asleep when the train pulled into the Cincinnati station for a scheduled stop. But before the train could leave the station, all the black passengers had to move to the car behind the engine, where the fumes, the soot, and the noise were worst. This was done because the Jim Crow laws required that all black passengers be seated in the car behind the engine when the train crossed over the Ohio River into Kentucky, where segregation was still firmly enforced. This minister's earliest memories of life in America are of being aroused out of his sleep to experience the discomfort and humiliation caused by living under a no room policy.

In many countries today there are severe no room policies for Christians. In fact, Christians today are the most persecuted religious group in the world and that persecution is intensifying. There are eleven countries that practice the systematic persecution of Christians. In China, for example, the police destroyed at least 15,000 religious sites in the first half of 1996, and routinely sentence believers to its religious gulags. Two Catholic bishops are currently in a Chinese prison. Vietnam frequently arrests Christians, and more than one million non-Muslim people in the Sudan are reported to have been killed. The *Baltimore Sun* has proved the existence of a slave trade that abuses Christian boys. Saudi Arabia (an American ally) admits that freedom of religion does not exist there and that the government prohibits the practice of other religions: there is no room for other religions.

Finally, consider this report from the Children's Defense Fund which gives statistics on how the United States ranks among industrial countries using a number of different social indicators:

We [the United States] are number one in the following categories: military technology, military exports, Gross Domestic Product (GDP), the number of millionaires and billionaires, and health technology. In the gap between rich and poor children, however, we rank eighteenth; in living standards among the poorest one-fifth of our children, sixteenth; in efforts to lift children out of poverty, seventeenth. And we are last in protecting our children against gun violence.

In other words, we are richer than anyone else and stronger in terms of military power and technological knowledge. But we are at or near the bottom when it comes to care and protection for our youngest and most vulnerable citizens.

Indians, blacks, Christians, children—no room for them in our inn. If all of this makes us uncomfortable, John the Baptist would be smiling. But smiling, of course, only if it leads us to do something, to begin making room for others:

> making room for the Spirit through our prayer life;
> making room for the unfortunate through our giving;
> making room for enemies through our forgiveness;
> making room for the poor through our sharing;
> making room for minorities through our acceptance;
> making room for tolerance through our attitude;
> making room for Christ by our public discipleship.

In 1998, in the sixth year of the administration of Bill Clinton, when Alan Greenspan was head of the Federal Reserve Board and Christie Whitman was governor of New Jersey and Rudy Giuliani mayor of New York, during the high priesthood of Pope John Paul II, the word of the Lord was spoken to…to…to whom?

To you and me.

4

REJOICE

PHILIPPIANS 4:4–7

"Rejoice in the Lord always; again I will say, rejoice." So begins the second reading from St. Paul. But before we declare that he is some kind of Pollyanna, living in a cozy, comfortable, make-believe world, we should know one thing. Paul writes these words from prison. There he is: uncertain of his future and cut off from his mission. He even hears that some preachers are preaching the gospel out of false motives; that news is breaking his heart. Yet Paul tells us to "rejoice."

Paul's letter from prison points out the distinction between happiness and joy. One of the motivating principles in the founding of the United States was the right to pursue happiness. Yet Scripture invites us to receive joy. What is the difference? Happiness generally depends on the quality and the quantity of material goods; it comes from the outside. Joy can thrive even in the midst of deprivation; it comes from the inside.

Still, there is a problem here. I mean, the notion of joy seems almost irreverent in a world where so much is going wrong. Who can be joyful while babies starve and teenagers shoot each other and whole tribes of people try to wipe each other off the face of the earth? It's hard to be joyful about any of that.

The message of joy in this kind of world would be almost cynical—

except that joy has never had very much to do with what is going on in the world. That is what makes joy different from happiness or pleasure or fun. All of the others depend on certain conditions—good health, a good job, a happy family, lots of toys and possessions. The only condition for joy is the presence of God. And so joy can break forth in a depressed economy, in the middle of a war, in an intensive care waiting room, or in the slums.

Jonathan Kozol has written a book, called *Amazing Grace*, about the life of poor people in the Bronx. The title comes from the gospel song, which Kozol often heard sung at various churches in the Bronx. But more than that, it reflects the author's amazement that in the midst of the most dire unhappiness something very much like joy still flourishes. As with Paul, the joy of these citizens of the Bronx depends on the confidence that God is present even in their pain and deprivation.

One pastor tells Kozol that the third stanza of "Amazing Grace" is the motto and anthem of the people whom the pastor serves:

Through many dangers, toils, and snares,
I have already come,
'Tis grace that brought me safe thus far,
And grace will lead me home.

Take another deprived person, Mary. She arrived, pregnant and unwed, at her cousin Elizabeth's door. Well, whatever she expected, a joyous blessing was what she got. Elizabeth's excitement ignited Mary's, and Mary started singing in the hallway, before she had even taken her coat off. She started to praise God for turning the world upside down, for looking with favor on her, a nobody from nowhere with no status, no privilege, no power; a minority woman in occupied territory. Yet, like Paul in prison, she felt an inner joy and sang of a God who brings down the powerful and lifts up the lowly, who fills the hungry and sends away the rich, empty.

You see, joy doesn't happen when we get what we want. It is much more likely to happen when we do *not* get what we want and we find ourselves laughing because God's ideas are so much better than ours. Usually, though, we have a hard time seeing that until our own wishes have crashed and burned. Yet it is there, in that wilderness, in empty-handed surrender, that joy is most likely to occur.

Let me share some other joy-while-in-prison stories.

A soldier was on duty one Christmas morning during World War II. It had been his custom to go to church each Christmas with his family, but now, stationed in an outlying district of London, that was impossible. So with some of his soldier buddies, he walked down the road that led to the city as dawn was breaking. Along the way they came upon a old, gray, stone building over whose main door were carved the words, "Queen Ann's Orphanage." So they decided to knock and see what kind of Christmas celebration might be taking place inside.

In response to their knock, a matron came and explained that the most of the parents of these particular children had been killed in one of the many bombings that had taken place in London. The soldiers went in just as the children were tumbling out of bed. There was no Christmas tree in the corner. There were no presents. The soldiers moved around the room wishing the children "Merry Christmas," and giving them whatever they had in their pockets: a stick of gum, a piece of candy, a nickel, a dime, a pencil, a pocketknife, a good luck charm.

Then the soldier who had gotten his buddies together noticed a little fellow alone in the corner. This little fellow looked an awful lot like his nephew back home, so he approached him and said, "And you, little guy, what do you want for Christmas?" The child replied, "Will you hold me?" The soldier, with tears brimming in his eyes, picked up the little boy and held him in his arms, very close.

War, homesickness, death, orphans, no tree, no presents—but like Paul in prison, the soldier had experienced joy. Here is another story, told by a woman:

One day, I answered a knock at my door and found two children, in ragged outgrown coats, huddled inside the storm door. "Any old papers, lady?" I was busy, preoccupied with my own worries and poverty. I wanted to say no—until I looked down at their feet. Thin little sandals, sopped with sleet. "Come in and I'll make you a cup of hot cocoa."

There was no conversation. Their soggy sandals left marks upon the rug. I served cocoa and toast with jam to fortify them against the chill outside. Then I went back to the kitchen and started back on my household budget....The silence in the front room struck through to me. I looked in. The girl held the empty cup in her hands, looking at it. The boy asked in a flat voice, "Lady, are you rich?" "Am I rich? Mercy, no!" I looked at my shabby slipcovers and rundown apartment.

The girl carefully put her cup back in its saucer. "Your cups match your saucers." Her voice was old, with a hunger that was not of the stomach. They left after that, holding their bundles of papers against the wind. They hadn't said thank you. They didn't need to. They had done more than that. Plain blue pottery cups and saucers. But they matched.

I tested the potatoes and stirred the gravy. "Well," I thought, "Potatoes and brown gravy, a roof over our heads, my man with a good steady job, faith and love. These things match, too." Suddenly, I felt a strange peace, an awareness of God in the small things of my life. I moved the chairs back from the fire and tidied the living room. The muddy prints of small sandals were still wet upon my rug. I let them be. I want them there in case I ever forget again how very rich I am.

Finally, this story comes from a doctor:

I had a young man come into my practice with bone cancer. His leg was removed at the hip to save his life. He was twenty-four years old when I started working with him and he was a very angry young man with a lot of bitterness. He felt a deep sense of injustice and a very deep hatred for all well people because it seemed so unfair to him that he had suffered this terrible loss so early in life.

I worked with this man through his grief and rage and pain using painting, imagery, and deep psychotherapy. After working with him for more than two years there came a profound shift. He began coming out of himself. Later, he started to visit other people who had suffered severe physical losses and he would tell me the most wonderful stories about these visits.

Once he visited a young woman who was almost his own age. It was a hot day in Palo Alto and he was in running shorts so his artificial leg showed when he came into her hospital room. The woman was so depressed about the loss of both her breasts that she wouldn't even look at him, wouldn't pay attention to him. The nurses had left her radio playing, probably in order to cheer her up. So, desperate to get her attention, he unstrapped his leg and began dancing around the room on one leg snapping his fingers to the music. She looked at him in amazement and then burst out laughing and said, "Man, if you can dance, I can sing."

It was a year following this that we sat down to review our work together. He talked about what was significant to him and then I shared what was significant in our process. As we were reviewing our two years of work together, I opened his file and there discovered several drawings he had made early on. I handed them to him. He looked at them and said, "Oh, look at this."

He showed me one of his earliest drawings. I had suggested to him that he draw a picture of his body. He had drawn a picture of a vase and running through the vase was a deep black crack. This was the joyless image of his body and he had taken a black crayon and had drawn the crack over and over again. He was grinding his teeth with rage at the time. It was very, very painful because it seemed to him that this vase could never function as a vase again. It could never hold water.

Now, several years later, he came to this picture and looked at it and said, "Oh, this one isn't finished." And I said, extending the box of crayons, "Why don't you finish it?" He picked up a yellow crayon and putting his finger on the crack he said, "You see, here—where it is broken—this is where the joy comes through." And with the yellow crayon he drew light streaming through the crack in his body. He settled back, artificial leg and all, and radiated that joy.

Joy is an inner sense of God's presence and God's abiding love for us. It is a profound belief that God will have the last word; it is a still point in the storm of life. No wonder Paul, confounding the jailers who censored his letters, could write, "Rejoice....The Lord is near. Do not worry about anything...the peace of God, which surpasses all understanding, will guard your hearts and your minds in Christ Jesus."

5

SECOND THOUGHTS

MATTHEW 3:1–12

John the Baptist, a remarkable man in many ways, is the dominant figure in today's readings. We know that he received a call from God, and he answered it.

And so, Matthew's gospel starts off: "In those days John the Baptist appeared in the wilderness of Judea, proclaiming, 'Repent, for the kingdom of heaven has come near.'…But when he saw many Pharisees and Sadducees coming for baptism, he said to them, 'You brood of vipers! Who warned you to flee from the wrath to come? Bear fruit worthy of repentance…every tree that does not bear good fruit is cut down and thrown into the fire.'"

This obviously is not a man unsure of himself. On the contrary, this is a man on fire with purpose, God's prophet aiming for the jugular; a strong, confident man. John was called. He reacted without hesitation and began his mission, a straight man on a straight line. But somewhere along the way—we don't know when—doubt began to creep in. Was he right? Was he really called by God or was this self-delusion, all his fervent preaching for naught? Was his cousin Jesus really the one he was paving the way for?

John wasn't so sure anymore. Maybe after so many years, he was at a low point. Things weren't working out well. After all, at this time, he was no longer found along the Jordan but languishing in jail, detained in Herod's fortress of Machaerus situated on the lonely desert heights overlooking the Dead Sea, awaiting who knows what. Or, as Matthew writes sparingly a few chapters later, "John was in prison." He had time to think. Maybe he had been all wrong, chosen the wrong path, bet on the wrong Messiah. Doubts made for troubled dreams, and so John decided to act.

Matthew gives us the account: "When John heard in prison what the Messiah was doing, he sent word by his disciples and said to him, "Are you the one who is to come, or are we to wait for another?" There it was, plain, simple, and direct. "Just like John," Jesus might have thought to himself.

And so Jesus answered the delegation sent by John in the best way he could: "Go and tell John what you hear and see: the blind receive their sight, the lame walk, the lepers are cleansed, the deaf hear, the dead are raised, and the poor have good news brought to them." And then he pointedly added with softness and compassion, "And blessed is anyone who takes no offense in me." Jesus looked long after the departing disciples of John and then, when they were out of sight, commented: "Truly I tell you, among those born of women no one has arisen greater than John the Baptist."

John of Advent is many people throughout the ages. He is one of those who at first, say yes to God, but then have second thoughts. He is like those of us who say things like this: I have been faithful to God. I have kept trust. I have prayed. I have been active in ministry. I read all the right books, faithfully go to Mass, and give to the poor. Yet my life has not turned out all right.

A woman recently sent me a letter filling me in on her family. The boys are doing fine, but the girls! One is living with a man and is planning to marry him outside the church. The other married a Jewish man, had the children baptized Catholic, and now is converting to Judaism. This daughter is going to raise the kids—my grandchildren—Jewish. Why me? How could my daughters desert the faith after all the years I spent raising them to be good Catholics?

"Are you the one who is to come, or are we to wait for another?" Throughout the ages, how many people have asked this question with grief or bitterness or disappointment? How many people have wondered to themselves: was it wrong to have been so faithful? Worse, have I been a fool? People prayed for my son, we had a prayer chain going, we believed he would be healed, pleaded for a miracle. He died anyway. Some whispered it was because I didn't have enough faith. If only I had believed more firmly!

To come to terms with this dilemma, listen to the words of a fine and insightful Southern Baptist minister named Al Staggs:

> My wife died in April of this year following a twelve-year battle with cancer, a particularly malignant melanoma. Comments from well-meaning but misguided friends about the healing power of faith have compelled me once again to rethink my theology of healing. I confess that I have extremely low tolerance for the so-called faith healers or for the peddlers of healing. I'm aghast that anyone would dare to claim to understand the mind of God about any particular person or any particular illness.
>
> What these folks do to people is to hold out hope for a complete reversal of a person's physical condition. When the miracle does not occur, the lack of miraculous action can be attributed to a person's lack of faith, which only compounds the person's problems. Not only are these people terminally ill, but they are also being taught that they are not good Christians. In my weaker moments I am reminded of the passage from Matthew 7:22–23, where Jesus says, "Many will say to me on that day, 'Lord, Lord, did we not prophesy in your name, and in your name drive out demons and perform miracles?' Then I will tell them plainly, 'I never knew you. Away from me, you evildoers!'"
>
> A few weeks prior to my wife's death, a couple with whom we had been friends visited and recounted story after story of "miraculous" answers to their prayers. After hearing a steady diet of incidents in which people were healed of their infirmities or found better paying jobs, my wife looked over at both of them and said simply "It hasn't worked that way for us."
>
> Sometimes I just want to ask these people who become so excited about miraculous healing, "Has your vaunted prayer program yet kept anyone alive forever?" Eventually we all die, including those who were healed of their particular disease. No one has yet managed to avoid the grim reaper. So why save our success stories for just those precious few who have been

allowed a few months or years longer than they would otherwise have had?

There needs to be a major emphasis on God's grace and sufficiency for every illness and every situation. The Christian community should talk just as loud and long about God's presence in the most hopeless situations as we do about the "miraculous healings."

[Henri] Nouwen had this to say about death: "Death does not have to be our final failure, our final defeat in the struggle of life, our unavoidable fate. If our deepest human desire is indeed to give ourselves to others, then we can make our death into a final gift. It is so wonderful to see how fruitful death is when it is a free gift." Nouwen's words and his own approach to his life and to his recent death are a counterbalance against those whose "healing" hit-and-run ministries suggest that death is a defeat and that only miraculous cure is a victory.

Stories of miraculous healings have their place. The miracle of a believer's faith, however, in the face of terminal illness, and the faith of a loving family, is just as important as any story of a miraculous cure of an illness. Very few people experience a total reversal of illness. Most people diagnosed with terminal illness struggle through it to the very end. So let us hear the stories of the miraculous presence of God in the lives of these saints who are faithful to the end.

Amen. There is the key to dealing with our doubts. It is holding on to the faithful presence of God in our worst moments, clinging to belief in the ultimate victory of God's love which will make all things new again. No one is free of second thoughts, especially in times of crisis. Not even John the Baptist; not even Jesus. "Father, if it is possible, remove this cup from me." "My God, my God, why have you forsaken me!" But there is a response, and in it our life lesson: "Nevertheless, not my will but thine be done....Into your hands I commend my spirit—my gift."

In other words, as Staggs has said, be assured of and hold on to, the miraculous presence of God in times of seeming abandonment, in times when we are tempted to look for someone or something else to believe in. Recall the distraught woman who cried out to the priest, "Where was God when my son died?" The priest answered softly,

"The same place as when his son died."

If John was one who received the call, reacted with certainty, and then lapsed into doubt, he is legion. But he gave his life for truth and God was present in John's fidelity, despite his doubt. Truly, no greater man was born of a woman.

And so it is for us. Yes, pray for the miracle, the sudden cure: it happens. But also pray to discern the divine presence in the rhythmic pain, suffering, and death of human existence and offer them as a gift, a gift which will be forever accepted by a love that never falters, in a place where there are no more tears.

6

EMMANUEL

MATTHEW 1:18-24

Matthew, the author of today's gospel, has a favorite literary device he uses to get across his point: he "bookends" his narrative. That is to say, he introduces a motif at the very beginning of his gospel and then repeats it at the end, tying the story together. For example, at the beginning of his gospel, he tells us of the magi who seek the "King of the Jews," causing the authorities alarm. At the end of his gospel, the very same phrase appears written on Jesus' cross: "Jesus of Nazareth, King of the Jews."

Likewise, at the beginning of the gospel, the magi are the Gentiles who make an act of faith in Jesus while his own people do not. It is the same at the end of the gospel. When the Jews, Jesus' own people, deliver him up it is a Gentile, the Roman centurion, who makes an act of faith: "Truly this man was the Son of God."

There is another bookend in today's gospel. After the angel came to Joseph and told him to take Mary as his wife, Matthew states that this action fulfilled the Lord's words: "The virgin shall be with child and give birth to a son and they shall call him Emmanuel," a name, he says, which means "God is with us." At the very end of Matthew's gospel, the name "Emmanuel" travels to the last line, when Jesus speaks these words: "And remember, I am with you always to the end of the age."

Matthew teaches us that Emmanuel, "God with us," is what Jesus is all about. This tells the story of the presence of God in our lives from beginning to end. Yet often we do not sense or believe that God is with us, and this is especially true in times of crisis. Let me illustrate with the poignant story of a woman struggling with her faith, seeking to find God's presence in her time of crisis. The woman's name is Anne Donovan, and she tells her story in the September 19, 1998 issue of *America* magazine. The title of her article is, "The Painful Effort to Believe," and it is an account of the birth of her stillborn daughter.

Donovan opens her article by telling us that she had forced herself to go to the baptism of her sister-in-law's baby—a sister-in-law who never went to church and was not even married in church. Yet here was her sister-in-law, having her baby baptized with the priest calling the baby "a gift from God," while she, Anne Donovan, a faithful, practicing Catholic, had just lost her stillborn daughter whom she had gathered in her arms, still warm from her body—soon to grow cold—and peeked at her peaceful face and perfect little body before they took away her lifeless form to prepare her for burial. Life is truly unfair, isn't it?

The article continues as Donovan describes the birth of her baby:

> Those things I had relied on—modern science, women's intuition, God's mercy—had failed, and I had nothing to hold on to. Medical staff, family members, my husband, they all shifted around me as I was induced and slowly dissolved into labor. There was nothing anyone could do except help me deliver the baby. When a chaplain forced herself into the room to talk about God, I yelled at a nurse to get her away from me.
>
> All my multi-layered, carefully constructed faith was stripped away as I focused on one thing: the injustice that our little girl didn't have a chance to take even a single breath. It never occurred to me to pray, not from the moment we first heard the news, not when I was in labor, and not a month later as I sat at home sorting through my emotions and preparing for a memorial Mass of the Angels.
>
> Prayer seemed so futile, even unnecessary, like throwing a glass of water on a burning house. I had prayed my entire pregnancy for the baby to be healthy and she was. Carly was perfect but she wasn't alive, cooing in my arms. How could I not feel betrayed? It wasn't that I was angry at God. It was, and still is, more a sense that I have to be alone and focused to work through this spiritual crisis.
>
> My grief is so intimate. I carried Carly; I gave birth to her; I

endured aching arms and breasts for months afterwards whenever I heard an infant cry. As much as others tried to comfort me, their words only succeeded in alienating me more. I remember telling my husband that I felt like I was on a ship pulling away from a dock where our friends and family stood waving good-bye.

Donovan was looking for faith, for dialogue, for someone who could help her in her struggle with the God issue. Instead, she continues:

In the weeks following Carly's death, well-meaning friends and relatives called and sent hundreds of cards and letters offering helpless words of condolence. Most of their efforts said the same thing: "It was God's will. We cannot understand God's will." Those words kept me up at night for months, spinning through my frantic mind, tying me in philosophical knots.

I know they were trying to help, but every time the issue of God's will sprang up, I was miserable. It got to the point where I couldn't even numbly smile or nod any more when the phrase inevitably popped up. I just clenched my teeth to keep from saying something I'd regret.

Anne Donovan was aching for answers, for partners in grief and search. She writes:

What worries me about all of this is that I realize only a few people are willing to have a dialogue with me that explores the tangled, dark, and frightening mess of our doubts and fears and anger over Carly's death. Many of my friends and family lapse into embarrassed silence when I mention her name, as if I have just told a distasteful joke.

I started to notice a distinct difference between most of the letters from our Christian friends and those from our Jewish friends. The letters of Jewish friends expressed a genuine exploration of the sense of injustice and pain that the news of Carly's death stirred in them. They acknowledged their confusion and wished that time would be kind to us. They did not try to placate us with the idea that someday we would understand why this happened. They spoke from the heart, telling us only: "This is unfair, it is so painful, it is so tragic, we are thinking of you." We grew to treasure their honesty and their willingness to explore.

Now listen to the way friends tried to help her, saying to her perhaps the very same things we would say. They are pious thoughts, but in the end, of no help to someone struggling with faith, struggling to find God. Donovan comments:

I have been told some remarkable things in the interest of consolation. I've been told to rejoice that my daughter went to heaven unmarked by sin, her soul clean and pure, perfect. That God has a special place reserved for her. I have been told that I should feel privileged: I have my very own baby angel, my own divine connection. To me, these are cartoonish images. They are about as comforting as imagining God as a robed elderly man with a long white beard, floating around on a cloud. These are images used to reassure a child, and they feel frozen in time.

Anne Donovan rejects platitudes. In her ongoing grief she is searching, searching. She resonates with the words found in a letter which Harriet Beecher Stowe wrote to a friend: "When the heart strings are suddenly cut, it is, I believe, a physical impossibility to feel faith or resignation; there is a revolt of the instinctive and animal system, and though we may submit to God, it is rather by constant painful effort than sweet attraction."

Donovan, a woman who lost her child and almost her faith, ends her long article with these plaintive words: "Some may wonder why, after our experience, I still want to make the painful effort to believe. I can only respond that, despite my doubts, having seen the breathtaking perfection of my daughter's peaceful face, it is impossible to think God was not there."

And so we come back to the Emmanuel of Matthew's gospel. The God whose birth we anticipate at Christmas is named Emmanuel, God is with us. Somehow in the darkness God is there. The whole point of the incarnation is this: God is with us from beginning to end. God is with us like a faithful spouse, for better or worse, for richer or poorer, in soul-sickness or in health, in life and in death, and beyond.

Those of you who carry dark memories and heavy burdens, whose hearts are hurting, whose faith is weak, whose doubts are strong, whose anger is justified—remember Matthew's bookend message about Jesus:

"They shall name him Emmanuel," which means, "God is with us....And remember, I am with you always to the end of the age."

7

LOVE AMONG THE RUINS

JOHN 1:1–18

So solemn and captivating is this feast of Christmas the ancients held that cattle in stables fall to their knees at midnight, birds sing all night long, and trees and plants, especially those along the Jordan River, bow in reverence toward Bethlehem. On Christmas Eve, the water in wells and fountains is said to be blessed by God with healing powers. Mysterious bells chime joyfully in the depths of mines, while cheerful lights can be seen in caves.

It was once believed that at midnight the gates of paradise are opened and anyone who died at that hour would enter heaven at once. Children born on this night are especially blessed; they are believed to have the power to see spirits and even command them. Animals are thought to be able to talk like humans at midnight—in Latin, no less!—while witches, evil spirits, and ghosts have their powers suspended and can work no harm on humans, beasts, or homes.

Legends like this one abound:

On the first Christmas night the animals were given the power of speech. Thus they could praise God and tell everyone about the birth of Jesus. The first animal to speak was the cock, who flapped his wings and chanted, "Christ is born."

And the crow heard the cock, and wanted to know what time it took place. So he cawed, "When, when?" In the forest, the mighty lion heard the news of Christ's birth, and roared with all his might, "Today Christ is born." The cow wanted to know where the Christ Child was born, so she lowed, "Where, where?"

The sheep heard the angels telling the shepherds the good news of great joy and bleated the answer, "He is born in Bethlehem." The donkey wanted all to visit the stable at Bethlehem and see the Holy Child, so he brayed, "Let us go to Bethlehem." A little lark rose high in the air, as if to lead the way, and trilled, "To adore him." The dogs barked, "We should go to Bethlehem," and the horse whinnied, "Wheeeee...he is born in Bethlehem." All the animals offered their services to the Holy Infant and the Blessed Mother Mary; the lowliest of all God's creatures, the worm, was the first to do so.

It was so dark in the stable that Mary could not see to put on the little garments of the Baby Jesus. A little worm, seeing how hard it was for her, crept along the floor to a slit in the door through which the moonlight was shining. He took a ray of light and carried it along until he reached the Blessed Mother. Then he climbed up her cloak and settled on her knee so that she could see by the light.

The little Savior was so pleased, he said to the worm, "Dear little worm, your kindness to my mother shall be rewarded. I make you a present of the light. You shall never lose it." Then the little worm was placed on the edge of the manger bed where it took the place of a nightlight. And ever since, it has been known as the glowworm.

In Act 1, Scene 1 of *Hamlet*, Shakespeare echoed some of those same beliefs:

Some say that ever 'gainst that season comes
Wherein our Savior's birth is celebrated,
The bird of dawning singeth all night long:
And then, they say, no spirit dare stir abroad;
The nights are wholesome; then no planets strike,
No fairy takes, no witch has power to charm,
So hallow'd and so gracious is the time.

From this ancient awe, we moderns have spun a different version of Christmas. We have commercialized this feast and sanitized it. Take, for example, the Christmas card image of the nativity, a scene which is always presented as a tableau of angelic choirs, a babe in a manger, Mary and Joseph in clean clothes, humble, sweet shepherds with well scrubbed and properly posed animals, and richly dressed Wise Men with fabulous gifts. That scene may look like a Radio City Musical Hall production, but it is not an accurate portrayal of the first Christmas.

To begin with, take the shepherds: they were the dregs of the earth. These were people who couldn't find a better job. On the whole, shepherds were conniving thieves, several steps below our own proverbial used-car salesmen, a rather nasty lot. Then there were the magi, certainly wise men of a sort, but not Jews, not people of the prophecies or people of the promise; in a word, they were outsiders.

Mary and Joseph were not physical models of perfection, like Barbie and Ken, but poor peasants of the countryside who wore trav- el-worn, dusty, dirty clothes. The stable animals were not sanitized, and people had to walk around their droppings. Bethlehem was not Greenwich, Connecticut, but a scruffy village of no account. And the manger? We are not talking about a nice crib from Toys R Us, but a feeding station for animals. In dressing up the Nativity story to look like a set designed by Disney, we miss the point of the Incarnation.

And just what is that point? It is that God came into and among human existence with all of its limitations and flaws. Christmas is a potent and palatable sign of God's desire to embrace our brokenness. After all, Jesus is the Word made flesh who dwells among us. Among us, not some paid actors in a play; among us, nasty, untrustworthy people like the shepherds, outsiders like the magi, the different, the oddball, the out-of-step folk, the poor peasant parents who smelled from the journey. And it is no accident that this God who desired to be with us as we are, with all of our flaws, was born in a feeding sta- tion. Because that is why God came into our lives: to nourish our bro- kenness, to feed our hungry souls. Christmas truly shows us love among the ruins of our lives.

Well, let me tell you: this child of the manger grew up and didn't change one bit. He was criticized for hobnobbing with the marginal, the outcasts, and those outside the pale. He broke bread to feed sinners and publicans and hypocrites, and had the temerity to say, "I have come to call sinners, not the just." He flirted with the Samaritan prostitute at the well, he gave a second chance to Zacchaeus, a corrupt politician, he actually touched an untouchable, a leper, and he died between two thieves, who were probably a couple of shepherds. From the cradle to the grave, the Word has dwelt among us. How's that for consistency!

The big question for Christmas is, why don't we pay attention to all this? Why do we allow ourselves to fall for the commercial sentimentality of this season, when God made incarnate in Jesus echoes Dostoyevsky's words: "Love is a harsh and dreadful thing." Harsh is being born among the scum of the earth, and dreadful is dying naked on a cross with holes in your body.

That same great Russian writer, Dostoyevsky, got the Christmas message right in his story called "The House of the Dead," where he describes the coming of Christmas day in a Siberian camp.

> It was a dingy little settlement among frozen wastelands. From the grim prison at one end of a single muddy street the convicts peered through barred windows at the small cathedral on a hill at the other side of town. The bells rang merrily as that Christmas dawn arrived and villagers trooped in happy procession to the early church service. It was Christ's mass, Christmas. "But not for us, who are cut off from all humanity," the ragged prisoners wept, huddled together for comfort from the cold.
>
> Finally, however, when the long cathedral service was ended, a priest came to the prison, set up a crude altar, and began the service of worship.
>
> "Now God has come to us!" the convicts shouted in surprised joy.
>
> "Oh, yes," replied the priest. "This is where he lives all year long. You see, he goes to the cathedral only on special occasions."

The truth is, God lives all year long among us. But often, in practice, we deny it. We think we are beyond his concern, his care, his love. We array Jesus in royal trappings and place him high atop a stage setting, under strobe lights. This makes us think that he is removed from our shepherd lives, and so we do not experience his care and embrace.

How can we think this about a God who ached so badly to be among us that his first audience was the dregs of society?

Let me mention Marilyn Monroe in this Christmas homily, not just to get your attention, but because she figures here. As you know, she has become a kind of icon, a symbol of the empty sexuality of our time. In his autobiography *Timebends*, playwright Arthur Miller, one of Monroe's husbands, mentions that he watched Marilyn descend into the depths of depression and despair during the filming of the movie *The Misfits*. He feared for her life, as he watched their growing estrangement, her paranoia, and her growing dependence on barbiturates.

One evening, after a doctor had been persuaded to give Monroe yet another shot, she finally fell asleep. Miller stood watching her, reflecting. He wrote: "I found myself straining to imagine miracles. What if she were to wake and I were able to say, 'God loves you, darling,' and she were able to believe it. How I wish I still had my religion and she hers." How sad that Arthur Miller and Marilyn Monroe, a couple of shepherds, didn't know God was partial to them.

I suggest that the only way we will find the meaning of Christmas is to jettison the pretty Christmas card images of the birth of Jesus and rediscover that Christ is here where he has always wanted to be: among the small and among the straw, hanging out there, so to speak, because he knows that is where we hang out. That is what the stable scene of Jesus' birth is all about. The Word became flesh among us and for us. Jesus wanted to be close to us: he brought Love among the ruins.

Author Ian Maclaren tells a true story of a young woman in his book, *Beside the Bonnie Briar Brush*. This woman was raised in a Christian home in Ireland, but she wanted to find her freedom: freedom from all the rules, freedom from religion, freedom from puritanism, freedom from God. And so she goes away and finds the kind of life she thinks is free. She gets for herself all she has ever desired. But it is never enough. And what she possesses begins to possess her. Now she doesn't even know what it means to be free.

Well, one day, like a prodigal daughter, this woman decides to go home. When she gets near the cottage of her birth, she wants to turn around. What is she looking for anyway? She's left this place behind! And her footsteps falter. She begins to turn her body. But then the dogs in the yard catch scent of her. They haven't forgotten her, even though it has been so long. Then the light comes on at the door, and she knows she's been caught.

When the door opens, all she can see is her father bathed in the light. And he calls out her name, even though he doesn't have a reason to expect her. He calls out her name, and suddenly her feet take her running to him. And he takes her in his arms, and he sobs out blessings on her head.

Later, when the woman tells her neighbor what happened, she says, "It's a pity, Margaret, that you don't know Gaelic! That's the best of all languages for loving. There are fifty words for 'darling,' and my father could be calling me every one of them that night I came home."

Jesus has fifty-plus words for us—that is what the stable scene is all about, what Christmas is all about. But to hear them, we have to get close and find our rightful place among the shepherds, the wise men, the animals, and all the other outcasts Jesus came to save. We have to go to the trough, to the feeding station.

It comes down to this: if you look to the media and popular culture, there is no way that you will find anything other than a tinseled tableau of the first Christmas. But gathered in a faith community, where Jesus still humbly comes in the spoken word and in a small piece of bread, we know he is here for the shepherds, the outcasts, the glowworms. In Christmas he has fulfilled his desire to be near us, to be with us.

Remember: Christmas is not a tableau in a store window. Christmas is the celebration of the Word made flesh, our flesh. It is the celebration of Love among the ruins of our lives.

8

TENDING TO YOUR TREASURE

MATTHEW 2:13-15, 19-23

Most of us envision the Holy Family as shown in those wondrously famous Renaissance paintings or on the front of beatific Christmas cards. Joseph is usually off to one side, Mary and the Baby are clean and lovely, and everyone has a halo around his or her head.

The truth of the matter is that such paintings, great art though they may be, are a long way off from the scene depicted in Matthew's account of Jesus' birth. In fact, Joseph is the central character in these first stories. Further, he is a visionary and a man of action. He takes Mary to be his wife even though she is already pregnant. And when Jesus is born Joseph whisks the family away to Egypt, out of the reach of the tyrant Herod.

Even to this day, if you go to the old town in Cairo and duck through the walls of the old fortress known as Babylon, you can ask for directions to the church of St. Sergius. It's one of a clutch of Coptic churches huddled together along the tiny streets, hidden behind ordinary-looking doors a few steps down from a muddy alleyway. Once inside you can climb down—if the floods have not been too bad—into the crypt, an arched room just a few feet across. And this, you will be told, is the place where the Holy Family stayed for a month as refugees from Herod while Joseph found work as a carpenter on the new Roman fortress.

While standing in the old church, perhaps you will sense something of the tension that most likely existed in the life of the young refugee family. This is fairly easy to do, because the Copts of Cairo are nowadays a persecuted and fearful minority, and wariness looks out from every face around you. The Holy Family, like these persecuted Copts, was alert and ready for action. They were vigorously, riotously human, very much a family on the move as they went from Bethlehem to Egypt and back to Judea, then on to Nazareth in Galilee.

Eventually, as we discover later in Matthew's gospel, there were other kin—we can count five boys and at least two or three girls. When he has grown, Jesus works out of Capernaum on the shores of the Sea of Galilee. Joseph is apparently dead, and when his mother and relatives catch up with Jesus they are apparently unconvinced by his teaching. Later on, however, two of the boys—James and Jude—become leading figures in the young church. So did Jesus' cousin Simeon, son of his uncle Clopas and his aunt Mary, who was among the women standing at the foot of the cross.

Also a part of this family were Mary's kinsfolk, Elizabeth and Zechariah and their son John. It was quite a clan. A troop of strong-willed, visionary people who appear and reappear throughout Jesus' life—and not always in happy, harmonious agreement. Indeed, they were a very human family.

All of this brings us back to today's liturgy. The point of the feast of the Holy Family is not primarily to extol families and family life, but to remind us that Jesus was part of a family, as most of us are. Further, he was deeply affected and shaped by his family. Therapists tell us that we are molded by our experiences as children in a family. Thus, we can never underestimate the importance of family background. A woman gives us this example:

As the family of a career soldier in the Air Force, my parents, my brother, and I became quite adept at packing up our belongings and moving to a new place. By the time I graduated from high school, I had attended twelve different schools. While there are obvious disadvantages to such a mobile existence, there are also positive opportunities for growth.

Our seemingly rootless way of life proved to be a catalyst for developing a rootedness in one another as family. At each new base, we all formed friendships but each new assignment required that we loosen those ties and go on to welcome a new network of relationships. The only stable and dependable bonds were those we shared among ourselves.

While I never gave much thought to our unusual circumstances, one experience in particular made me gratefully aware of the treasure which is family. I was eight years old when my father received orders for Japan. During the three years that we were stationed there, we saw, up close and personal, the ravages of the Second World War and the devastating toll that war had taken on so many families.

Within very close proximity to our base, there were dozens of orphanages. Each one was filled to capacity with children whose parents had died as a result of the bombings of Hiroshima and Nagasaki or whose relatives had lost the means to care for them. There were also hundreds of Nisei, or Japanese-American children, who had not been claimed by their American G.I. fathers and were not readily accepted into Japanese society.

Each squadron on base was assigned an orphanage; each family within the squadron was responsible for several of the orphans. There were visits each weekend and special celebrations for both the Japanese and American holidays.

When my mother baked cookies, she always made several dozen more for our friends at the orphanage; when she bought soap, toothpaste, or other toiletries, she purchased extra for the same reason. As we learned to speak Japanese, the children learned English. While we gave willingly and happily of all we could, there was one gift we could never impart; that was the security and joy of family. As I matured, I learned that the sad plight of the orphans in Japan was not unique. Nor was this kind of suffering unique to children.

As a young adult, I worked as a nurse's aide on the geriatric floor of a large general hospital. The experience of one woman remains with me. She was elderly and had been in a comatose state for months; not able to speak, she did, however, respond to gentle voices and tender treatment. Since she never had any visitors, I was shocked to learn that she had nine adult children, most of whom lived nearby.

All over the world, families are broken and their members are orphaned by divorce, continuing wars, famine, ethnic cleansing, the debilitating effects of old age, and diseases such as AIDS....Of course, our commitment to Christ compels us to provide for them; we have been taught that we are to revere each member of the human family as our brother and sister, parent and child. While tending to their needs, we cannot help but be grateful for the blessed experience of our own families.

Family life is a high calling indeed. Those of us who are parents should check what kind of blessed experiences we are giving our children. It is not simply enough to feed and clothe our children; we must nurture their minds and hearts and souls. For it is in our families that our children first discover who they are. To help them in this discovery is holy work.

Go to a playground where you will see little daily miracles. When Susie falls over and runs to Mom, and Mom kisses her to make her better, the crying stops and the smile comes back. What kind of healing is this that takes pain away with a kiss? For most of us, our families are the closest thing we have to heaven. Family can be a place where we are made one by love, where we discover that we are part of each other, where we begin to come close to God. We can all aspire to live in holy families.

Today's feast offers each of us an occasion for recognizing and appreciating the treasure which is family. Perhaps this special day might also prompt us to consider how well we are tending to that treasure. Even though our experience of family may not have been good, most of us value the gift of family and understand its nuclear and essential importance for both society and the church. Some of us become caught up in the pressures of daily living, however, and do not take the time to tend the treasure that is ours. For this reason, the church gives the gathered assembly selections from Scripture intended to renew and deepen our familial commitments.

Some years ago, the late Harry Chapin had a popular song called, "Cat's in the Cradle." It was a ballad about the relationship between a father, who spent his time and energy being successful, and his son who wanted to share in his father's life. "When you comin' home, Dad?" the son would repeatedly ask, only to receive the reply, "I don't know when. But we'll get together then, Son." As the boy grew to manhood and the father grew wiser, he began to pose the same question to his son, "When you comin' home, Son?" only to receive the sadly predictable reply, "I don't know when. But we'll get together then, Dad."

Chapin's song and today's readings remind us that "then" may never come. Therefore, we are challenged to take the time now to tend to the treasure of family. For the message of Christmas is that we are given a savior who appeared not with trumpets and clouds, but who was born into a family. Families are holy communities, and we are all called, in one way or another, to help create holy families. Because this, quite literally, is where the gospel of Christ begins.

9

FEAR OF GLORY

LUKE 2:41-52

.

The story of Jesus in the Temple besting the teachers belongs to a long list of ancient stories of children who get the better of adults. Kids, naturally, love such stories. Jack outsmarts the giant, a symbol of all adults who, in children's eyes, are giants; Little Red Riding Hood puts one over on the wolf. Little David gets the best of the big man, Goliath.

And here is Jesus, from a hick town, with no formal schooling, who had not read the great books of the world, confounding the university people. All those who don't do well on the SATs, who have no access to power and wealth, should love this story.

Still, why is this incident in Scripture? Do we need another story of a wise kid putting down adults? (In the Bible, yet.) Doesn't this story belong to fairy tales? No. It belongs to grace. It tells the ancient God-story that the small, the weak, the vulnerable have God and have glory, and should never settle for less. As the boy's mother sang of her own nothingness before he was born, "God has looked upon the lowliness of his handmaid for he who is mighty has done great things for the likes of me....He has scattered the proud, brought down the powerful and lifted up the lowly...and all generations shall call me blessed."

And that's what I want to talk to you about: about all generations calling you blessed, about calling yourself blessed—provided you claim God and claim glory and stop denying it. To get what I'm driving at, let me begin, as I shall end, with the splendid words of Nelson Mandela in his 1994 inaugural speech:

> Our deepest fear is not that we are inadequate. Our deepest fear is that we are powerful beyond measure. It is our light, not our darkness, that frightens us most. We ask ourselves, who am I to be brilliant, gorgeous, talented and fabulous?
>
> Actually, who are you not to be? You are a child of God. Your playing small doesn't serve the world. There is nothing enlightened about shrinking so that other people won't feel insecure around you. We were born to make manifest the glory of God within us.
>
> It is not just in some of us; it's in everyone. And, as we let our own light shine, we unconsciously give other people permission to do the same. As we are liberated from our own fear our presence automatically liberates others.

Mandela is right. And his magnificent words are scriptural. Deep down inside, we are afraid, not of our inadequacy, but of our glory; not of our darkness, but of our light. And so we play it small. What a shame, what a pity. And, someday, what a judgment. We play it small to escape our glory which may make others feel insecure, and we embrace what an insecure world tells us to embrace. We wear the same designer clothes, drink the same Starbucks coffee, collect the same accessories, strive for *Baywatch* bodies, embrace our careers rather than our children, cut the same corners to get ahead, talk the same talk, value the same commercially induced values—and in the process of it all, we lose our identity.

Sooner or later, we no longer make manifest the glory of God within us—indeed, we suppress our glory and can no longer name it. The light no longer shines for us because, fearful of our own light, we have become a part of the attractive darkness.

Glory, of course, cannot be completely suppressed—after all, we are children of God no matter how much we try to cover it up. And so at times we find ourselves flirting with New Age paraphernalia, watching *Touched by an Angel* on TV, and even going to church on Christmas. But this is not enough, not nearly enough. Something is wrong and Mandela puts his finger on it. We act and live the way we do because it is our light, not our darkness, that frightens us most. How dare we be brilliant, gorgeous, talented, and fabulous, a child of God?

How dare we be the kid who slays the giant, the little girl who bests the wolf, the backwoods boy who confounds the university teachers in the Temple?

How dare we be civil in a vulgar world, chaste in a sex-saturated media, sober in a besotted place, honest in a bottom-line economy, simple in a city that offers us fifty kinds of mustard at the supermarket, selfless and compassionate while living in a culture of greed?

How dare we be bold enough to pull the plug on the mechanical attachments—the telephone, the laptop computer, the FAX machine, the cell phone, the beepers—which keep us attached to the marketplace, but also detached from human relationships? How dare we liberate ourselves from the machines that were supposed to be our servants but which have become our masters?

How dare we honor our marriage vows in a divorce culture, embrace a lifestyle that says "I have enough" in a consumer culture?

How dare we feed the hungry, give drink to the thirsty, clothe the naked, visit the sick, comfort the sorrowful, and publicly state our aching need for a God of infinite concern, forgiveness, and love?

How dare we embrace that which makes manifest the glory of God within us when the world tells us, programs us to believe, that we really have no time for godly, fundamental ways—after all, our career is a god that demands total allegiance? Who do we think we are trying to play it big when everyone else is playing it small? Do we want to make others feel insecure? We're no kid in the Temple letting his light shine through. We cannot admit that we are brilliant, gorgeous, talented, and fabulous. If we did admit that, would we—could we—live the way we do now?

Let's go back to the gospel. Now what do you see there? A budding adolescent confounding the establishment? Or do you see a young man from poor parents and a backward town who simply knows who he is: powerful beyond measure, brilliant, gorgeous, talented, and fabulous? Jesus had it right when he asked, "Did you not know I must be about my Father's business?" Relationships, care and concern for others, peacemaking, forgiveness, healing, love: these are the Father's business.

There is one more question to ask: are we about our Father's business? Or are our fears exposed, the fear that maybe we are children of God, the fear of the glory within us?

That grand old musical, *Man of La Mancha*, tells the story of Don Quixote, who lives with the illusion that he is a knight of old, battling windmills which he imagines are dragons. Near the end of the musical, Don Quixote lies dying. At his side is Aldonza, a worthless slut he had idealized by calling her Dulcinea, "sweet one," much to the howling laughter of the townsfolk. But Don Quixote loved her in a way unlike anything she had ever experienced. When Quixote breathes his last, Aldonza begins to sing the haunting song, "The Impossible Dream." As the last echo of the song dies away, someone shouts to her, "Aldonza!" But she proudly pulls herself up and responds, "My name is Dulcinea."

This gospel is like that story. It reminds us that, although the culture calls us Aldonza and wants us to live as such, God calls us Dulcinea—my beloved—and asks us to live accordingly. God wants to liberate us from what we fear and remind us who we are and how we must live. What or who made us forget who we are, urged us to settle for less? Who made us settle for being called "Aldonza"?

Maybe our New Year's resolution, our theme for a new year, should be this: that we reclaim our dignity, recognize our fears, be about our Father's business by living as who we are, the sons and daughters of God who were put here on earth to liberate others from rejection, separation, loneliness, and hurt.

So now, I will close as I began, with an excerpt from Nelson Mandela's inaugural speech. This time, close your eyes and listen carefully. Listen as one who has discovered a new truth:

> Our deepest fear is not that we are inadequate. Our deepest fear is that we are powerful beyond measure. It is our light, not our darkness, that frightens us most. We ask ourselves, who am I to be brilliant, gorgeous, talented and fabulous?
>
> Actually, who are you not to be? You are a child of God. Your playing small doesn't serve the world. There is nothing enlightened about shrinking so that other people won't feel insecure around you. We were born to make manifest the glory of God within us.
>
> It is not just in some of us; it's in everyone. And, as we let our own light shine, we unconsciously give other people permission to do the same. As we are liberated from our own fear our presence automatically liberates others.

Amen.

10

THREE RESOLUTIONS

LUKE 2:16–21

Traditionally, of course, New Year's Day is the time for resolutions. Why? Because last year, although there were indeed good deeds and good moments, there were some less than glorious aspects in our moral and human lives. Instinctively, we know that we should be better—some bad habits or personality quirks or the way we treated certain people or last year's tepid prayer routines—things like this need attention, need our determination to improve.

Well, whatever your conscience tells you about New Year's resolutions, I would like to suggest three. I hope these will not seem too abstract or grand, but give us food for thought. And as I am wont to do, I will begin by sharing a few stories:

Edward Bok, onetime editor of the *Ladies' Home Journal*, came to this country as a child, from Denmark. Many years back, his grandfather had been commissioned by the King of Denmark to lead a band of soldiers against pirates who were playing havoc with shipping along a certain coastal area.

The elder Bok set up his headquarters on a rocky, desolate island just off the coast, and after a few years was able to clear the pirates out. Upon returning to the mainland, Bok reported back to the King. The King was very pleased with his efforts, and offered Bok anything he wanted. Bok told the King that all he wanted was a plot of land on the island where he had just lived and fought for so many months. The island was barren, the King noted: why would he want to live there? I want to plant trees, was Bok's reply. I want to make the island beautiful.

The King's aides thought he was crazy. The island was constantly swept by storms and high winds; he would never be able to grow trees there. Bok, however, insisted, and the King granted him his wish.

Bok went to live on the island, built a home, and was eventually able to bring his wife there to live. For years they worked industriously, persistently, planting trees, shrubs, and grass. Gradually the vegetation took hold and the island began to flourish. One morning the couple arose to hear birds singing. There had never been any birds on the island before. Eventually the island became a showplace, and is now visited by thousands of tourists each year. When he died, the grandfather requested that the following words be inscribed on his tombstone: "Make you the world a bit more beautiful and better because you have been in it."

But the story doesn't end there. Edward Bok, the grandson, believed that anyone who was able to do so should retire at the age of fifty and spend the rest of his or her life making the world a more beautiful and better place to live. And he was as good as his word. He retired at fifty and bought Iron Mountain, the highest point in Florida at an elevation of 324 feet above sea level. There, he set out to repeat what his grandfather had done.

Edward Bok was more than successful. Iron Mountain is now called Mountain Lake Sanctuary, Florida. Upon his death, Edward Bok willed the land to the State of Florida, and it is now a major tourist attraction. On the younger Bok's grave is the same inscription as is on his grandfather's: "Make you the world a bit more beautiful and better because you have been in it."

So there we have it, the first resolution: to make the world a better and more beautiful place because we have been in it. Does this inscription sound too grand to be a resolution? I don't think so. There are many ways to make the world a more beautiful and better place:

plant a tree, bring flowers to the nursing home, spend time with a teenager, read a story to a child, clean up the neighborhood, send cards to the sick. Take something that is rough or unfinished or ugly and make it beautiful.

The second resolution is this: pick up on what others have started. Most of us have known losses. We have lost spouses or children, relationships or health, or maybe only our equilibrium. However we may name our losses, they are out there scattered all over the landscape. But we can choose what to do about these losses. We can either turn in on ourselves and forever cry "woe is me"; or we can pick up on those who turn tragedy into discipleship.

For example, think of Sadako, a little Japanese girl caught in the bombing of Hiroshima. She saw her mother and father and the rest of her family destroyed right before her eyes; she herself had severe radiation burns. She was in a hospital, essentially waiting to die, and she knew she did not have long to live. But instead of bemoaning her tragedy, she said: "This can never happen again to people. People cannot be this cruel to one another. So each day I am going to cut out and make a white crane, and I am going to send it to somebody and ask them to be a disciple for peace."

Well, Sadako did this every day for 683 days, and then she died. And those who knew this little girl had their choice. They could be so outraged over the bombings that they would be consumed by a desire to go out and bomb the rest of the world in revenge, or they could pick up on what she started. And so they made a 684th white crane, and a 685th, and a 686th, ad infinitum. Each of those white cranes goes throughout the world with the message that life can be better than it is now.

Build on the good works of people you know, but also of people you don't know. Instead of getting angry and blowing up the world, get involved with organizations that are trying to make the world a better place. Perhaps you can join MADD (Mothers Against Drunk Driving), or Amnesty International, or Pax Christi. Do something to make life better for us all. There are homeless people to house, there are hungry people to feed, and lonely people to visit. There are cranes to be cut out and sent.

This is a good resolution, isn't it? Pick up on what others have done. Continue the love and spirit of good and decent people, which will turn the world around.

The third resolution: this year, show someone what God is like.

A man relates that when he was a little boy, he was forever coming home late from school, which meant he was late for dinner every day. His parents finally got fed up and said, "Look, next time you come late for dinner, you will get bread and water. That's it!"

Sure enough, the next day the boy came home late from school. He walked into the house and there were his mother and father, with plates with meat and potatoes and vegetables set in front of them. In front of his place, however, were a plate of bread and a glass of water.

The boy was crushed. His father waited for the full weight of the lesson to sink in, then silently took his own full plate and put it in front of his son. He took his son's empty plate and put it in front of himself. And this man, the boy who is now a man, said to me: "All my life I have known what God is like by what my father did that night."

It's as simple as that.

People learn about God not because they figure out the Trinity, not because they tune into what the Vatican is doing, not because they are great theologians, not because they understand Greek. People learn about God from Godlike people. Even people who have done some evil, even people who have messy corners in their lives; you can still share a full plate with someone who has nothing, so to speak. You can be God to someone who will remember what God is like because they remember what you are like.

So those are my three suggestions for New Year's resolutions. First, make the world a bit more beautiful, better because you have been in it. Secondly, pick up what others have started—you *can* make a difference. Thirdly, show somebody this year what God is like, without letting them know that's what you're doing.

If we all half keep these three resolutions, this will be a very happy new year indeed.

11

GOD SHOWS NO PARTIALITY

ACTS OF THE APOSTLES 10:34–38

The second reading from the Acts of the Apostles catches our eye this morning. In the heady days after the resurrection, while the embolden apostles were preaching the news of Jesus, Peter had a vision about kosher and non-kosher animals. Then a heavenly voice told him to eat the non-kosher, or unclean, meat. Peter protested, until the voice said, "What God has made clean, you must not call profane."

Peter was pondering this dream when word came that a centurion of the Roman guard named Cornelius, a Gentile and therefore an unclean man, wished to be baptized. Peter hesitated at first. After all, this man was defective in nearly every way. He was a foreigner, a Gentile, a soldier of the occupying force. No way could God be calling him. But then Peter recalled his dream, caught its meaning, and commented: "I truly understand now that God shows no partiality." And so Peter took this unclean Gentile, this foreigner, this ritual sinner, into the faith community through baptism.

From this incident and from Peter's words, we can reflect on two truisms. The first is that all of us are Cornelius. And we know that, don't we? We are "unclean," sinners, defective in one way or another, spiritual quislings, unlikely candidates for holiness. Like Peter, we can't imagine that we would be called to live a life of quiet heroism

52

and holiness. Let others, made of more noble stuff, take that on. Grace will not settle on the likes of us.

A pagan once asked the rabbi, "Why, of all things, did God choose the humble thornbush as the place from which to speak to Moses?" The rabbi replied, "If he had chosen a carob tree or a mulberry bush, you would have asked me the same question. Yet it is impossible to let you go away emptyhanded. That is why I am telling you that God chose the humble thornbush to teach you there is no place on earth bereft of the divine presence, not even a thornbush."

This little parable tells us that we are all indeed candidates for holiness. The divine presence wants to settle in our miserable, thornbush lives. As Jesus himself said, "I have come to call the sick, not the well." And through the ages, he has done precisely that.

Who else would have called Peter, the one who denied, as head of the apostles? Paul, the persecutor, to spread the gospel? Cornelius, the Gentile outsider, to be a convert? Augustine, the libertine, to teach the masses? Merton, the playboy, to popularize the contemplative life? Dorothy Day, the communist, to care for Christ's poor? All of these were thornbush people, all flawed, all partial; but like Cornelius, all subject to the Spirit.

"I truly understand now that God shows no partiality," exclaimed Peter. In other words, our partiality, our flaws, our imperfections, our uncleanliness, our state in life, our sins; none of these can be used as excuses to duck God's call to grace, to holiness, to sainthood, to conversion. However true the prayer, "O Lord, I am not worthy," it is no ground for living small, settling for spiritual mediocrity, being a sometime disciple.

Imperfect people—perhaps especially, imperfect people—are subject to the Spirit. And we must let the Spirit breathe where it will in us without any lame excuse that we are not worthy of its attention. No; we are called to holiness simply as who we are. God shows no partiality.

The second truism is this: our imperfect gifts must be joined to the imperfect gifts of others in order to make the world whole. All of us, as I said, are partial, unfinished, deprived in one way or another. But again, that is no excuse to sit back and feel sorry for ourselves or worse yet, to settle for half a life, a tepid spirituality, an ungiving posture. Our talents and gifts, however small, however fractured, must be joined to another's for the sake of life, love, and redemption.

This is the concept behind MADD, Mothers Against Drunk Driving. Here parents who have suffered the terrible loss of their children, who could sit in a corner all their lives buried in sorrow, have chosen to use their grief for something useful. This is also the story of Alcoholics Anonymous: addicted people creatively sharing their wounded lives for mutual help and healing. Or take the story of these two delightful ladies:

> In the spring of 1983, Margaret Patrick arrived at the Southeast Senior Center for Independent Living to begin her physical therapy. As Millie McHugh, a long-time staff member, introduced Margaret to people at the center, she noticed the look of pain in Margaret's eyes as she gazed at the piano. "Is anything wrong?" asked Millie. "No," Margaret said softly. "It's just that seeing a piano brings back memories. Before my stroke, music was everything to me."
>
> Millie glanced at Margaret's useless right hand as the black woman quietly told some of the highlights of her music career. Suddenly Millie said, "Wait right here. I'll be back in a minute." She returned moments later, followed closely by a small, white-haired woman in thick glasses. The woman used a walker.
>
> "Margaret Patrick," said Millie, "meet Ruth Eisenberg." Then she smiled. "She too played the piano, but like you she's not been able to play since her stroke. Mrs. Eisenberg has a good right hand, and you have a good left, and I have a feeling that together you two can do something wonderful."
>
> "Do you know Chopin's Waltz in D-flat?" Ruth asked. Margaret nodded. Side by side, the two sat on the piano bench. Two healthy hands—one with long, graceful black fingers, the other with short, plump white ones—moved rhythmically across the ebony and ivory keys.
>
> Since that day they have sat together over the keyboard hundreds of times—Margaret's helpless right hand around Ruth's back, Ruth's helpless left hand on Margaret's knee, while Ruth's good hand plays the melody and Margaret's good hand plays the accompaniment. Their music has pleased audiences on television, at churches and schools, and at rehabilitation and senior citizen centers.

And on the piano bench, more than music has been shared by these two. For it was there, beginning with Chopin and Bach and Beethoven, that they learned they had more in common than they ever dreamed—both were great-grandmothers and widows, both had lost sons, both had much to give, but neither could give without the other.

Sharing that piano bench, Ruth heard Margaret say, "My music was taken away, but God gave me Ruth." And evidently some of Margaret's faith has rubbed off on Ruth as they've sat side by side these past five years, because Ruth is now saying, "It was God's miracle that brought us together." And that is the story of Margaret and Ruth, who now call themselves "Ebony and Ivory."

Remember that wonderful film, *Driving Miss Daisy?* A proud Jewish woman and an illiterate black man learned to consolidate their individual weaknesses—her physical weakness and his educational weakness—into communal strength and friendship.

Each of us has a small voice, but united we can sing God's praises. Each of us has a hand or foot or an eye that we can join with others to feed the hungry and comfort the sorrowful. Each of us has a poor gift, but connected with others, we make a rich tapestry of God's mercy and love. Each of us has a tiny talent, but with others we can form a mosaic of beauty and truth.

Looking at the hated soldier, the oppressor, the unclean Gentile, Peter was forced to swallow his pride, his prejudice, and admit, "I understand now that God shows no partiality." Peter discovered—as we must—that Cornelius and all unclean, oppressive, less than perfect people, are also subject to the call of the Spirit. Secondly, our partial gifts, be they meager or great, must be joined to the gifts of others in order to make the Spirit present, and the world whole. Peter has given us a lot to think about today.

LENT, EASTER *and* PENTECOST

12

THE SCANDAL OF THE CROSS

I have a favor to ask you today. I want you to use your imagination. Imagine that you have just met the new neighbors who moved in next door. They seem like very nice people.

After you have gotten to know them a bit better, they invite you to worship with them on Sunday. You have never heard of their religion; it is something entirely new and different. On the other hand, you feel a bit honored that they want to share their faith with you. And so, perhaps as much out of curiosity as out of friendship, you go to their place of worship.

Well, imagine your surprise if you enter the front door, look into the sanctuary, and don't see an altar. In fact, what you do see shocks you, utterly shocks you. The whole sanctuary is bare except for an electric chair, placed dead center! My God, you feel like turning right around and running for your life.

At the very least, you feel like excusing yourself, as you wonder what in the world you have gotten into. What kind of strange cult is this to have such a bizarre item in their place of worship? What kind of people are these? And yet, for some reason, you hesitate. You hesitate between disgust and interest, between fear and curiosity. You find yourself torn because these people, as well as everyone else present in the church, don't seem weird at all.

In fact, as you look around, they seem to be rather nice; more than nice, they seem to be rather loving people. It is obvious from the others who have gathered with them that they show a great deal of love and concern for each other. They are obviously bringing a spirit of worship to this day. And so you are torn.

Finally, you decide to stay. Your host picks up a small pamphlet from the pew, and hands it to you. In the pamphlet is an explanation of the group's belief. You read that at the center of their faith and worship is a man who was strapped to the electric chair and put to death through the machinations of a political and a social system which saw this man as a threat to their lives of privilege and of power.

Subsequently, these followers have discovered that when they gather together, this man is present in spirit, pouring out his love and his grace into their lives. And slowly it begins to dawn on you that to them the electric chair—a horrifying symbol of the state's power over life and death, a symbol of disgrace and condemnation and fear—has been transformed for these people into something entirely different from its common meaning.

It's quite a shock, quite a reversal to make an electric chair a point of veneration and inspiration. You are baffled: how can something so monstrous represent the very power and wisdom of God to these people? Instead of a rich and famous lifestyle, instead of yachts and villas, perks and private jets, sleek automobiles and perfectly toned bodies, an electric chair is the symbol for life's meaning? It's beyond all explanation.

And now I want to tell you something. In imagining that moment of perplexity; in imagining the shock of walking into a worship space and seeing an electric chair placed center stage, you have put yourself back into the experience of certain people in the first century who walked into a gathering of people called Christians. At the center of the Christians' worship space stood what was the electric chair of that time: a cross. Visitors to a Christian church back then would be shocked to see that a cross—a hated, disgraceful, shameful, and feared symbol of death—would be cherished, would be a symbol of revelation, redemption, and inspiration for these people.

We have gotten so used to the symbol of the cross that we take it for granted. We decorate it, encrust it with diamonds, and make a bauble out of it, another rock concert artifact like an earring or nose ring. We have lost the ability to understand its shock value, to understand what it cost Jesus to die on cross and the demands which the cross makes on those who embrace it.

Look, there it is, above the altar. How often do you notice it? The cross is a powerful sign that the world has got it all backwards. Jesus does not appear to us on MTV or arrive in a shiny new Mercedes. Rather, Jesus comes to us in the most outlandish and scandalous way. He comes in sacrifice and self-giving and total love. Innocent of the charges against him, he nevertheless accepts the electric chair of his time—the cross—to show us how far he will go for us, how high he will be raised for us, and most importantly, where he expects us to follow.

The world puts forth a message of success: blessed are the rich and financially secure. Blessed are those who are proud and powerful. Blessed are the clever, the tricky. Blessed are the celebrities. Blessed are Donald Trump, Hugh Hefner, and Monica Lewinsky. But the cross gives an opposite message: blessed are the poor in spirit, for they will see God. Blessed are those who are sorrowful when they see the swollen bodies of children living through famine; when they see brother and sister killing each other in the war-torn countries of the world. Blessed are the homeless and the mentally ill, who wander the streets with no one to look after them.

Blessed are those who have a deep thirst for justice and are not content to live with injustice and pain. Blessed are those who do not pick up guns and kill, but who work toward peace for all people. Blessed are those who do not return hurt, an eye for an eye, but forgive. Blessed are the chaste, the faithful, the honest, those who keep their word. And blessed are those who are willing to put themselves on the line and suffer persecution, ridicule, and name-calling in order to embrace a Christian way of life.

This is what the cross means.

During these latter days of Lent, I suggest that we ponder anew what we take so lightly; that we discover a sense of scandal and outrage that the primary symbol of our religion is a cross. We must come to terms with the reality that the cross is not a pendant, not a decoration. It is the sign of a radical way of living that demands making choices. When we make the sign of the cross, we declare our radical stance to the world. We state that we are willing to die to self, we are willing to be countercultural.

In Robert Bolt's play, *A Man for All Seasons*, Henry VIII is trying to persuade his chancellor, Thomas More, to agree with his decision to divorce his first wife and marry Anne Boleyn. Henry says: "You must consider, Thomas, that I stand in peril of my soul. It was no marriage; she was my brother's widow."

More responds: "Your Grace, I'm not fit to meddle in these matters. To me it seems a matter for the Holy See." And Henry interrupts:

> Thomas, Thomas, does a man need a pope to tell him when he's sinned? It was a sin, Thomas; I admit it. I repent. And God has punished me; I have no son....Son after son she's borne me, Thomas, all dead at birth, or dead within the month; I never saw the hand of God so clear in anything....I have a daughter, she's my good child, a well-set child, but I have no son. It is my bounden duty to put away the Queen, and all the popes back to St. Peter shall not come between me and my duty!

Then he adds these powerful words: "How is it that you cannot see? Everyone else does." And More answers quietly, "Why, then, does Your Grace need my poor support?" And here comes Henry's answer, in effect a challenge to Thomas More to take up the cross:

> Because you are honest. What's more to the purpose, you're known to be honest....Look, there are those like Norfolk who follow me because I wear the crown, and there are those like Master Cromwell who follow me because they are jackals with sharp teeth and I am their lion, and there is a mass that follows me because it follows anything that moves—and then there is you.

The cross looms largely for More. He can reject the cross and live with fame and riches for the rest of his life, or he can defy the king and face certain death. More embraces the cross. He becomes one of those weird people whose leader died on a cross.

Let me tell you about another person who stood by her values. Most of you will not recognize the name Nichelle Nichols. She is the actress who played Uhura in the original *Star Trek* television program, and she was in six *Star Trek* movies.

What is significant about Nichelle Nichols is that she was one of the first black women regularly featured on a weekly TV show. As such, she had some obstacles to overcome. A few studio executives, for example, were hostile toward her. Often, her character would be diminished by script rewrites; the studio even withheld thousands of pieces of her fan mail. Nichols was well aware of the prejudice going on, and after one year on the program, she decided to quit.

Before she did, however, Nichols happened to go to a fundraiser for the National Association for the Advancement of Colored People (NAACP). There she happened to meet Dr. Martin Luther King, Jr., who urged her not to leave the show because she was a role model for many. Said Nichols sometime later in an interview, "When you have a man like Martin Luther King, Jr., say you can't leave a show, it's daunting. It humbled my heart, and I couldn't leave. God had charged me with something more important than my own career." She was, in effect, offered the cross.

The rest, as they say, is history. Not only did Nichelle Nichols become a fixture on *Star Trek*, she actually influenced NASA by challenging them to hire blacks and women for their astronaut corps. By embracing the cross, Nichols found the defining role of her career and influenced a nation through one of the most popular TV shows ever produced.

Like the electric chair, the cross is scandalous. Jesus died on it and we are asked to embrace it. So look at it for what it is. Don't sanitize it. Realize how bizarre you and I are to center our lives around a cross. Yet it is precisely this terrible, shameful symbol which is offered us by Jesus: "Whoever does not take up the cross and follow me is not worthy of me."

The cross is not a pendant. It is not a decoration. It is not pretty. It is a challenge—for Thomas More, for Nichelle Nichols, for you, and for me. It's a risky thing to sign yourself in the name of the Father and of the Son and of the Holy Spirit. Amen.

13

NO AND YES FOR LENT

MATTHEW 4:1–11

On Ash Wednesday, the Christian faithful around the world lift up their faces to be signed with ashes. This sign is meant to remind them both of their mortality and of the promise of new life through repentance. The ashes signal entry into the holy season of Lent, a time of fasting, an opportunity to deprive the body and consequently make room for the spirit.

Truth to tell, these days Americans harbor an extra motive for fasting; as a whole, we are much too overweight. In fact, the *Harper's Index of Statistics* states that, at the current rate of increase, all Americans will be overweight by the year 2059!

Still, while fasting from food can be good practice as an act of discipline—and nothing can be achieved without discipline—I challenge you to consider another view as you ponder the lenten season. It is as important to control what goes into your mouth as it is to control what comes out of your mouth. And so this year, I would like you to consider fasting from what comes out of your mouth.

There are four areas we might consider in this kind of fasting. The first is fasting from foul language. The air around us is full of it, and not just from the Howard Sterns and Jerry Springers of the media. The f-word is commonplace, monotonously and boringly so, in movies, in song lyrics, in novels and magazine articles, and in everyday conversation. Sometimes it seems as if everyone—from CEOs to detectives, presidents of colleges and banks, people with degrees up and down their arms can't say a single sentence without a dirty or vulgar word. All that education, and still, from the mouths of men—and in the spirit of equality, increasingly women—spew forth language unheard in public twenty years ago. Foul language has even become part of our children's vocabulary.

Crude talk and endless sexual double meanings pollute commercials, TV shows, and daily conversation. This has become so commonplace that we take it all in as part of normal discourse. But when locker room talk becomes the ordinary means of communication it coarsens us, devalues us. I suppose all this foul talk from children and adults alike is meant to signal sophistication and freedom—but to my mind, all it signals is poverty of vocabulary and a small mind, a small heart. Certainly, foul language has no place in the life of a disciple of Jesus.

I like the story of a college kid who brought his roommate home for dinner. At the meal, the guest accidentally knocked over his water glass, and without thinking, let out a stream of obscenities. Everyone at the table was aghast except grandma, who looked straight at the young man and said, "You eat with that mouth?"

So, the first practice for Lent—for all of us, young, old, and in between—is to watch our language. Watch what comes out of your mouth, for what comes out tells what is inside your heart. Using foul, dirty language or telling a smutty joke may make you feel like a big shot, one of the gang. But it belies the fact that you are not one of the gang. Remember, you are one of Christ's gang. You are God's child, and God's children don't talk like that.

The second lenten practice is to keep judgments from spilling out from your mouth. This might be hard to do for the whole of Lent, but maybe you can pick one day to keep your judgments to yourself. Friday is a good choice, in honor of Jesus' crucifixion. This was also the day when he also granted paradise to the man on his right, the good thief, whom we would have deemed unworthy of God's attention.

And so for each Friday of Lent, make no judgments about people: about their motives, their goodness or badness, their social standing, their defects, their clothes, their color, their jobs, their mistakes. Just see everyone as God's children, people for whom Christ died, fellow pilgrims. For one day a week during Lent, avoid letting negative judgments come forth from your mouth.

Thirdly, try to control the verbal negatives that so readily come from our mouths. Not just the hate language, but the put-downs, the jabs that hurt, the insults, the criticism, the condemnations, the sarcasm, the harmful gossip, the rumor that smears. Again, if it's too much of a challenge to do this on every day of Lent, make it just one day a week. You may want to choose Wednesday as your no-negative-words day, as tradition holds that this was the day Judas let the words which betrayed Jesus fall from his mouth.

Kathleen Norris, the prize-winning poet and spiritual writer, was a "Navy brat," as the phrase goes. She writes of the time she had moved with her family to Hawaii, where she had to attend a new school with other children of military parents. She was a new seventh-grader in a school where the other kids had been there together since kindergarten. These children "were less than receptive to a socially awkward, chubby, buck-toothed girl from the mainland who knew next to nothing about their world." Yet by the midafternoon of her first day in the school, Norris thought that things might work out well between her and the other students.

But as she was sitting in a bathroom stall, she heard several girls enter the bathroom. To her chagrin, it quickly became obvious that they were talking about her, and in the most unflattering terms. They busily dissected her, mocking her hair, her weight, her shoes, her clothes, her voice, and her manner—until one of them noticed her shoes in the stall. "Omigod, she's in here," one of them whispered, and they fled.

Norris writes:

> One of the hardest things I have ever had to do was to walk back into that classroom, knowing that three pairs of eyes would be watching me very intently. I did not then understand that those girls might feel some remorse. I did wonder if they would worry that I had recognized their voices. But I hadn't been at their school long enough to do that. Every girl in that room was suspect to me. And a few minutes in the bathroom had taught me that it was decidedly "their" school, and that I was an unwel-

come interloper....I had to struggle with myself not to run away that afternoon. I did not do so because I am stubborn, and proud. I refused to let my enemies know—already they had become my enemies—how deeply they had wounded me.

Words can hurt. Avoid the verbal negatives for the Wednesdays of Lent.

The fourth lenten practice is to let the word "no" fall more often from your mouth. After all, your "nos" define you every bit as much as your "yesses." Jesus is our guide. When he cured the man possessed of a demon and that man wanted to follow him, he said no. "Go home to your friends, and tell them how much the Lord has done for you, and what mercy he has shown you." You will give glory to God if you bloom where you're planted.

When Pilate questioned Jesus, he shook his head no and refused to answer, for he knew Pilate wasn't really after the truth. He said no to the pain-dulling hyssop offered to him on the cross. He would go all the way for us. And in today's gospel, Jesus said no to turning stones into bread for he did not come to serve himself. (On the other hand, when it came to giving bread to others, to the five thousand in the desert, he said yes.)

So, be like Jesus for Lent. Say no to drugs. Say no to premarital sex. Say no to infidelity. Say no to cheating. Say no to lies. Say no to over-consumption. But say yes to truth. Say yes to words that encourage and heal. Say yes to charitable deeds and sharing. Say yes to prayer time. Say yes to your family's need for your presence and time. Say yes to Jesus.

So let's repeat our four lenten practices: first, watch out for foul, dirty language; second, avoid judgments; third, avoid verbal negatives; and fourth, learn to speak the word "no." Cleaning up our mouths makes room for the positive words, for the encouraging word we all need, and for the prayer-word we must speak in sincerity and truth. All this is very hard work because we usually don't even think about what comes out of our mouths. But listen to yourself. Listen to your friends. Listen in on conversations and hear the vulgarities that weave through them. Then, like the grandma in our story, ask yourself, "I eat with this mouth?" More to the point: you eat the Body and Blood of Christ with that mouth? You take communion with that mouth?

The devil offered to turn stones into bread if Jesus would feed only himself, and Jesus opened his mouth and said no. The devil offered a magic show if Jesus would be popular, and Jesus opened his mouth and said no. The devil offered a mall full of goodies if Jesus would sell his soul, and Jesus opened his mouth and said no.

God offered Jesus the cross for our salvation. Jesus opened his mouth and said, "Father, not my will but thine be done."

14

MARK BECOMES A CHRISTIAN

During these forty days of Lent, as you know, the RCIA candidates—that is, those in the Rite of Christian Initiation of Adults—are going through several steps in a process which will culminate with their baptisms on Holy Saturday night. This process of initiation is a very ancient one, based on the catechumenate of the early centuries of Christianity. The catechumenate was a long training period that included instruction, prayer, fasting, and conversion, as well as learning how to live as a Christian. It was a spiritual internship.

Here is how it worked back then. Someone from the Christian community would sponsor a candidate and give the name of this candidate to the bishop. The sponsor testified to the candidate's honesty and worthiness. Bishops had to be careful in those days lest they unwittingly took in a Roman spy who would eventually turn in all the Christians of the area.

Over the years that followed, the sponsor worked, prayed, and fasted along with the candidate until the candidate made a final decision to become a Christian. This process could last for many years. To catch something of the spirit of this preparation, right through to the completion of the Christian initiation rites, let us follow an imaginary candidate through the steps. We'll call him Mark.

Mark is twenty-six now. For a long time, he has been distressed at the empty paganism in which he was brought up. Like many a young man in our own times, Mark has been searching for meaning in his life. Well, three years ago he heard about the new Christian religion. Carefully, he has ascertained a person to whom he could speak. With much caution, he found a sponsor to instruct, guide, and pray with him.

And so, for the last three years, Mark has met with the Christian community. First, he has undertaken a serious routine of prayer, scrutinies, and exorcisms. At the same time, he has been investigating the Christian community. Does he want to be like these people? Are they living what they profess? (It is worth remembering that the RCIA candidates today are doing the same with us, that is, putting us under investigation to see if it's worthwhile to become Catholic.)

Now Mark has arrived at the beginning of Lent. He has to decide whether he will become a Christian, whether or not to hand in his name and request baptism. After much prayer, he decides to do just that. Mark is now ready for forty days of intensive learning. He will be allowed to come to the first part of Mass to hear the Scripture readings, after which he will be dismissed for prayer, meditation, and fasting. Almost daily during Lent he and the other candidates are led before the bishop, who questions them as to the sincerity of their motives and the worthiness of their characters. This questioning is called the "scrutinies."

The bishop also asks the candidates' neighbors, "Does this man live a good life? Does he respect his parents? Is he a drunkard or untrustworthy?" Once the bishop finds that the candidate is free from all the faults about which he has questioned the witnesses, he writes down the candidate's name. As he watches the bishop write his name, Mark's heart gives a jump. Why? Because he knows full well that in these times of persecution, should this book be found, it would be his death warrant. To have one's name written down in the baptismal register is a most serious commitment. It means risking one's life. (Being a Christian back then was no small matter.)

The exorcisms follow the scrutinies. To the ancients, the spirit of evil was no abstraction. Evil existed then as it does now, in the form of hatred and war and famine and injustice and corruption. But exorcism then did not imply devil possession. Rather, it implied that the candidates were in the bondage of sin. Exorcism was meant to help the candidates break away from sinfulness, to dramatize their determination to "put on Christ."

At last, Holy Week, the time for the culmination of all this preparation, the great week, arrives. The candidates will actually be baptized on Saturday night, the Easter vigil. The joyful tension is mounting.

On Holy Thursday, as he has been instructed, Mark takes a bath— not an ordinary bath, but one done consciously as a sign of ritual purification. Then, on Good Friday and Holy Saturday, Mark fasts and prays. At about ten o'clock on Holy Saturday night, Mark goes to a preappointed place. There, along with about seventy-five other young boys and men (the women are meeting elsewhere), he is brought into a large room. The sponsors are there, along with the bishop. The room is darkened and the ceremony begins.

As a body, the seventy-five men rise and face west. (Mark's teacher has told him that the west is the symbol of darkness and therefore, the abode of Satan, the place of evil.) Then one of the deacons shouts, "Stretch out your hands!" As the men stretch out their hands in the dark they try to feel the evil spirits and ward them off. They then expel their breath in an effort to blow the spirits away. On cue, all the candidates speak firmly out loud with one voice: "I detach myself from you, Satan, from your pomp, your worship, and your angels." There is a collective sigh of relief at that bold declaration. Mark feels it, and knows there will be no more pagan games, pagan idols, or pagan devil worship in his life.

The group suddenly makes an about-face. They turn noisily to the east and say, with even more firmness and volume: "And I attach myself to you, O Christ!" Their faces are brighter now for they all know that the east is a sign of life and therefore, a sign of Christ.

It was in the east that the Garden of Eden had been planted, the place of original innocence to which they all aspire. As it rises in the east, the sun brings newness, life, and brightness, the very things which are the fruits of baptism. They all know the Scripture verse which reads: "As the lightening appears from the east, so shall the Son of man appear." Turning away from the west (Satan) and toward the east (Christ) is a dramatic way of spelling out conversion, a word which means "a turning around."

Having thus turned from west to east, from darkness to light, and professed their faith, the men now stand with hands at their sides. Mark watches the bishop approach him and the others. He anoints Mark on the head with some oil. This is the seal, the *sphragis*. This is the mark of Christ, his brand. After all, shepherds put their mark on their animals and owners on their slaves. Why should it not be so for Christ?

The group now moves further into a pre-chamber to the baptistry. Here they strip off all their clothing to symbolize the words of Paul: "You have stripped off the old self with its practices." This is also a sign of returning to the primitive innocence of Adam and Eve, who went naked and felt no shame before sin entered into the world. Taking off one's clothes is a decisive gesture which means putting off vanity, frivolous ornaments, luxury, bad habits—in a word, anything that is incompatible with new life as a Christian. After the baptism, the candidates will be clothed with linen robes, a sign of new life.

Deacons now approach Mark and begin to anoint him once more with oil, this time from the top of his head to his toes. Oil is a preservative, and this anointing is a sign of preservation from sin. Rubbing the body with oil is common among the Greek athletes, especially wrestlers. Because these new Christians will have to wrestle with the power of evil, they too are rubbed all over and made, in Paul's words, "athletes for Christ."

After this anointing, Mark and the other candidates are led to the baptistry itself. While he awaits his turn, Mark notices how the shape of the pool is like a tomb or even a womb, a sign of rebirth in water and the Spirit. He recalls Jesus' words: "Unless a man is born again of water and the Spirit he cannot be saved." There is a brief blessing of the pool by the bishop; now the baptism is at hand.

Just before midnight, so it will be finished by the first moments of Easter Sunday, the baptism begins. Mark steps into the water, which comes up to his chest. The bishop kneels by the side of the pool and puts his hand on Mark's head. He applies a little pressure. Taking his cue, Mark ducks under the water and comes up. The bishop asks, "Do you believe in the Father?" Mark answers yes, and is ducked into the pool. "Do you believe in the Son?" "Do you believe in the Holy Spirit?" Mark answers yes to these questions, too. And so the bishop says, "Mark is baptized in the name of the Father and of the Son and of the Holy Spirit."

Mark comes out of the pool. It is now Easter. He is dried off and then anointed with myron, a special perfumed oil, on his five senses. This anointing is given with the prayer that Mark receive the Holy Spirit. The very name "Christ" is Greek for "anointed one," and so in this last anointing, Mark is reminded that he has received the Spirit of Jesus. Now Mark is clothed in a white linen robe which denotes the risen Christ, purity of life, and the forgiveness of sin. This robe will be worn for a full week until Low Sunday.

Mark is handed a lighted candle and given a kiss of peace. On this Easter Sunday morn, like the risen Lord, Mark is now radiant with his new life of faith. With the others, Mark is led to the awaiting assembly—the same people who had so impressed him with their style of living—to be greeted by them and partake, for the first time, in eucharist with them. And this is the completion of Mark's initiation into the Christian religion.

So that's the way it was back in the second century. And this is still the way it is today for hundreds of thousands of converts throughout the world who are preparing to be received into the church. We cradle Catholics take all this for granted. But by following the story of Mark through the process of initiation into the church, I hope you get a renewed sense of what means to be a Christian. Know what it costs, what it promises, most of all, the importance of your role as witnesses to Jesus Christ.

15

FAITH: RISKY BUSINESS

GENESIS 12:1–4

Let's start today with a story, this one from Max Lucado's book *And the Angels Were Silent*:

> They called him Artful Eddie, and he was the slickest of the slick lawyers. He was, as they say, one of the "roars" of the Roaring Twenties. A crony of Al Capone, he ran the gangster's dog tracks. He mastered a simple technique for fixing the races by over-feeding seven dogs, then betting on the eighth. Wealth. Status. Style. Artful Eddie lacked nothing. Then why did he eventually turn himself in? Why did he offer to squeal on Capone? What was his motive? Didn't Eddie know the consequences of ratting on the mob?
>
> He knew, but he had made up his mind. What did he have to gain? What could society give him that he didn't already have? He had money, power, prestige. What was the hitch? The hitch was his son. Eddie had spent his life with the despicable. He had smelled the stench of the underground long enough. He wanted more for his son. He wanted to give his son a name. But in order to give his son a name, he would have to clear his own. Eddie was willing to take a risk so that his son could have

a clean slate.

Artful Eddie never saw his dream come true. After Eddie squealed, the mob remembered. Two shotgun blasts silenced him forever. Was it worth it? It was for the son. Artful Eddie's boy lived up to his father's sacrifice. His became one of the best known names in the world.

But before we finish the story about Eddie's son, let's talk about the principle involved here: risky love. This is love that takes a chance, love that goes out on a limb. It's love that makes a statement and leaves a legacy, sacrificial love which is unexpected, surprising, and stirring. Risky love prompts actions that steal the heart and leave impressions on the soul, acts of love which are never forgotten, as we find in today's first reading.

If you count them up in your Bible, God made seven big promises to Abraham. This sounds like a wonderful deal until you consider that Abraham was at the not-so-tender age of seventy-five. He and his wife Sarah were not going to get the rest they deserved. Couldn't God have found a younger couple and commanded them to pack up and leave the land they knew and loved for a land they neither knew or loved? Abraham and Sarah were too old to pull up roots and start all over again; they were too old for risk-taking.

But God was never good at listening to arguments. He hassled another elderly couple, Elizabeth and Zechariah, in the same way. Why did God bother Abraham and Sarah just when they should have been settling down into old age? Why does God bother us just when we thought we were safe? God continually calls us to risk everything in love; Christianity is risky business.

Mrs. S. J. Brooks, a telephone operator in Folsom, New Mexico and a devout disciple of Jesus, took a risk. When warned to flee for her life from a flood that was speeding to engulf the town, she rejected the opportunity to save herself. Instead, she began calling up the towns-people and warning them of the imminent danger from the flood. More than forty families subsequently acknowledged that their lives were saved through the magnificent courage of one frail woman, whose lifeless body was found twelve miles down the canyon, with the telephone headpiece still attached to her ears.

A priest friend of mine, Fr. Vincent, is stationed at a parish in Manhattan. Every morning, my friend would have breakfast at a little deli downtown. And every morning, he would see the same crowd who also started their day at that deli. One day, Fr. Vincent walked into the deli and introduced himself to the crowd, then asked everyone there to also introduce themselves to each other. In doing so, he was just hoping for a more friendly atmosphere in the place—and it worked.

But interestingly, it worked for everyone but the owner. All he would reveal of himself was his name, Harry. After a few weeks, all the regular customers had become friends, and Fr. Vincent continued to pressure Harry to reveal a little more about himself. Finally, after much persuasion, Harry decided to take a risk. He reluctantly announced to all that Harry wasn't his real name: it was Hazim, and he was from Baghdad, Iraq.

The risk which Harry took was considerable. He could lose his customers—the majority of whom were Jewish—and the business he had spent so many years building up. You see, this was at the time when Saddam Hussein was a real threat to world security, and he had missiles trained on places like Tel Aviv. Tensions between Arabs and Jews were running high. Naturally, all the customers in the deli froze when Harry announced his national origin. No one said anything, but people drifted out one by one.

The next morning, as Fr. Vincent was shaving, he heard a radio report that the U.S. had begun bombing Baghdad. Father Vincent dropped what he was doing and ran to the subway, hoping to reach the deli before Harry opened that morning. Above all, he wanted to reassure the man of his friendship and love—and perhaps even protect him from the crowd.

As Fr. Vincent rounded the corner to the deli, he saw the regular morning crowd lining the sidewalk, waiting for Harry. When Harry arrived, he hesitated, almost turning back. Why had he taken the risk of revealing his real name? But while he was deciding what to do, all of his Jewish customers ran toward him and surrounded him with hugs and words of affection and encouragement. He wasn't the enemy; he was Harry. Wiping a tear from his eye, Harry said gruffly, "You know, you still have to pay for the doughnuts. But from now on, the coffee will always be free."

Mrs. Brooks, Harry, the customers—all these people took risks. Sometimes it's necessary to take risks, especially when it comes to the spiritual life. Remember, Jesus told a parable about three people to whom the king gave money. Two took risks and doubled the money. The other one refused to take a risk for the Master and buried the money away in the ground where it stayed and did nothing. Ultimately, this servant was condemned for not taking a risk.

Sometimes, the risky, extravagant gesture is needed, like the woman who took expensive perfume and poured it over the feet of Jesus. Jesus said to those who feigned shock, "Why are you troubling this woman? She did a good thing for me. This is the time for extravagant gestures, this is the time for risky love. This is the time to pour out your affections on one you love." Abraham and Sarah, the woman with the perfume, Jesus himself—all took risks. The Abraham story we heard today drives home this point: be a risky Christian.

Don't take part in drugs even if it means ridicule. Be chaste in a world that will mock you for it. Leave the room when they show an X-rated video and be called a lot of names. Give time to the poor and needy in a self-centered society. Give to charity and pass up spending more on yourself. Do something daring for Jesus or, to use Mother Teresa's words, "Do something beautiful for God." Be serious about your faith. Take risks with your life, your love, as Jesus risked his life for us.

Which brings us back to Artful Eddie, the Chicago mobster:

Had Eddie lived to see his son Butch grow up, he would have been proud. He would have been proud of Butch's appointment to Annapolis. He would have been proud of his commissioning as a World War II Navy pilot. He would have been proud as he read of his son downing five enemy bombers in the Pacific night and saving the lives of hundreds of crewmen on the carrier Lexington. Eddie's name was cleared. The Congressional Medal of Honor which Butch received was proof.

When people say the name O'Hare in Chicago, they don't think gangsters—they think aviation heroism. And now when you say this name, you have something else to think about. Think about the undying dividends of risky love the next time you fly into the airport named after the son of a gangster gone good—the son of Eddie O'Hare.

16

HOLY MOSES!

EXODUS 3:1-8, 13-15

Former Massachusetts congressman Tip O'Neill tells the story of a man called Honest Jake:

> Jake became well known in the Boston area because of his assistance to three generations of immigrant families. He owned a little variety store and would extend credit to the poor immigrants to help them get started in their new land.
>
> As Honest Jake neared his sixtieth birthday, a group of people he had helped decided to give him a party and a generous gift of money. Jake received the money gratefully and began to use it for a makeover. He had his teeth capped, and bought a hairpiece. He invested in a diet and exercise program and lost a lot of weight. He purchased a whole new wardrobe.
>
> Then he boarded a plane, and a few hours later the new Honest Jake hit the beach at Miami. There he met a beautiful young woman, asked her for a date, and she accepted. But before they could go out together, a thunderstorm came up. Honest Jake was struck by a lightning bolt and died instantly. In heaven, he said to God, "After all those years of hard work, I was just trying to enjoy myself a little. Why? Why me?" And God said to him, "Oh, is that you, Jake? Sorry, I didn't recognize you."

Jake's story is not unlike that of Moses. Moses had been raised in Egyptian affluence, in the palace of the pharaoh, a privileged lad. But one day, in a fit of passion, he killed an Egyptian overseer who was abusing the Hebrew slaves. He then fled, becoming a fugitive. Like so many other outlaws he went into the desert, changed his identity, and became a shepherd.

While tending to his sheep, he met the daughter of a very wealthy and influential man. Moses married this woman and so recovered the good life, with nobody the wiser, as he took on the role of a rich shepherd and landowner. Like Honest Jake, Moses had a makeover. He was safe and secure in his new role—until that day when he spied the burning bush. Or, more accurately, when the burning bush, like some divine bounty hunter, spied him.

Further on in the passage from Exodus, Moses declined four times to take part in God's plan to "go save my people." He wanted to remain anonymous; he wanted to duck God's call. First, Moses protested, he was nobody: "Who am I that I should go to the Pharaoh and bring the Israelites out of Egypt?" Second, he did not know God's name: "They will ask me, what is his name? What shall I say to them?" Third, no one would believe him: "But suppose they do not believe me or listen to me but say, 'The Lord did not appear to you?'" Fourth, Moses claimed he was not a public speaker: "O my Lord, I have never been eloquent...I am slow of speech and slow of tongue....Please send someone else."

Isn't it remarkable how enduring those objections have been? Why, they are the very same ones we use today to remain anonymous Catholics, to duck the call of God.

First excuse: I am nobody. "Who am I that I should go and bring the Israelites out of Egypt?" Well, who was Peter but a traitorous fisherman that he should lead the band of apostles? Who was Magdalene but a woman of the streets that she should become a saint? Who was Zacchaeus but a corrupt official that he should be called by Christ? Who was Augustine but an out-of-wedlock father that he should become a great bishop and theologian? "I am nobody" doesn't wash with God. It never has. For us to use that excuse, out of a sense of false humility, to duck our call to holiness is as lame as it was for Moses.

Second excuse: I do not know your name. Whose fault is that? Do you read Scripture? Have you ever read a spiritual book? We know all about Princess Di and Leonardo DiCaprio, the latest sales at Wal-Mart, the standings of our favorite sports teams, and a million items of trivia. But do we know Jesus? Christian evangelicals ask the question, "Have you accepted Jesus as your personal Savior?" Most of us don't know how to answer because we haven't accepted Jesus, in any guise. And thus, it may be true when we say, "I do not know your name."

Third excuse: no one will believe me. "Suppose they do not believe me or listen to me but say, 'The Lord did not appear to you?'" asked Moses. Suppose they do not believe me or listen to me and say it's indigestion or "you're getting religion: you'll get over it." Or they simply won't let me change because I make them feel uncomfortable. No one will take this happy-go-lucky guy seriously if he talks about religion. No one will take this ordinary woman seriously if she starts helping out at the hospital. So I back away from the burning bush. I have my image, my reputation to think of.

Fourth excuse: I am no public speaker. "O, Lord, I have never been eloquent...I am slow of speech and slow of tongue." Our version of Moses' objection is: I am ungifted, unimportant, slow of speech. So I will bury what little talent I have in the ground. Call someone else.

Excuses, objections, rationalizations: we use them all to ward off the Lord. And do you know what? We succeed at doing it, we duck our call. And yet...and yet...there is a burning bush inside us, a fire in our guts that won't be stilled; a hunger for God, for the divine in our lives; a dreadful need for meaning, commitment, acceptance, and love. Like Moses, we can offer what objections we might but the fire will not go out. The bush will continue to burn and beckon to us.

Actor Robert Duvall caught fire from the bush. He wrote, directed, and starred in that remarkable movie, *The Apostle*. Duvall tells the story of how he came to write this film. While on a trip down South, Duvall came across a church, about which he writes:

> I had never seen such an extraordinary outward expression of faith as I witnessed in the Pentecostal church. I had never seen a church like that. People could barely contain the joy of their faith. Folks were alive with it, imbued. Folks were on their knees singing praises and clapping, shouting to God! The air cracked with the Spirit. It was impossible to be a mere observer.
>
> I wanted to sing and shout with them. I couldn't explain it, but I knew the people in that church had a gift, a story to share. Somehow, someday, I would tell that story....What was most

important to me was to make a movie where Christianity was treated on its own terms, with the respect it deserves. Hollywood usually shows preachers as hucksters and hypocrites, and I was sick and tired of that. I wanted to show the joy and vitality I had seen with my own eyes and felt in my heart and in my life, the sheer, extraordinary excitement of faith. I especially wanted to capture the rich flavor, the infectious cadences and rhythm of good, down-home, no-holds-barred preaching.

As I began to write it, the story seemed to flow from me. I wasn't getting anywhere with Hollywood, yet my work on the movie filled my soul. One Sunday in New York City, I visited six churches, ending up at Harlem's vast Abyssinian Baptist Church. There, in a packed congregation before a huge choir, we all began to sing "What a Friend We Have in Jesus."

I found myself connected to the Lord in a way I had never felt before, deep within me. Yes, I thought, we're all kin through Jesus. Not just what we read about him in the Bible, but who he is. That was the secret to powerful faith, the power I wanted to convey in my movie.

The Pentecostal church which he found down South was Duvall's burning bush. He became a man on fire who answered the call.

The Moses story is our own. We are called to a mission of faith, and we give four good reasons why someone else should be called, not us. We try to deflect the heat, duck the summons, settle for being just an average, nondescript Catholic. But in our hearts we know, like Moses, that our objections are hollow.

Lent is a good time to expose such shallowness. God calls to us from the burning bush. We are chosen for holiness. Like Moses, we are people with a past, trying to blend into the general population, the secular background. But it's no use. The bush is burning and refuses to go out. But, as the gospel warns, we'd better give an answer before *we* go out.

17

YOU ARE MY SUNSHINE

JOHN 11:1–45

Love is stronger than death. So we are told in the striking words of Ezekiel: "I will open your graves." So we are told by St. Paul: "The one who raised Christ from the dead will give life to your mortal bodies also." And so we are told in the very human and powerful story of Lazarus returned from the dead. Each of the three readings today brings home the truth that love is stronger than death. In that light, let me share three true stories with you today.

Like all good parents, when Karen and her husband found out that another baby was on the way, they did what they could to help their three-year-old son, Michael, prepare for a new sibling. They found out the baby was going to be a girl, and so day after day, night after night, they gather Michael in their arms, and Michael sings to his sister in Mommy's tummy. He sings the only song he knows, "You are my sunshine." He sings it day after day, night after night.

The pregnancy progresses normally for Karen, an active member in her church. Then the labor pains come: every five minutes, every minute. But complications arise during delivery. Hours of labor; would a C-section be required? Finally Michael's little sister is born, but she is in serious condition.

With its siren howling in the night, the ambulance rushes the infant to the neonatal intensive care unit at St. Mary's Hospital.

The days inch by. The little girl gets worse. The pediatric specialist tells the parents, "There is very little hope. Be prepared for the worst." Karen and her husband contact a local cemetery about a burial plot. They had fixed up a special room in their home for the new baby; now they plan a funeral. Michael keeps begging his parents to let him see his sister. "I want to sing to her," he pleads.

Week two in intensive care: it looks as if a funeral will come before the week is over. Michael keeps nagging his parents about singing to his sister, but children are not allowed in the ICU. Finally, Karen makes up her mind. She will take Michael to the hospital whether they like it or not, figuring that if he doesn't see his sister now, he may never see her alive.

So she dresses Michael in an oversized scrub suit and marches him over to the ICU. He looks like a walking laundry basket, but the head nurse recognizes him as a child and bellows, "Get that kid out of here now! No children are allowed!" The mother instinct rises up strong in Karen, and this usually mild-mannered lady glares steely-eyed into the nurse's face, her lips a firm line. "He is not leaving until he sings to his sister!" Karen tows Michael to his sister's bedside. He gazes at the tiny infant losing the battle to live, and he begins to sing. In the purehearted voice of a three-year-old, Michael sings: "You are my sunshine, my only sunshine, you make me happy when skies are gray...."

Instantly, the baby girl responds. Her pulse rate becomes calm and steady. Keep on singing, Michael! "You never know, dear, how much I love you. Please don't take my sunshine away." The baby's ragged, strained breathing becomes as smooth as a kitten's purr. Keep on singing, Michael! "The other night, dear, as I lay sleeping, I dreamt I held you in my arms...." Michael's little sister relaxes as rest—healing rest—seems to sweep over her. Keep on singing, Michael! Tears conquer the face of the bossy head nurse. Karen glows. "You are my sunshine, my only sunshine....Please don't take my sunshine away."

Funeral plans are scrapped. The next day—the very next day—the little girl is well enough to go home!

In an article about this incident, *Woman's Day* magazine called it "the miracle of a brother's song." Karen called it a miracle of God's love. The medical staff simply called it a miracle. We call it the Lazarus story all over again. Love is stronger than death.

Some years ago, then-Vice-President George Bush spoke at a prayer breakfast. He told of his trip to Russia to represent the United States at the funeral of Leonid Brezhnev. The funeral was as precise and stoic as the communist regime. No tears were seen and no emotion displayed—with one exception.

Mr. Bush told of how Brezhnev's widow was the last person to witness the body before the coffin was closed. For several seconds, she stood at the side of the coffin. Then, in atheistic, communist Russia, she reached down and traced the sign of the cross on her husband's chest. In the hour of her husband's death she went not to Lenin, nor Karl Marx, nor Khrushchev. In the hour of death she turned to a Nazarene carpenter who had lived two thousand years ago, a man who had dared to cry out, "Lazarus, come forth!"

Finally, I want to tell you this story about my niece, who teaches brain-injured children. She really does a lot of wonderful things with them. One of my most poignant memories of her and the children was when she had her class stage a production of *My Fair Lady*.

My niece gave the lead role to a little girl in a wheelchair. In so doing, it never occurred to my niece that the audience—so conditioned by our self-imposed boundaries of what is possible and not possible—would weep, myself among them, when the little girl rolled herself across the stage singing, "I could have danced all night."

"Did I not say that if you believe you will see the glory of God?" These stories hearken back to something Jesus said: "If you, evil as you are, can give good things to those who ask you, how much more your Heavenly Father?" In other words, true stories such as I have just shared make credible the Lazarus story.

A little boy's song which brought his sister back to life; Brezhnev's widow marking the sign of the cross on her husband in a country that had outlawed religion; a crippled girl who innocently sang about dancing all night: if these things can happen on a mere human level, then how much more so with God? If such love as these stories attest to can indeed be present among us, why couldn't a more powerful love make life, not death, the last word to be uttered?

If we, evil as we are, can sing "You are my sunshine," why can't God sing "Untie him and let him go?" If the sign of the cross can make its appearance at the highest levels of official disbelief, why can't God say, "I am the resurrection and the life. Whoever believes in me, even if he die, will live, and everyone who believes in me will never die?" If a crippled girl can "dance" and sing, why can't God say, "Take away the stone?" If human love is fruitful, how much more so is God's?

Michael's song becomes Jesus' song raised to new heights. The widow's faith becomes Jesus': "whoever believes in me will never die." The crippled girl's song becomes Jesus' promise that we will all dance all night. Why is all this possible? The crowd had it right when they observed of Jesus, "See how he loved him."

18

BY THE SEASHORE

JOHN 21:1–19

How many of us recognize ourselves in the gospel we just heard? Well, we are there, right in the boat along with the fisherman. And we, too, are given a specific instruction: cast your net on the other side, that is, change your life. Move beyond your present bondage.

Psychologist Robert Johnson says, "Each person's psyche has an inborn evolutionary urge to grow, to integrate the contents of the unconscious, to bring together all the missing parts of the total individual into a complete, whole, and conscious self." Have we done that? Are we growing into mature, whole people? "By middle life most of us are accomplished fugitives from ourselves": do these words of John Gardner apply to us?

Indeed, many of us have become fugitives from ourselves as we strive to become somebody else, clones of the media which dictates how we should live, look, act, think, and dress. Spending twenty-eight percent of our free time with "the tube," we are easily made subject to the marketplace and advertisers who tell us that we are but rational animals, beasts with implanted computers, creatures with no future, no heaven, no God. All is now.

Anyone who doesn't sport Nikes, who drives a five-year-old car, or who hasn't bade farewell to virginity by age eighteen is a loser. We are told to live by the virtue extolled in the words of Frank Sinatra: "I did it my way." The result, as Marya Mannes writes, is that, "Certain words are too troublesome for us now: sacrifice, nobility, courage. Only suckers give up something they want for something others need. Only suckers act purely from moral conviction. Only suckers stick their necks our for what they believe, when what they believe makes others uncomfortable."

I remember a man coming to me—a very successful man who earned a lot of money—and he was miserable. He hated his job, and was sorry he was ever promoted. I asked him what his life was like *before* the promotion. Oh, he said, it was great. He actually looked forward to going to work every day. He enjoyed what he did, and he was good at it. He was liked by his coworkers. But then the company promoted him and now he's miserable. He forces himself to go to work. He's not sleeping well. His family is unhappy.

I asked him why he didn't go to his boss and ask to have his old job back. Well! He couldn't do that, he said; he needed the money. He had bills to pay. It seemed to me that a man who made so much money could get by with less but no, he just could not bring himself to do it. What would people think? In America, you don't go backward. You keep fishing off the same side, even if you keep coming up empty.

We are molded by our educational system to be cogs in the economy, technical units in the vast machinery of consumption, working all week and pigging out on the weekends. No time to reflect on what kind of people we are becoming, what kind of relationships we have, or whether we might be missing certain values in our lives.

Yet there is more to life than the sum total of our possessions, more than being like Leonardo DiCaprio or Cindy Crawford. There is more to life than casual sex and drugs and endless busyness, more than a career and worldly success. And so Jesus tells us: cast your nets, into the waters of prayer, into a world touched by God. Find your center in Jesus, in life beyond your own, in healthy relationships with family and friends, into the suffering and pain of self-giving that is the requisite for real happiness. Cast your nets into the other side of life.

Jesus' words are also meant for the many people who get caught in the game of "if only": if only I had been born to different parents; if only I were rich; if only I were taller (or shorter); if only I hadn't done this or that. We play the "if only" game over and over again. But unless we can learn to live with things as they are, we will continue to live in an illusion.

The way to become more human is to accept ourselves as what we are, along with the tangled webs that surround us: our wounds, past mistakes, contrary agendas, unexpected setbacks, and the like. Jesus said, cast your net on the other side. There is life and abundance there but we will never discover either one if we stay on the safe side, crying "if only!"

This story is echoed on the shoreline by the disciples. If only they hadn't fallen asleep in the garden of Gethsemane; if only they hadn't fled when the going got tough outside Pilate's chambers; if only they hadn't abandoned Jesus beneath the cross. And there is Peter, leader of the pack; if only he hadn't denied knowing Jesus—three times, no less.

In speaking to Peter, however—and to us all—Jesus did not accuse: "Why did you leave me? How could you have betrayed me? Why did you do it?" He said nothing of the past, for he accepted the past as past. What mattered was here and now. Jesus simply asked, "Do you love me?" Forget the past; forget the "if onlys"; forget the same tired, fruitless side of your life that you've been fishing from. Forget the guilt and the shame and forever wishing things didn't happen as they did or that you weren't as unlucky as you are. Cast your net on the *other* side.

Stephen Hawking's twisted body did not prevent him from becoming a brilliant scientist; blind and deaf Helen Keller became one of the noblest human beings ever; widowed and poor, Elizabeth Ann Seton became a teacher of teachers and a saint; adopted child Dave Thomas became the founder of Wendy's; New Jersey multimillionaire Charles Feeney gave away all his money to the poor. These people cast their nets out on the other side.

Jesus is speaking to those who are stuck in a rut—even when the rut is glamorous, fast-paced, and psychedelic, filled with perks and six-figure salaries. There is another side to life, a richer side, a more fulfilled side. Forget your past, forget your fruitless "if onlys."

Cast your net on the other side, into the wide sea of family, relationships, nobility, sacrifice, and service; cast your net into humanity, rather than material goods. What will you find if you cast your net on the other side? Exactly what the disciples found: a full net.

19

ORDINARY FOLK

LUKE 24:13–35

The appeal of this marvelous Emmaus story is that it talks about where we live. It's not about a high-falutin' revelation, or about great saints, or about exotic places and people. The Emmaus story is about ordinary, everyday despair and ordinary, Monday-morning drudgery. It's about bumping into a stranger on the way to work, about sitting down at a table, about sharing a meal. It's about our commonplace lives as we go through the motions of our day, vaguely wondering where God is in all of this, wondering, does my life matter? Will things get better? What's it all about, anyway?

You know the story. A couple of unknown, down-in-the-mouth followers of Jesus are trudging along a dusty road, chatting as they head back home and back to work. Their conversation is full of despair and discouragement, small talk, disappointment: life is a burden and doesn't live up to its promises.

Immediately, the readers of this tale know that these disciples are not just on the road to Emmaus, but they are on the road of life and have just experienced one more hurt, one more letdown. Where is God in all of this? When they meet the stranger, he asks them about their conversation and they recite their woes. Their conversation is ours, the everyday stuff: the kids, the economy, world crisis, spouses, lovers, school, the job, the boss, and so on, the threads of the daily fabric of our lives.

Then the two men add their disappointment. They say, "We were hoping...." Hoping for what? For answers to their questions, the same thing we all hope for as we move through life. Where is God? Does my life count? Does anything make any sense? Why should I have this sickness or betrayal or accident or death of a loved one? Why don't I have some sign that God is near? I could put up with anything if I felt the presence of God, I'm sure of that.

The Emmaus story picks up on the lives of every man and every woman and every child. We are all on the road of life: some just beginning their journey, some in the middle, and others near the end. Along the way we gossip, we win a few and lose a few, we enjoy the company of family and friends, and we despair when our enemies seem to win. And that is all part of the conversation on the road to Emmaus. Then the disciples sigh: "We were hoping for a God of justice and compassion to make sense of it all. And suddenly, into this routine conversation, this wandering and wondering, comes God, the stranger with the holes in his hands who shares food, shares himself.

And that is the point of the story: God is here. God penetrates our everyday lives, but we don't always know it. Just as our friends going to Emmaus finally recognized the Risen Christ—not in some fabulous technicolor explosion, but in the simple breaking of the bread—they remind us that God is there in our lives, too, although we don't see it most of the time. God loves us and wants to be near us; this story invites us to see that God's love can be found everywhere. Easter moments abound.

Let me share with you two true stories.

A man named Tom Long was once asked to be a speaker at a conference. On the plane headed home, he sat next to a older man who had also been at the conference, and they struck up a conversation. At one point, the man told Tom that he and his wife were the parents of several children, one of them a son in his thirties who was confined to a nursing home. This son had been injured badly in an automobile accident several years before and he was in a permanent comatose state.

The man startled Tom when he said, "We stopped loving our son. We visited him every week because it was our duty as parents, but we had stopped loving him. Love is a reciprocal relationship, giving and receiving. Our son could not receive, our son could not give. We went to see him, but we had stopped loving him. Until one day when we went to visit our son.

"We were surprised that he already had a visitor in his room. We did not know this person; he was a stranger. It turned out that this man was a eucharistic minister from the local parish who routinely visited patients in the nursing home. As we waited outside in the hall, we saw this visitor talking to our son, like they were engaged in a conversation. I thought to myself, 'As if my son could appreciate a conversation.'

"Then the man took out a Bible and read my son a psalm—as if my son could appreciate a psalm. Then he prayed a prayer as if my son could appreciate a prayer. And then he gave him communion as if my son could appreciate communion.

"And then it dawned on me that the man does know. Of course, he knows. He sees my son not simply through clinical eyes, but through the eyes of faith; he treats my son as a child of God."

This was a moment of grace for the man with the son, an Easter scene. The eucharistic minister was the stranger on the road to Emmaus, revealing the presence of God. God, who loves us deliriously, is in our lives and cares about us. Sometimes, it's a matter of practice to be able to discern him. I am reminded of my second story, the story of an old man dying of cancer:

The old man's daughter had asked the local priest to come and pray with her father. When the priest arrived he found the man lying in bed with his head propped up on two pillows and an empty chair beside his bed. The priest assumed that the old fellow had been informed of his visit. "I guess you were expecting me," he said.

"No, who are you?"

"I'm the new associate at your parish," the priest replied. "When I saw the empty chair, I figured you knew I was going to show up."

"Oh, yeah, the chair," said the bedridden man. "Would you mind closing the door?"

Puzzled, the priest shut the door.

"I've never told anyone this, not even my daughter," said the man, "but all my life I have never known how to pray. At Sunday Mass I used to hear the pastor talk about prayer, but it always went right over my head. Finally I said to him one day in sheer frustration, 'I get nothing out of your homilies on prayer.'

"'Here,' says my pastor, reaching into the bottom drawer of his desk. 'Read this book by Hans Urs von Balthasar. He's a Swiss theologian. It's the best book on contemplative prayer in the twentieth century.'"

"Well, Father," said the man, "I took the book home and tried to read it. But in the first three pages I had to look up twelve words in the dictionary. I gave the book back to the pastor, thanked him, and under my breath whispered 'for nothin'.'

"I abandoned any attempt at prayer," he continued, "until one day about four years ago my best friend said to me, 'Joe, prayer is just a simple matter of having a conversation with Jesus. Here's what I suggest. Sit down on a chair, place an empty chair in front of you, and in faith see Jesus on the chair. It's not spooky because he promised, "I'll be with you all days." Then just speak to him and listen the same way you're doing with me right now.'

"So, Padre, I tried it and I've liked it so much that I do it a couple of hours every day. I'm careful though. If my daughter saw me talking to an empty chair, she'd either have a nervous breakdown or send me off to the funny farm."

The priest was deeply moved by the story and encouraged the old guy to continue the journey. Then he prayed with him, anointed him with oil, and returned to the rectory. Two nights later the daughter called to tell the priest that her daddy had died that afternoon.

"Did he seem to die in peace?" he asked.

"Yes. When I left the house around two o'clock, he called me over to his bedside, told me one of his corny jokes, and kissed me on the cheek. When I got back from the store an hour later, I found him dead. But there was something strange, Father. In fact, beyond strange, kinda weird. Apparently just before Daddy died, he leaned over and rested his head on a chair beside his bed."

In the simple breaking of the bread; in the care of a comatose son; in the empty chair; in all of the routine comings and goings of our life along our own road to Emmaus, the Stranger—who is no stranger— is there.

And you know what? He loves you.

20

THE RAGMAN

JOHN 10:27–30

Three weeks ago, we heard the story of Peter and John running to discover an empty tomb. Two weeks ago, we listened as Thomas touched Jesus' wound. Last week, Jesus asked Peter, three times: "Do you love me?" This week, the Risen Shepherd promises that no one shall snatch us, his sheep, out of his hand.

What do all these post-resurrection accounts add up to? The answer is that they are not just about Easter, but about Jesus' entire life, death, and resurrection. Further, they are the story of our redemption. These gospels tell us that Jesus is the last word—not the frightening words like evil, darkness, and despair.

Jesus took all our anxieties, fears, and sins into the Garden of Gethsemane, infused them with love, and made hope the last word instead. Jesus took our hurt, suffering, pain, disillusionment, and betrayal upon himself in his passion, infused them with love, and made wholeness the last word. Finally, Jesus took death, our most dreaded enemy, upon himself at Calvary, infused it with love, and made eternal life the last word.

All the words to describe the limitations which confine human existence have become next-to-the-last words. Our redemption means that a love so full, so rich, so universal, so powerful, and so complete has shattered these human barriers, these human words, once and for all. "Jesus died for our sins" means that human limitations, including sin, are not final: life is. Jesus took our limited human condition upon himself and transformed it by his unlimited love.

Because we have heard it so often, perhaps this message doesn't affect us much anymore. So let me retell the Easter story, the story of our redemption, in another way. Listen.

Early before dawn one Friday morning, I noticed a young man, handsome and strong, walking down the alleys of our city. He was pulling an old cart filled with clothes both bright and new, and he was calling in a clear, tenor voice, "Rags! Rags! New rags for old! I'll take your tired rags!"

Now this is a wonder, I thought to myself, for the man stood six-feet-four, and his arms were like tree limbs, hard and muscular, and his eyes flashed intelligence. Could he find no better job than this, to be a ragman in the inner city? I followed him. My curiosity drove me. And I wasn't disappointed.

Soon the Ragman saw a woman sitting on her back porch. She was sobbing into a handkerchief, sighing and shedding a thousand tears. Her knees and elbows made a sad X. Her shoulders shook. Her heart was breaking.

The Ragman stopped his cart. Quietly, he walked to the woman, stepping around the tin cans, dead toys, and Pampers.

"Give me your rag," he said so gently, "and I'll give you another." He slipped the handkerchief from her eyes. She looked up and he laid across her palm a linen cloth so clean and new that it shone. She blinked from the gift to the giver.

Then, as he began to pull his cart again, the Ragman did a strange thing. He put her stained handkerchief to his own face and then he began to weep, to sob as grievously as she had done, his shoulders shaking. Yet she was left without a tear.

This is a wonder, I breathed to myself, and I followed the sobbing Ragman like a child who cannot turn away from mystery.

"Rags! Rags! New rags for old!"

In a little while, when the sky showed gray behind the rooftops, the Ragman came upon a girl whose head was wrapped in a bandage, whose eyes were empty. Blood soaked her bandage. A single line of blood ran down her cheek. Now the Ragman looked upon this child with pity, and he drew a lovely yellow bonnet from his cart.

"Give me your rags," he said, tracing his own line on her cheek, "and I'll give you mine."

The child could only gaze at him while he loosened the bandage, removed it, and tied it to his own head. The bonnet he set on hers. And I gasped at what I saw: for with the bandage went the wound! Against his brow ran a darker, more substantial blood—his own!

"Rags! Rags! I take old rags!" cried the sobbing, bleeding, strong, intelligent Ragman. The Ragman seemed more and more now to hurry.

"Are you going to work?" he asked a man who leaned against a telephone pole. The man shook his head.

The Ragman pressed him. "Do you have a job?"

"Are you crazy?" sneered the other. He pulled away from the pole, revealing the right sleeve of his jacket—flat, the cuff stuffed into the pocket. He had no arm.

"So," said the Ragman, "give me your jacket, and I'll give you mine." Such quiet authority in his voice.

The one-armed man took off his jacket. So did the Ragman— and I trembled at what I saw: for the Ragman's arm stayed in the sleeve, and when the other put it on, he had two good arms, thick as tree limbs, but the Ragman had only one.

"Go to work," he said.

After that he found a drunk, lying unconscious beneath an army blanket, an old man, hunched, wizened, and sick. He took the blanket and wrapped it round himself, but for the drunk he left new clothes.

And now I had to run to keep up with the Ragman, though he was weeping uncontrollably and bleeding freely at the forehead, pulling his cart with one arm and stumbling for drunkenness, falling again and again, exhausted, old, and sick—yet he went with terrible speed.

On spider's legs he skittered through the alleys of the city, this mile and the next, until he came to its limits and then he rushed beyond.

I wept to see the change in this man. I hurt to see his sorrow.

And yet I needed to see where he was going in such haste, perhaps even to discover what drove him so.

The little old Ragman—he finally came to a landfill. He came to the garbage pits. And then I wanted to help him in what he did, but I hung back, hiding. He climbed a hill. With tormented labor he cleared a little space on that hill. Then he sighed. He lay down. He pillowed his head on a handkerchief and a jacket. He covered his bones with an army blanket. And then he died.

Oh, how I cried to witness that death! I slumped in a junked car and wailed and mourned as one who has no hope because I had come to love the Ragman. I sobbed myself to sleep.

I did not know—how could I know?—that I slept through Friday night and Saturday and its night too. But then, on Sunday, I was awakened by a violent light.

Light—pure, hard, demanding light—slammed against my sleeping face and I blinked and I looked and I saw the last and first wonder of all. There was the Ragman folding the blanket most carefully, a scar on his forehead but alive! And, besides that, so healthy!

There was no sign of sorrow or of age, and all the rags he had gathered shined for cleanliness.

Well, I lowered my head and, trembling for all that I had seen, I myself got out of the junk car and walked to the Ragman. I told him my name with shame, for I was a sorry figure next to him.

Then I stripped myself of everything and I said to him with yearning in my voice, "Dress me. Make me new again!"

He dressed me, my Lord. He put new rags on me and I am a wonder beside him.

The Ragman! The Ragman! The Risen Christ!

21

KNOWING WHO YOU ARE

1 PETER 2:4–9

"You are a chosen race, a royal priesthood, a holy nation, God's own people, in order that you may proclaim the mighty acts of him who called you out of darkness into his marvelous light."

There is a story in Buddhist literature about a man who came up to a monk and said, "When I look at you, I see a pig!" And the monk said, "And when I look at you, I see the Buddha." The man said, "How is that?" The monk replied, "Well, what you see is what you are on the inside. If you see the Buddha, then you are the Buddha. If you see a pig...."

The Talmud tells us that "We do not see things as they are. We see things as *we* are." The spiritual life begins with knowing who you are. Your deeds then flow from this identity. Radio "shock jock" Howard Stern was discussing the Albanian refugee situation, which occurred during the war in Kosovo, on his program one day. Because of war and hate, these refugees have seen their homeland ravaged, their homes destroyed, their wives and daughters raped, members of their families tortured and killed; they have fled with only the clothes on their backs and now live in unsanitary camps, dying from hunger.

So what does Howard Stern say about these people? I quote from an article on this show that appeared in the *Wall Street Journal*: "The

Serbs are just having a good time...Those Albanian women are hot...look at this influx of hot chicks...look at those haunches." Stern's take on the tragedy at Columbine High School in Littleton, Colorado? "Some of those girls fleeing the school were really good looking." And then he wondered whether the suicide gunmen tried to have sex with any of the good-looking girls. Quote: "At least if you're going to kill all the kids, why wouldn't you have some sex?"

That is what Howard Stern sees because that is what he is. While other people who have compassion see traumatized kids in need of great and tender healing, he sees pigs. You do not see things as they are; you see things as you are.

All day, all night, all year long, advertisements try to tell you who you are and set your identity as a consumer of endless choices. Take, for example, a recent ad featuring Levi's jeans which ran across six full magazine pages. Using various photographs of five young couples, the ad portrayed the shifting sands of young love. The captions under each picture told us how long (or briefly) each couple stayed together: Callie and Ty, three years; Callie and Noah, one year, five months; Noah and Kim, two and a half years; Jeremy and Kim, eleven months; Jeremy and Andrea, a week and a half.

The final photograph shows Andrea hugging an unnamed girlfriend, while just behind the two girls a poster declares, "My parents got divorced." The caption underneath this picture reads: "At least some things last forever. Levi's: they go on." The message is clear: love doesn't last. Relationships come and go. Marriages don't last either, not even your parents' marriage. The only thing that lasts in life is the brand name you purchase from our company. Buy our product. It will tell you who you are.

Advertisers see kids as a commodity, a source of enormous profit. Here is a quote from the *New York Times*: "The 1999 version of a sixth grade math textbook currently used in about fifteen states remains drenched with product shots and trivia about everything from Barbie dolls, Cocoa Frosted Flakes, Sony Playstations, Spaulding basketballs, characters and entertainment sites owned by Disney and Warner Brothers, and fast-food fare from Burger King and McDonald's. Those who oppose salting a textbook with brand names say this is the most egregious example of advertising's steady march through public education."

What do you think using name brand items in textbooks teaches a captive audience of impressionable children? It teaches them that you are what you own and what you consume. The students don't see math, but brand names—because they are not students learning math but consumers learning brand names.

There is a violent video game called Postal which revolves around the killing of innocent adults and children. The creators of this game have worked it out so that the only way a player can exit the game is to put a simulated gun in his or her mouth and pull the trigger. The game's creators see the players not as chosen, holy, royal, or one of God's own, but as disposable.

In a current college textbook on marriage and the family, you can read the following in the first chapter, titled "One Hundred and One Choices on Relationships": "There is no one model for individuals, relationships, or marriages....Family diversity includes two parents, single parent families, same sex partners, opposite sex parents, step-families...multigenerational families...single-parent families headed by a woman or a man, child-free families and communal families.... Awareness of these alternative families expands the range of choices." These words well describe who we are today: rootless people incapable of commitment.

The Talmud is correct. We do not see things as they are. We see them as *we* are. And this is why the question "who are we?" is so important. Day and night, there are negative messages all around us from people who want to tell us who they think we are. The Howard Sterns of this world see us as objects; the imagemakers offer so many options and endless lifestyle choices that we never discover life itself; the advertisers preach a slick gospel which says that their products give us our identity.

But the words from Peter quoted before cut through all of this. Peter tells us a different story. We are a chosen race, he says, because God has called us by name; we are royalty because God calls us "beloved"; we are holy because Jesus told us so. We are God's own people because God gathers us as a mother hen gathers her chicks. Further, Jesus no longer calls us servants but friends. He goes to prepare a place for us, and he will come back and take us to himself. Jesus and Jesus alone is the way, the truth, and the life.

From day one, we need to teach our children who they really are deep down inside: beloved by a God who will leave a hundred dollars to search for a penny; who leaves ninety-nine sheep to seek out one lost little lamb; who is humble enough to wash their feet; who is "crazy" enough to suffer and die for them; who forgives them over and over again; and who is forever and ever the God of second chances.

A child can be the most unpopular, untalented, awkward nerd in the world, but no one—no one—can touch their inner dignity and worth. Each child, each one of us, is the beloved son, the beloved daughter in whom God is well pleased. There is nothing greater than that.

"You are a chosen race, a royal priesthood, a holy nation, God's own people." The scriptural writer is only passing on an ancient spiritual wisdom with these words. We must see ourselves and the world as who we are. And then we—chosen, royal, holy, God's own people—will act righteously towards others and toward ourselves.

22

MARY'S FIFTEEN MINUTES OF FAME

ACTS 1:12–14

"All these were constantly devoting themselves to prayer, together with certain women, including Mary, the mother of Jesus." Isn't that interesting? The writer of these lines from the Acts of the Apostles has brought Mary back into the picture.

Mary is not mentioned much in Luke's gospel. Luke features her, of course, as a model of faith and obedience during the time before and up to Jesus' birth. Here, Mary is center stage, and Luke gives us a lovely portrait of her as the one who said yes to God's messenger, the one who sang exuberantly of God's goodness to her, the one who treasured all these things in her heart.

Mary's presence is noted at the Presentation in the Temple, as well as when the twelve-year-old Jesus is lost for three days. But that's it. Unlike the other evangelists' accounts, in Luke we hear no more about Mary—until this passage from Acts which we just heard. And so we have Mary present at two significant births: the birth of the Messiah and, some thirty-three years later, the birth of the church. What did Mary do in the time between these two births?

People handle the loss of fame and recognition in different ways. One case stands out in my mind, a story about a girl named Ellen and her brush with fame:

She was very pretty, as I found out later from her photograph. A lovely, talented girl, she did some work in a little theater in New York. One of the writers who used to write for the old *Saturday Evening Post* saw her. He liked her and he had connections. He had a friend in Los Angeles, and he had arranged for her to go there for an interview.

Ellen bought a whole new wardrobe and all the rest. She was very excited. This was the beginning of a glorious career. Well, the day came for her to leave for the west coast. She said goodbye to her family and, before she left, she stooped down to say goodbye to her pet dog. In his frolicking, the dog put out his paw and accidentally scratched her a little bit on the cheek, but it didn't matter because a little makeup would cover that.

She arrived at Los Angeles and, as sometimes happens, her luggage was lost. She was unnerved by that. The man who was supposed to meet her was late. She was starting to get nervous and somewhat unstrung. Finally he came, but she had gotten so upset that she began to cry. And on top of that, her cheek where the dog had scratched was infected.

So between the crying and the infection and not having a wardrobe, the poor girl was in no mood to see anybody. The people out there were kind to her. They tried to calm her down. They told her, "Look, get yourself together and come back."

But she didn't come back. Instead she took the train back home. And back home she retreated into herself and fell under the protection of her doting widowed mother. She would see nobody. She began to eat and got very heavy. This alarmed her because her father had died from obesity. So she went to the other extreme: she went on a starvation diet.

When I met her, she was like skin stretched over bone. I talked to her. I suggested that she was at a point where she needed psychiatric care, but both she and her mother were very offended at that. Finally, she went to a psychiatrist I knew. But he said that at this stage, he couldn't do anything for her. He suggested that they try to get her on some vitamin regimen and build her up.

She died. She died of starvation with plenty of food on the table. And her mother said she died talking of the interview that went wrong like it happened last week instead of thirty years ago.

Well-known author and pastor Frederick Buechner writes sadly of his mother, who died a very lonely death as an old woman. Let me share his words with you:

> Being beautiful was her business, her art, her delight, and it took her a long way and earned her many dividends. But when, as she saw it, she lost her beauty…she was like a millionaire who runs out of money. She took her name out of the phone book and got an unlisted number.…
>
> With her looks gone she felt she had nothing left to offer the world, to propitiate the world. So what she did was simply to check out of the world as an old, last rose of summer, the way Greta Garbo and Marlene Dietrich checked out of it, holing themselves up somewhere and never venturing forth except in disguise.
>
> My mother holed herself up in her apartment…then in just one room of that apartment, then in just one chair in that room, and finally, in the bed where one morning a few summers ago, perhaps in her sleep, she died at last.

The artist Andy Warhol once made a comment that every person has fifteen minutes of fame in their lives. Ellen and Buechner's mother missed the invitation to reinvent love and fame in the eyes of God after their fifteen minutes of fame were over. Jesus' mother Mary, after her fifteen minutes, moved into a hidden life of care and service. For years she quietly nurtured Jesus, taught him, buried her husband, and finally let her son go as all mothers must. Then she stayed home to help others, going about unrecognized, growing deep into prayer and, most of all, being a special help to the has-beens.

Mary nurtured and inspired those whom age or sickness or changing tastes and fortunes had made obsolete, widows and widowers, orphans, the formerly employed, the one-time powerbrokers, and people of influence, all decent people who, for one reason or another, fell from grace. Mary devoted herself to showing these has-beens how to grow beyond what they once were.

Finally, after years of obscurity, after years of a deepening spiritual life, she is summoned to be present at birth of the church. She, old and venerable, would become mother to that church. Mary's fifteen minutes of fame, then her long obscurity, gained for her the position of the patron saint of the has-beens—the lost, those who have strayed, the hopeless sinners, anyone striving to reinvent ways of loving and living again after their fifteen minutes of fame are over. Through her long apprenticeship, Mary became for them the mother of hope, renewal, and compassion. This story, told by Max Lucado in his book, *No Wonder They Call Him Savior*, will illustrate:

The small house consisted of one large room on a dusty street. Its red-tiled roof was one of many in this poor neighborhood on the outskirts of a Brazilian village. For all that, however, it was a comfortable home. Maria and her daughter, Christina, had done what they could to add color to the gray walls and warmth to the hard dirt floor.

Maria's husband had died when Christina was an infant. The young mother stubbornly refused opportunities to remarry. Instead, she got a job and set out to raise her young daughter. Now, fourteen years later, the worst years were over. Though Maria's salary as a maid afforded few luxuries, it was reliable and provided food and clothing. And now Christina was old enough to get a job and help out.

Some said Christina got her independence from her mother. She recoiled at the traditional idea of marrying young and raising a family. Not that she couldn't have had her pick of husbands. But it was her spirited curiosity that made her keep all the men at arm's length. She spoke often of going to the city. She dreamed of trading her dusty neighborhood for exciting avenues and city life. Just the thought of this horrified her mother. Maria was always quick to remind Christina of the harshness of the streets. "People don't know you there. Jobs are scarce and the life is cruel. And besides, if you went there, what would you do for a living?"

Maria knew exactly what Christina would do, or would have to do for a living. That is why her heart broke when she awoke one morning to find her daughter's bed empty. Maria knew immediately where her daughter had gone. She also knew immediately what she must do to find her. She quickly threw some clothes in a bag, gathered up all her money, and ran out of the house.

On her way to the bus stop she entered a drugstore to get one last thing. Pictures. She sat in the photograph booth, closed the curtain, and spent all she could on pictures of herself. With her purse full of small black-and-white photos, she boarded the next bus to Rio de Janeiro.

Maria knew Christina had no way of earning money. She also knew that her daughter was too stubborn to give up. Knowing this, Maria began her search. Bars, hotels, nightclubs, any place with the reputation for streetwalkers or prostitutes. She went to them all. And at each place she left her picture taped on a bathroom mirror, tacked to a hotel bulletin board, fastened to a corner phone booth. And on the back of each photo she wrote a note.

It wasn't too long before both the money and the pictures ran out, and Maria had to go home. The weary mother wept as the bus began its long journey back to her small village.

It was a few weeks later that young Christina descended the hotel stairs. Her young face was tired. Her brown eyes no longer danced with youth but spoke of pain and fear. Her laughter was broken. Her dream had become a nightmare. A thousand times over she had longed to trade these countless beds for her secure pallet. Yet the little village was, in too many ways, too far away.

As she reached the bottom of the stairs, her eyes noticed a familiar face. She looked again, and there on the lobby mirror was a small picture of her mother. Christina's eyes burned and her throat tightened as she walked across the room and removed the small photo. Written on the back was this compelling invitation: "Whatever you have done, whatever you have become, it doesn't matter. Please come home." And Christina did.

Maria. Mary. The same message, the same person, really. The same invitation to new beginnings. Mary, who knew the ups and downs of life and the changing fortunes of fame, has the same message for us all: "Whatever you have done, whatever you once were, whatever you have become, it doesn't matter. Please come home."

In the end, of course, Mary did gain fame all over again, this time not as the biological mother of Jesus, but as a true disciple, a faithful follower, the mother of the church. The woman who was wrapped in silence for so many years became the mother of compassion, pity, reconciliation, and new beginnings. She became someone whom we all could turn to in time of need.

"All these were constantly devoting themselves to prayer, together with certain women, including Mary the mother of Jesus." Oh, yes: Mary, the mother of Jesus. You remember her....

23

SIGNS OF A HEALTHY PARISH

ACTS 2:1–11

Pentecost is often considered the birthday of the church. Actually, the church was born out of the side of Christ on Calvary. But we can say that Pentecost celebrates the church "going public."

Tradition teaches that there are four marks of the church: it is one, holy, catholic, and apostolic. The documents of the Second Vatican Council state that the local parish is not merely a franchise of the universal church, but the whole church realized locally in itself. And when the church is seen as the local parish, the four marks can be translated differently. They become the four Ms: melding, ministry, mirth, and mission, and they are the marks of a healthy parish. Let's define these words within the context of today's Scripture readings.

Take the first reading. It speaks of melding into a new community. "They asked in utter amazement, 'Are not all these men Galileans? How is it that each of us hears them in his native tongue? We are Parthians, Medes, and Elamites. We live in Mesopotamia, Judea, and Cappadocia, the province of Asia, Phrygia, and Pamphylia, Egypt and regions around Cyrene. There are even visitors from Rome....Yet each of us hears them speaking...about the marvels God has accomplished."

The cry must be the same in a healthy parish: "We are from Staten

Island, Bergen County, Manhattan. We grew up in Hackensack, the Oranges, Nutley, Jersey City, Hoboken, Bloomfield, Brielle, Point Pleasant, and the regions around Delaware and Maryland. There are even visitors from England, Ireland, and Australia. Yet each of us hears about the marvels God has accomplished."

And what marvels should all these expatriates hear? The answer to this question leads us to the second reading and the second M: ministry. "There are different gifts but the same Spirit; there are different ministries but the same Lord; there are different works but the same God who accomplishes all of them in everyone." Could there be a better description of a healthy parish? Look around a healthy parish and you will note the many gifts, the extraordinary ministries, the outreach, the care and concern of parishioners. From a wonderful religious education program to the liturgical ministries, from the social committee to social justice group, from counseling services to the Monday night novena, a healthy parish makes the words of the Pentecost Sequence, which we hear today, very real:

In our labors rest most sweet,
Pleasant coolness in the heat.
Consolation in our woes.

Cleanse our soiled hearts of sin,
Arid souls refresh within,
Wounded lives to health restore.

Bend the stubborn heart and will.
Melt the frozen, warm the chill.
Guide the wayward home once more.

This is the charism of a healthy parish. Any such parish, founded on shared and collaborative ministry, serves as a model of "different gifts but the same Spirit."

That brings us to the gospel, and two pregnant sentences from it that speak of the third and fourth marks of a healthy parish. The first sentence is, "At the sight of the Lord, the disciples rejoiced." Added to melding and ministry, what has always made a parish healthy is mirth, rejoicing. No parish, of course, is a stranger to tears and grief, to sorrow and loss, to tragedies and death. But beneath and between the tears lies the bedrock of faith that justifies rejoicing.

"At the sight of the Lord, the disciples rejoiced." Holy laughter in the corridors of a healthy parish has always taken the edge off sorrow. Like my embarrassment once as I was customarily greeting people after Mass, and rather jauntily said to one lady, "Mary, where is your husband this morning?" She answered (rather tartly, I thought), "Where's my husband? Right where you buried him last week." Oh God, how could I have forgotten! (I might add that this woman has since forgiven me.)

And then there is the teacher who told me about the time she read the parable of the Good Samaritan to her class. After reading the story, she asked the class why the priest did not go over and help the man by the wayside. A little girl answered, "Because he saw that the man had already been robbed."

You may appreciate this story which George Bush once told. While he was president, Bush made a public relations visit to a nursing home. There he came upon a wizened old man hobbling down the corridor. President Bush took the man's hands in his own, looked into his eyes, and said, "Sir, do you know who I am?" The man replied, "No, but if you ask one of the nurses, she'll tell you."

Then there was the teacher who asked her third-graders to write about their personal heroes. One little girl brought home her essay and showed it to her parents. Her father was flattered to discover that his daughter had chosen him as her hero. "Why did you pick me?" he asked expectantly. The little girl replied, "Because I couldn't spell Schwarzenegger."

The following dialogue is taken from an actual court transcript:

Q. Mrs. Smith, do you believe that you are emotionally unstable?
A. I should be.
Q. How many times have you committed suicide?
A. Four times.
Q. The truth of the matter is that you were not an unbiased, objective witness, isn't it? You, too, were shot in the fracas.
A. No sir, I was shot midway between the fracas and the navel.

Do you hear the sound of laughter here? That is the sound of disciples rejoicing. Because even though our individual sorrow may be great, the pentecostal spirit of our parish has always made us laugh because here we are taught that God will have the last word. At the sight of the Lord, *we* disciples rejoiced—always a sign of the Risen Presence.

And finally, there is this sentence from today's gospel: "Jesus came and stood among them and said, 'Peace be with you.' After he said this, he showed them his hands and his side. Jesus said to them again, 'Peace be with you. As the Father has sent me, so I send you.'" These words speak of mission, our last characteristic of a healthy parish. They remind us that the task is far from finished. Years of what has been points to what must yet be, what lies ahead.

Jesus still shows his hands and his side today. He still bears his wounds in the poor and downtrodden. He still testifies to the terrible hunger for God which many people feel, yet which they don't know how to satisfy. And so they look for satisfaction in the slick, counterfeit ways of drugs and sex and material consumption.

Jesus still stands before this parish, as he does before every faith community, and shows us his wounds. Each and every one of us needs to tend to these wounds, for Jesus will not allow complacency to set in. Thus the parish's mission continues.

And so, to sum up, the four marks of a healthy parish are melding, ministry, mirth, and mission. These four qualities must be part of every parish's past, present, and future; its faith, hope, and love; its pride, joy, and challenge; its goal and its Pentecost.

24

THE JANITOR'S HANDS

JOHN 20:19–23

I would like to tell you two stories from my childhood which will help shed light on this feast of Pentecost.

When I was a child, my parish church of the Sacred Heart in New Brunswick was an attractive semi-Gothic building, with pillars that formed arches inside the body of the church and the nave. In the highest part of the arch in the sanctuary was a very large triangle with rays of lights emanating from it. Inside this triangle was a single, enormous eye. I went to the school behind the church, and since my home was only a block away, an apartment above our bakery shop, I would, as Sister urged us, stop in for a quick visit on the way home from school. Although I liked the church and its smells and sights, I was, like any little boy of six or seven, always intimidated by that large eye high above the altar always looking at me.

One day when I shot in for a quick visit, an old lady was there saying her rosary. She noticed me gaping apprehensively at the eye and she motioned me to come over to her. "You're one of the Bausch boys, aren't you?" she asked. I nodded. She sat me down beside her and held my hand. Looking up at that eye she said, "Son, some people will tell you that that eye means God is always watching you to see when you are doing wrong, so he can punish you." Then she paused and looked at me. "I don't want you to think of it that way. Every time you see that eye, I would rather have you remember that God loves you so much he can't take his eyes off you."

What a difference it made to look at the eye in that way! God was in love with me, just like my mother and father loved me. I was the apple of his eye. And every time after that, when I went in for a visit, I would wave at the eye and say, "Here I am! It's me, Billy."

My other childhood memory is of the time that our pastor visited us in class one day. Much to our surprise, with the pastor was Mr. Curry, the janitor. The pastor said, "I want you children to look at this man's hands." The janitor, an obviously embarrassed but obedient member of the flock, held out his palms for us to see. His hands were calloused and dirty, the type of hands that warranted immediate dismissal from the dinner table in my house.

The pastor then held up Mr. Curry's right hand for us to see. "These hands do the Lord's work," he said. We all looked at each other. Some of us were thinking that these very same hands grasped a mop to clean up a third-grader's spilled lunch, and we wondered about the extent of the Lord's interest in the task. "This man's hands," the pastor continued, "have cleaned our church, kept your school running, and washed the statues of Jesus, Mary, and Joseph that grace our lawn. This man's hands—this man's life—are dedicated to the Lord in each and every thing he does. Take a good look at your hands and see that they do the same."

These two stories underscore a misunderstanding we have about Pentecost. When we say that this feast is the birthday of the church, what most of us are really thinking, the image that immediately pops up, is that Pentecost is the birthday of the hierarchical church. Pentecost, we feel, is the feast of the institutional caretakers—popes, cardinals, archbishops, bishops, pastors, priests—who form less than one percent of the total Catholic population.

And so many of us think that the more we imitate the ordained—the more we do what they do, the closer we are to the altar, so to speak—the more holy we are. Likewise, a reverse statement follows: the less time we spend on "church" things—like teaching in the religious ed program, or becoming a lector or eucharistic minister, or cleaning the church—the less near we are to God.

The result of this mindset is that holiness seems to move in a descending order of unworthiness. And it's all based on what you do for the church, not anything to do with how you live out your faith at home, or work, or in the neighborhood.

As a kid, I remember that the most we non-church folk could hope for was to sneak into purgatory with a scorched rump when our time came. Even retreats for the laity implied this message with the usual focus on prayer and the sacraments. One would seldom, if ever, hear anything about using the gifts of the people for public witness and service in the midst of the world. And so the equation came down to this: church activity equals heightened spirituality; worldly activity equals danger.

Even our good works can unintentionally give the wrong message. For example, we are called out of our daily lives and neighborhoods to work in soup kitchens, homeless shelters, AIDS residences, nursing homes, peace groups, and so forth. Which, by all means, is a wonderful and noble response to Christian service. But what often happens is, ordinary people conclude that ministry and service and gospel living all fall into a category apart from their everyday lives. There is an implication that gospel living is only found outside of our ordinary, daily work and routines.

And so we have never developed a spirituality of everyday-ness, an understanding of a God who is planted where you are, a sense of calling and mission, of co-creation, a sense that God loves us so much at every moment that he cannot take his eyes off us. A sense, in short, of being church.

I like to remind parents that above all other people, they have the best chance of salvation. Why? Because in the well-known passage from Matthew, Jesus gives us the only requirements for salvation. These requirements are known as the corporal and spiritual works of mercy. The beautiful part is that they are built right into normal family life.

In raising children, parents cannot avoid heaven. Feed the hungry, give drink to the thirsty, clothe the naked: each work of mercy is found right in the boring routines of everyday living. Not in the sanctuary, not in the foreign missions, not in the hierarchy, but right there in the home and neighborhood. How, you say?

With the 2:00 AM bottle: giving drink to the thirsty.
Diapering: clothing the naked.

Cough medicine to the bedroom: visiting the sick.

Preparing meals: feeding the hungry.

"Dad, can you help me with my homework?": instructing the ignorant.

"Mom, what'll I wear?": counseling the doubtful.

The cat died: burying the dead.

Hearing the kids' prayers: praying for the living and the dead (endlessly).

"Are you still in the bathroom?": visiting the imprisoned.

This is being church; this is what church is all about; this is where we find church. The Spirit fell on us at baptism to both uncover and witness to God in our daily lives, in our world. Mystery writer Dorothy Sayers was on target when she once remarked that it is unfortunate that at church on Sunday morning, a carpenter hears, "Don't get drunk on Saturday night, and be sure to give enough in the collection," instead of hearing "Be the best carpenter you can be."

But we resist the notion that we are church, ordinary folks doing everyday things. We think that holiness has to be found elsewhere, not in our home, neighborhood, school, or workplace. But God has loving eyes on us at every moment. God has given us blessed hands to be church where we are, right here and now, not somewhere or sometime else.

During a weekend retreat some years ago, I listened to a successful lawyer talk about the ministries in which he was involved, for example, the Cursillo movement, RCIA, and so on. At one point I asked this obviously good-willed man about the workaday world of his professional life. Did he encounter values and practices contrary to the gospel there? And if so, what did he as a Catholic do about them?

The man's answer was revealing: "I don't even want to look at that question," he said. Somewhere along the line, like so many other people, he had interiorized the erroneous idea that being church was confined to church activities—not something that should be the witness and fabric of our everyday life.

Actually, early Christian tradition gives us an almost exclusively lay church. Some people were indeed called to follow Jesus, to be disciples; but most of those New Testament people were grounded and remained grounded in their world. Think, for example, of Zacchaeus, or Simon's mother-in-law, or Jairus and his daughter, the Jericho blind man, the woman with the hemorrhage, the woman at the well, even Martha, Mary, and Lazarus.

God established the church as a people, as all of us, not just a clerical few. The church is you and I, called to live decent, moral lives and bear witness to the gospel. And we are called to do this right here, in the trenches of everyday living, loving, hurting, struggling, and dying. Recall, after all, St. Paul's words in today's second reading: "Now there are varieties of gifts, but the same Spirit....To each is given the manifestation of the Spirit for the common good....For in the one Spirit we were all baptized into one body...we were all made to drink of one Spirit."

So it comes down to this: today is *our* feast, not a feast of the hierarchy. Pentecost is a public declaration that God loves each of us so much he cannot take his eyes off us. As a result, God has poured out his Spirit on all of us and has given us, so to speak, a janitor's hands to share that love. Pentecost is God's official delegation of us as church in the everyday-ness of life.

"They were all filled with the Holy Spirit and began to speak in different tongues as the Spirit enabled them to proclaim." We ourselves are filled with the Holy Spirit so that we, the church, can speak the hope-filled message of love and redemption in our different tongues, that is, in our various walks of life and in our different accents.

My advice today? Go home, look in the mirror, and exclaim, "Happy birthday, church!"

FEASTS *and* CELEBRATIONS

25

NO COMPROMISES

JOHN 18:33-37

The gospel today gives us a rich tapestry of a scene fraught with drama and color as the two protagonists square off. Pilate is nervous. He has been in and out of the praetorium seven times, between the people and the prisoner. In his heart he knows Jesus is innocent—after all, his wife had a dream about that. But in his mind he knows he must play the game of politics, and so he mixes up a compromise: he washes his hands and then sends Jesus off to his death.

And so Pontius Pilate comes down in history as the great compromiser. He represents all who compromise their principles and so continue to sentence Christ to his death. On the other hand, there are those who do not compromise, those who demonstrate by their lives that Christ is king and they will follow him. When Christ is king, when Jesus really matters to people, the compromises fall away before the truth. Let me share some stories about people who would not compromise.

In April, 1940, Nazi Germany invaded Denmark. There was little resistance because the Danes felt it would be hopeless. A puppet Danish government got on as best it could. But then, in 1943, German policy toughened. It was decided to impose on Denmark the same "final solution" of exterminating Jews, as elsewhere.

Suddenly, there was a remarkable transformation within Denmark. German officers leaked the plan to the Danish resistance. Escape routes were quickly organized. Jewish people tell how complete strangers approached them in the streets with the keys to their houses so they could hide. Train guards and boat captains joined the plan.

Within a few weeks, all but a few of the 7000 Jews had been whisked over the Oresund to safety in Sweden. Some even tell how their escape boats were boarded and searched by German patrol vessels, yet the Germans let them through. For many Danes it eventually meant the concentration camp and death. But faced with the very human need of the Jews, it seemed that a whole nation—and many Germans, too—turned their back on political compromise and performed a true and great act of love.

This story tells of the remarkable courage of one man:

Private Joseph Schultz, a loyal, young German patrol soldier, was sent to Yugoslavia shortly after it was invaded. One day the sergeant called out eight names, Schultz's among them. They thought they were going on a routine patrol, and as they hitched up their rifles, they came over a hill, still not knowing what their mission was.

There were eight Yugoslavians there, standing on the brow of the hill; five men and three women. It was only when they got about fifty feet away from them, when any marksman could shoot out an eye of a pheasant, that the soldiers realized what their mission was.

The eight soldiers were lined up. The sergeant barked out, "Ready!" and they lifted up their rifles. "Aim," and they got their sights. And suddenly in the silence that prevailed, there was a thud of a rifle butt against the ground.

The sergeant, and the seven other soldiers, and those eight Yugoslavians, stopped and looked. And Private Joseph Schultz walked toward the Yugoslavians. His sergeant called after him and ordered him to come back, but he pretended not to hear him. Instead, he walked the fifty feet to the mound of the hill, and he joined hands with the eight Yugoslavians.

There was a moment of silence, then the sergeant yelled,

"Fire!" And Private Joseph Schultz died, mingling his blood with those innocent men and women. Later found on his body was an excerpt from St. Paul: "Love does not delight in evil, but rejoices in the truth. It always protects, always trusts, always hopes, and always perseveres."

Finally, a story from the early 1960s:

During the prime days of the struggle for racial integration in the South, black civil rights workers—"freedom riders," they were called—would travel on buses from city to city, challenging segregationist laws. Sometimes they were greeted with violence; often they were arrested. In one town, a bus was halted by the police, and the passengers were booked and jailed.

While they were there, the jailers did everything possible to make the freedom riders miserable and to break their spirits. They tried to deprive them of sleep with noise and light during the nights. They intentionally oversalted their food to make it distasteful. They gradually took away their mattresses, one by one, hoping to create conflict over the remaining ones.

Eventually the strategies seemed to be taking hold. Morale in the jail cells was beginning to sag. One of the jailed leaders, looking around one day at his dispirited fellow prisoners, began softly to sing a spiritual. Slowly, others joined in until the whole group was singing at the top of their voices.

The puzzled jailers felt the entire cellblock vibrating with the sounds of a joyful gospel song. When they went to see what was happening, the prisoners triumphantly pushed the remaining mattresses through the cell bars, saying, "You can take our mattresses, but you can't take our souls."

It was the hymn singers who were in jail, but it was the jailers who were guilty. It was the prisoners who were suffering, but the jailers who were defeated. It was the prisoners who were in a position of weakness, but it was the broken and bigoted world of the jailers and of all the Pontius Pilates of history that was perishing.

What makes people take such stands in life when others do not? What makes them spurn the role of Pilate when others embrace it? I don't think there's much of a mystery here. The answer is as simple as it is true—as this little bit of wisdom tells us:

When you thought I wasn't looking, I saw you hang my first painting on the refrigerator, and I wanted to paint another one.

When you thought I wasn't looking, I saw you feed a stray cat, and I thought it was good to be kind to animals.

When you thought I wasn't looking, I saw you make my favorite cake just for me, and I knew that little things are special things.

When you thought I wasn't looking, I heard you say a prayer, and I believed there is a God I could always talk to.

When you thought I wasn't looking, I felt you kiss me good night, and I felt loved.

When you thought I wasn't looking, I saw tears come from your eyes, and I learned that sometimes things hurt, but it's all right to cry.

When you thought I wasn't looking, I saw that you cared and I wanted to be everything that I could be.

When you thought I wasn't looking, I looked, and wanted to say thanks for all the things I saw when you thought I wasn't looking.

In her book *Out of Africa*, Isak Dinesen tells the story of a young man from the Kikuyu tribe who worked for her on her farm for three months. He suddenly announced that he was leaving her to go to work for a Muslim man nearby. Surprised, Dinesen asked him if he was unhappy working for her. He told her that all was well, but that he had decided to work for a Christian for three months to study the ways of Christians, and then work for a Muslim for three months to study the ways of a Muslim. After experiencing both, he was going to decide whether to be a Christian or a Muslim.

What about that? What would this young man choose if he lived among us and saw, when we thought he wasn't looking, what we did and how we acted and how we treated each other? I wonder. Would he see Pontius Pilate or Private Schultz?

As always, the gospel comes back to haunt us. Light and darkness, right and wrong, principle or compromise, Pilate or Jesus: it was all there then, just as it is all here now. Every day. "For this I came into the world, to testify to the truth." That is what we are here for, too—isn't it?

26

A RELATIONSHIP OF LOVE

JOHN 16:12–15

I want to start off today by talking about General Ulysses S. Grant. As you may know, Grant had a terrible drinking problem. The only friend who was really close to him was a lawyer friend named John Rawlins. Rawlins convinced Grant to take a pledge to stay sober, particularly during the Civil War. And when Grant fell off the wagon and went back to drinking, it was John Rawlins who went to him as a friend, confronted him, and reminded him once again how many people depended on him.

If you go to Washington, D.C., you can look in front of the Capitol and you'll see an heroic statue of General Grant on his horse. But if you go down Pennsylvania Avenue to the other end, south of the Capitol, you will find a park called Rawlins Park. In that park is a very nondescript statue of John Rawlins. Yet the truth is, literally and figuratively, the only reason Grant stayed on his horse was because of John Rawlins.

Let me share another thought, this time from the movies. A poignant film called *There Were Times, Dear,* with Joanne Woodward, tells the story of a woman who had to cope with her husband's progressive Alzheimer's disease. The film shows her watching him as he becomes more and more lost; she watches him become a dazed and drooling invalid; she worries when she wakes up in the morning and he's missing and she doesn't know where he is. But she doesn't keep her distance. She stays with him, cares for him, bathes him, and dresses him. And she does all this with the knowledge that not only will he never be the same again, but there will come a point when he will not even know who she is. Yet she has no thought of leaving him or divorcing him or staying away.

Another powerful film, *Brian's Song*, told the story of two great football players, Brian Piccolo and Gayle Sayres. Gayle was black and Brian was white, and in all of professional sports history they were the first black man and white man to room together. And so the world watched carefully to see how they would get along together. What kept them together was their great sense of humor. At one point, Brian Piccolo was asked, "How do you two get along? How is it living with a black man?" He answered, "It's okay as long as he doesn't use the bathroom."

When Brian got cancer, he wasn't able to take part in the playoffs. Gayle Sayres did, and won football's most prestigious award, the George S. Halas Award. In the movie, Sayres stood up in front of everybody to accept the award, and said: "You flatter me by giving me this award. But I tell you here and now that I accept it for Brian Piccolo. Brian Piccolo is the man of courage who should receive the George S. Halas Award. I love Brian Piccolo, and I'd like you to love him. Tonight when you hit your knees, please ask God to love him too."

Why were we moved by that scene? Not just because it showed an extraordinary friendship between a black and a white man, but because it said something profound about the relationship: "I love this man."

Why do we resonate with these three stories, and what do they have to do with the Trinity? The answer is this: all these stories portray loving relationships. Instinctively, we know that we are at our best, our most moral, our most human, our most divine, when we are in loving relationships. But why? Because it is at those times that our true identity is revealed. What identity are we talking about here? Our identity as beings made in the image and likeness of the triune God, revealed precisely as a God whose very nature is a loving relationship.

The Trinity tells us that God is not solitary like the pagan gods. God is not capricious or cruel or immoral like the Greek gods. No, the

Trinity says that God is relationship—Father, Son, and Spirit—and the basis of that relationship is love. And we are made in that image. No wonder, then, that we are most godly, most divine, most happy, most fulfilled, when we, too, are in a loving relationship, are "Trinity."

Of course, if you flip it over to the other side, we are least ourselves and most unhappy and most inhuman when we are out of relationship, out of sync with the Trinity in whose image we are made. That is why the worst pain and illness in the world is to be out of relationship. Think of the raw emotions of a betrayal, a separation, the death of a spouse or a child, a divorce, of any severe breaking of a relationship. Some people commit suicide over a broken love affair. These situations hurt so much because they go against the grain of who we are.

On the other hand, the stories of John Rawlins and the wife of the husband with Alzheimer's disease and Gayle Sayres resonate with us, because they provide a mirror of the triune God in whose image we are made. They picture us at our godly best. They show us living in the pattern of the Trinity.

So the next time somebody says to you, "Well, you're a Catholic; you believe in the Trinity; what's it all about?" don't go into a long philosophical and theological discussion. Simply say: "It's about three Persons bound in a relationship of love—*and* it's about me, because I am the reflection of that relationship. The Trinity is the basis of the moral life which urges me to show in *my* life the glimpse I have of *God's* life: Father, Son, and Spirit in love."

27

GATHER, AFFIRM, AND CHALLENGE

LUKE 9:11–17

When I think of this feast day, traditionally called Corpus Christi, I think of three stories that I relate to the Eucharist. One begins with a verse that goes:

> I eat my peas with honey,
> I've done it all my life.
> They do taste kind of funny,
> But it keeps them on the knife.

Most of us have never known anyone who eats peas with a knife, but I do. It is quite a feat. I suspect I would scatter those little green things all around the dining room if I tried to do it. But my aunt on my father's side ate her peas with a knife. When we went to her house to visit we were both embarrassed and in awe of how she managed to do it. One day we had the courage to ask her—outside the earshot of my mother—and she told us this story:

She had grown up during the Depression. Her family was poor, like much of the rest of the country, but they had a vegetable garden which kept them from starving. Strangers passing through town in search of work were welcome at their table.

They never turned anyone away hungry.

Well, one day, her father brought home a man named Henry. Henry didn't know much English, but his gestures of gratitude toward the family were easy to understand. At dinner that evening, the family waited to let Henry start his meal first. Eagerly, he grabbed up his knife and dug into his peas. My aunt and the other kids in the family were astonished. Henry had an amazing ability to balance all the peas on his knife perfectly.

The children, of course, began to giggle and snicker at this strange eating habit. But my aunt's father, giving his children a silencing look, picked up his own knife and began eating his peas. Although he had much less success than Henry, he kept at it and eventually captured every last pea. His wife and kids followed suit.

That day, my aunt said, she saw a concrete example of acceptance, of treating people with dignity, in spite of their differences. So she kept up the practice as a way of passing down this message to her children and her grandchildren. Who knows how many generations can learn from the example of a father's acceptance of a man who ate peas with his knife?

The Eucharist gathers. It feeds the "five thousand," including women and children. As one of the eucharistic prayers reads, "It gathers people of every race, language, and way of life to share in the one banquet of Christ."

Most of you have heard of Dudley Moore, the successful movie actor. Did you know that as a youngster, Dudley was born with a clubfoot? He was smaller than the other children, and one of his legs was shorter than the other. Kids laughed at him and called him "Hopalong." "I felt unworthy of anything," says Dudley, "a little runt with a twisted foot." His parents felt guilty about his defect, and so Dudley felt that he had done something wrong. His home lacked love, and his parents seemed characterized by fear and anxiety.

When he was about six or seven, Dudley spent a lot of time in the hospital. There, a nurse named Pat once gave him a goodnight kiss. Forty years later, Dudley says, "I almost spin when I think about it. She was truly an angel of mercy, and that kiss was probably the first taste of real, unqualified, uncomplicated affection I had ever had. In many ways my entire life is based on recapturing that single moment of affection." How did Dudley Moore deal with his need for acceptance? He learned to make his classmates laugh. He became the class clown. And the rest, as they say, is history.

The Eucharist affirms. It is Christ's kiss to the marginal and unwanted and unloved.

Some of you know the story of Le Chambon, the "city of refuge." Its story is extraordinary and well worth reading; a TV program was made about it some years ago. During the the Second World War, Jewish people fleeing Nazi persecution were able to find refuge in Le Chambon, a village located in the mountains of southwest France. The story has become well known because the network for harboring refugees was not the work of single heroic households or of religious houses, but of a whole rural community.

The majority of the citizens of Le Chambon were Huguenot Protestants, a faith with a long history of religious persecution. When orders for the rounding up of Jews were issued by the German authorities via the French puppet government, the local leaders of the church urgently discussed what should be their response. They were accustomed to reading Scripture and praying about the right course of action at their regular meetings. Now, they knew they faced a critical decision. Led by their pastor, Andre Trocme, the Huguenot Protestants did not hesitate. They could not stand aside and allow innocent people to be rounded up and carried away to death.

The model for their response came from Scripture. They recalled the Law of Moses, which said that there should be "cities of refuge," places where a person accused of a crime could be sure of safety from arbitrary punishment until the case could be properly tried. If a refuge for suspected criminals was ordered by God, how much more should entirely innocent people be protected? So Le Chambon became a city of refuge, "lest innocent blood be shed," as the Bible said.

The whole village of Le Chambon was organized to receive the refugee Jews who were fleeing the Nazis. Forged papers were made. Jewish people—including many children—were placed in homes in the village and on outlying farms. Some were passed on to people who could get them out of the country, while others stayed throughout the occupation.

Amazingly, the village people refused to deny that they were sheltering Jews; they simply would not say who was and who wasn't a

Jew. Some Jews were caught and deported, and some villagers themselves died for the sake of those they sheltered. But in all, four thousand people were saved through the hands of the people of Le Chambon.

This story tells of the heroic work of hospitality. The village people shared already inadequate food and clothing with the newcomers, as well as their houses and their lives. They did not hesitate, because as Christians they believed that God had called them to give what they had and to trust that God would make it sufficient. At the same time, other people throughout Europe—kindly, decent people—who saw the plight of the persecuted Jews, said, in effect, "It's not our problem. Send them away, they can go to farms and villages elsewhere. Someone else will see to their welfare." Given the terrible danger as well as the massive propaganda against the Jews, it is hard to blame these people. Would any of us have done better?

In the gospel today, Jesus and his friends and those who had come with him gathered in "a lonely place" obviously not suitable to minister to the needs of a hungry crowd. But like another lonely place, a remote French village with few material resources, a miracle took place. As God said to the people of Le Chambon, he said to the disciples two thousand years earlier: "Give them something to eat yourselves." Instead of protesting that they had little, the disciples simply gave what they had.

The Eucharist challenges.

Let me say it again: the Eucharist gathers, affirms, and challenges. We too have gathered here today in this "out of the way" place for respite from a pagan world, to pass judgment on it, to state that its ways are not our ways, to redeem it by our love. We, too, are leaven for the world as we announce: "This is my body given for you."

28

SEEING AS SAINTS

MATTHEW 5:1–12

Before I became a priest, I worked in a mental hospital. During my first week on the job, I went with one of the psychiatrists to a back ward where I met a patient named Irma.

Irma was as certifiably crazy as could be. She told everyone, whether you asked or not, that she was the daughter of an African princess and a black tiger. (She was white.) I was young at the time, and therefore confident I could persuade her that her belief was irrational. So I approached her and struck up a conversation.

After half an hour of talking with her, I had made absolutely no dent in her crazy notions. On the other hand, I was amazed at how her construction of her inner world was so integrated. Only her starting point was bizarre; but once you accepted the starting point, her logic was perfect. Everything flowed from it. The psychiatrist later explained to me that mental illness lies in the starting point, in the imagination, in the seeing, and not in the logic. What made Irma sick of mind was that she only absorbed information that reinforced her flawed way of seeing life.

We can be much like Irma, locked in our own closed world, in our own blindness. And that can make us sick of soul, if not of mind. Think of how we are trained. From the moment we are born, we are bombarded with images of the "good life": expensive cars, exotic travel, constant entertainment, beautiful houses, lots of electronic toys. We are told that the perfect lifestyle consists of total freedom, with no rules and endless consumption. Any dissident images, perhaps of people who are poor or starving or needy, are filtered out, much like the absence of windows in a casino keep out any view of the real world. There is no end to the gambling; life is a ball.

What does all of this have to do with the feast of All Saints? A saint, after all, is really just someone who has broken out of the world, out of the marketplace, and who has learned to see the way Jesus sees. Simply put, a saint sees differently. Robert Barron, a fine theologian, reminds us of a great truth:

> Christianity is, above all, a way of seeing. Everything else in Christian life flows from and circles around the transformation of vision. Christians see differently, and that is why their prayer, their worship, their action, their whole way of being in the world, has a distinctive accent and flavor. What unites figures as diverse as James Joyce, Caravaggio, John Milton, the architect of Chartres, Dorothy Day, Dietrich Bonhoffer, and the later Bob Dylan is a peculiar and distinctive take on things, a style, a way, which flows finally from Jesus of Nazareth.

Origen of Alexandria once remarked that holiness is seeing with the eyes of Christ. Teilhard de Chardin said with great passion that his mission as a Christian thinker was to help people see, and Thomas Aquinas said that the ultimate goal of the Christian life is a "beatific vision," an act of seeing.

As Rabbi Harold Kushner writes in his book, *Who Needs God?* "Religion is not primarily a set of beliefs, a collection of prayers or a series of rituals. Religion is first and foremost a way of seeing. It can't change the facts about the world we live in, but it can change the way we see those facts, and that in itself can often make a difference."

Saints, then, are those who see and act on what they see. They are men and women who see with the eyes of Christ. In so doing, they see what is important, what matters, what takes priority, and hints of the divine. Are there any saints around today? Thousands, perhaps millions. And all of us are probably fortunate enough to know a few people, a few saints, whose lives inspire us and reflect the divine goodness.

A fitting tribute to saints of our time can be found on the west face of Westminster Abbey in London. There had been ten empty niches in the face, but now those niches are filled with statues of those known as modern-day saints. There is Dietrich Bonhoeffer, a German Lutheran minister killed by the Nazis, and Maximilian Kolbe, the Polish Franciscan priest who gave his life to spare another's in a Nazi extermination camp. There is Martin Luther King, Jr., the Baptist pastor known so well to all Americans, who was assassinated in 1968. There are two bishops: one is Anglican, Janani Luwum, and he was murdered in Uganda by Idi Amin. The other bishop is Oscar Romero, a Catholic from El Salvador, who was gunned down and killed by right-wing forces in 1980, while Romero was saying Mass. What all of these people had in common was that they saw a world in need of justice and compassion, and they decided to do something about what they saw.

Many, many people lead saintly lives, but some are truly heroic. For example, I remember Sister Mary Cleophas who taught high school and college math for fifty years. She made math comprehensible and enjoyable for even the most reluctant student. When she could no longer teach, Sister found another ministry. She organized a group of people to collect day-old bread from a bakery and distribute it to the poor. When even this work became too much for Sister, she retired to her provincial house.

One day, a younger sister was walking quickly down the hall and passed Sister Cleophas shuffling along with her cane, her body bent from osteoporosis. Despite her frailty, the older nun greeted the younger one as she sped by. When the young nun reached the end of the hall she stopped, and going back to the bent figure, said, "Sister Cleophas, I want you to know how much your smile means to me." Without a trace of self-pity, Sister Cleophas said, "My smile is all I have left to give."

All saints, past and present, see things differently. They see with the eyes of Christ. Here is another example:

Joey Russell's most prized possession used to be a 1912 postcard of the original Titanic, signed by an actual survivor of the ship's sinking. Four years ago, when he was nine years old, Joey had saved up all his chore money to buy the postcard at an auction. The mania surrounding the release of the movie about the Titanic assured Joey an excellent deal if he ever decided to sell his card.

And he did decide to sell it—but not for his own benefit. He saw something else; he saw that the mother of his best friend Kate needed a bone-marrow transplant. That's when Joey offered to sell his card to raise money for the procedure. The mother would need at least $60,000 in order to get the transplant, and without it she might die. But it didn't stop there.

When talk show host Rosie O'Donnell heard about Joey's act of kindness, she invited him on her show. There, she introduced him to the cast of the musical *Titanic*. But that wasn't the only reason she had invited him on her show that day. O'Donnell, along with the *Titanic's* producers, had arranged to buy Joey's postcard for $60,000. Now his best friend's mom could get her transplant.

Joey Russell could have seen all the things he could buy for himself with his Titanic postcard profits. But in the tradition of sainthood, he saw otherwise.

Here's another story:

The shocked family was standing on the sidewalk in front of their house, watching the firemen swarming in and out. A grease fire had severely damaged the kitchen and smoke was saturating everything they owned. They watched in dismay as the fire was put out—holes in the walls, scorched beams, broken dishes—a real mess awaited them.

Suddenly a pizza delivery car pulled up next to the curb, and a young man hopped out bearing a large pizza. The father of the family looked annoyed and said sharply, "Look I'm afraid you've got the wrong address. Obviously," gesturing toward the damaged house, "none of us ordered a pizza and, besides," he said wearily, "my wallet was in my jacket—in the kitchen."

The pizza guy smiled, shook his head, and said, "Oh, I know you didn't order this but I saw you all just standing there and I had to do something. There is no charge. Just try to take it easy and have something to eat." And with that he returned to his car and sped off as the astonished family watched.

How many saw the fire and just shook their heads or drove on? How many saw the people in need? At least one young man saw, and decided to do something about it. This qualifies him as a saint, at least for that day. Here we can remember the words from Matthew 25: "'Lord, when was it that we saw you hungry and gave you food, or thirsty and gave you something to drink?'...And the king will answer them, 'Truly I tell you, just as you did it to one of the least of these who are members of my family, you did it to me.'"

Seeing with eyes of Christ makes saints. Spiritual sight doesn't come easy in a world devoted to the maintenance of our blindness. But we can find a cure in prayer, good works, and the reading of Scripture. So let's open our eyes: we are the saints of today.

29

LEARNING TO LOVE

JOHN 13:31-33, 34-35

"I give you a new commandment, that you love one another. Just as I have loved you, you also should love one another." This is the summary of the Christian message: to love as Jesus loves us. That word, "as," pops up several times in Jesus' teaching: "Love one another as I have loved you...forgive us our trespasses as we forgive those who trespass against us...be compassionate as your Heavenly Father is compassionate." This is the standard by which our moral lives are to be measured. We are to love as Jesus did.

It is worthwhile to remember, however, that love is not instinctive, not inborn. It is a learned response. To make an analogy in the animal world, catching and eating prey is not automatic. The cubs have to learn that. And it is completely appropriate, on this day in particular, to ask: from whom do they learn how to catch and eat prey? Who protects the baby animals, moves them from den to den, defends them to the point of death, and teaches them survival skills? The answer is, their mothers.

Human mothers, it should be noted on Mother's Day, do the same. They teach us survival skills. But more than that, they teach love. And they teach it in the only effective way one teaches anything: by doing loving things for their children and for other people. They, like Jesus, become the measurement on how we are to love.

If Jesus said, "Just as I have loved you, you also should love one another," so every mother silently says the same. Watch me and you will learn how to love. Let me move you from inbred selfishness to sharing and concern for others. Watch me and I will show you how to do it. In this way, every mother furthers the gospel. As this little ditty by Ann Taylor tells:

> Who ran to help me when I fell,
> And would some pretty story tell,
> Or kiss the place to make it well?
> My mother!

Taylor could just as well have answered, "Jesus." Or how about this poem by Rudyard Kipling:

> If I were hanged on the highest hill,
> Mother o' mine, O mother o' mine!
> I know whose love would follow me still,
> Mother o' mine, O mother o' mine!
>
> If I were drowned in the deepest sea,
> Mother o' mine, O mother o' mine!
> I know whose tears would come down to me,
> Mother o' mine, O mother o' mine!
>
> If I were damned by body and soul,
> I know whose prayers would make me whole,
> Mother o' mine, O mother o' mine!

"Just as I have loved you, you also should love one another."

> Out of the French Revolution came the story of a mother who had wandered through the woods for three days with her two children, trying to survive on roots and leaves. On the third day, she heard some soldiers approaching and quickly hid herself and the children behind some bushes. The sergeant in charge prodded the bushes to see what was stirring behind them. When he saw the starving woman and children he immediately gave them a loaf of brown bread.
>
> The mother took it eagerly, broke it into two pieces, and gave one piece to each of the children. "She has kept none for her-

self," the sergeant said. "Because she is not hungry?" a soldier asked. "Because she is a mother," the sergeant replied.

"Be compassionate as your heavenly Father is compassionate." Love is taught by loving actions. Our first experience of love in this life comes from our mothers. We recognize that instinctively. What's the first thing someone says when they get in front of a TV camera? Of course, it's "Hi, Mom!" But I must hasten to add that love is taught by lots of "moms" and "dads"—even childless, single people like myself. And so Mother's Day and Father's Day really celebrate all those people who have mothered and fathered us, and taught us how to love.

I think of my fourth grade teacher, Mr. McElliott, who never married but who was a dear father to boys who sought guidance and understanding. I think of Miss Consolvo, who mothered many a teenager. Now that she is retired, she still gets invitations, letters, and visits from the many students who have never forgotten her kindness. People such as Mr. McElliott and Miss Consolvo have many children in the Lord.

Still, it's our natural mothers who preeminently teach us how to love. As one adult put it: "I finally found a Mother's Day card that expressed my feelings for my mother in real terms. The card said, 'Now that we have a mature, adult relationship, there's something I'd like to tell you. You're still the first person I think of when I fall down and go boom!'"

But perhaps nobody catches the mood, as well as the happy interplay of today's gospel and today's celebration, like the late Erma Bombeck. She writes:

On Mother's Day, all over the country grateful moms are pushed back onto their pillows. The flower on their bird of paradise plant (which blooms every other year for fifteen minutes) is snipped and put into a shot glass, and a strange assortment of food comes out of the kitchen, destined to take the sight from a good eye.

A mixer whirls, out of control, then stops abruptly as a voice cries, "I'm telling!" A dog barks and another voice says, "Get his paws out of there. Mom has to eat that!" Minutes pass, and finally, "Dad! Where's the chili sauce?" Then, "Don't you dare bleed on Mom's breakfast!"

The rest is a blur of banging doors, running water, rapid footsteps and a high pitched, "YOU started the fire, YOU put it out!" The breakfast is fairly standard: a water tumbler of juice, five pieces of black bacon that snap in half when you breathe on them, a mound of eggs that would feed a Marine division, and four pieces of cold toast. The kids line up by the bed to watch you eat and from time to time ask why you're not drinking your Kool-Aid or touching the cantaloupe with black olives on top spelling M-O-M.

Later in the day, after you have decided it's easier to move to a new house than clean the kitchen, you return to your bed where, if you are wise, you will reflect on this day. For the first time, your children have given instead of received. They have offered to you the sincerest form of flattery: trying to emulate what you do for them. And they have presented you with the greatest gift people can give: themselves.

That's the meaning and message of today's gospel: "Just as I have loved you, you also should love one another." It's a perfect gospel for Mother's Day. Why? Because love is what mothers do best.

30

STAND BY ME

JOHN 14:15–21

On this day, most preachers make some reference to Mother's Day even if it has nothing to do with our Christian tradition or liturgy. Still, going back to the origins of this holiday might give us some food for thought.

As you might know, the practice of celebrating Mother's Day comes from Civil War times. Mrs. Anna Reeves Jarvis wanted to organize a special day for mothers who had sons fighting on opposing sides in the Civil War. And so Mother's Day was meant to be comfort for a mother's worse nightmare: the possibility that her sons, on a battlefield somewhere, might be killing each other. In 1907, Jarvis's daughter began a movement to make Mother's Day a national event. Finally, in 1915, President Woodrow Wilson proclaimed the second Sunday of May as Mother's Day.

From there, the commercial interests took over. Today, Mother's Day is awash in slick sentimentality, and very few remember its painful origin. But perhaps we can recapture some of the original meaning of this day if we return to the image of children at war. And I am not talking just about the horrible reality of children killing other children, but also the cultural wars, the ones most parents feel they are losing to the all-powerful media. The good news is that teachers and parents in general, and mothers in particular, have one advantage in these cultural wars: they have the first chance to make a lasting impression. In the words of today's gospel, they are advocates, ones who "stand by" another as the "Spirit of truth."

And they stand by not silently, but with words of direction and wisdom repeated over and over again. As one mother puts it:

> On this Mother's Day, reading John's gospel, I am reminded of one of the main features of my mothering style. Like my own mother did, I talk to my children a lot! Since they were babies I have instinctively blanketed my three sons with songs, humming, whistling, and words. My mother's theory (as she explained it) went something like this: "You never know when your children are listening or what they will hear. So I say everything several ways, over and over. Perhaps one of the times or ways I speak will get through."
>
> I view my monologues with my children as a big part of my role as transmitter of values, and both general and specific operating instructions for life. I dare say that my children are not in the dark about my views, feelings, opinions, and wishes for them about almost anything from proper table manners to proper sexual conduct.

There you are. Raising moral children, guiding them through the cultural wars, comes from instruction and teaching. And, as that mother said, it comes from saying the same things over and over again.

When I was about eight or nine, my friends and I found a high mound from a house excavation. Of course, we simply had to climb it to see who was going to be "king of the hill." Once on top we surveyed our domain. That's when some girls walked by. The nerve of them to enter our territory! So we hurled dirt bombs down on them.

Needless to say, within hours the entire story had found its way through the neighborhood telegraph system right back home to my mother. Her reaction was instantaneous: "Did you boys throw dirt at the girls?" After some hesitation, I admitted that we had. "Well, that's not right. I will not have you doing that. You are marching down the street right now to apologize to the girls. And you are going to tell them that you won't do it any more."

Was this intervention really influential in my life? Well, I certainly still remember it! And I know I'm a little less inclined to throw dirt—in any sense—as a result of this childhood experience. Wise parents provide this sort of training all the time. They teach their children to act with virtue and thereby develop the ability to do so on a regular basis. Here are some examples of everyday advocacy:

I know you don't feel like doing your homework right now. You'd rather go out and play. But I want you to stick to the work for another half hour. Then you can join your friends down the street.

I know you don't like the sweater your grandmother sent you for Christmas. But she gave it to you out of love. So you will write her a thank-you note nonetheless.

I know you've received a last-minute invitation to go on this exciting weekend trip. But when you agreed to join the soccer team you made a commitment to your teammates. You don't have to play soccer next year if you don't want to. But for this year you made a commitment and you must fulfill it. So you cannot skip the game to go on the trip.

Would you say things like that to your children? If you don't, what kind of message are you sending? It's OK to break your commitments, your word, when something better comes along? Later on, when their marriage breaks up, you will wonder, where did they learn that? Parents don't have to be perfect to teach by telling. They can say to their children, "I do the best I can. I don't know everything. I've made my share of mistakes. You'll make some, too. But I want to tell you what I've learned."

At one time, parents used to try to have all the answers. But children resent and reject that approach. Now a lot of parents, unsure of themselves in a world of diversity and relativism, have lost their confidence and have gone to the other extreme: they don't give any answers. As a result, kids suffer from a lack of guidance and grow up without any values to live by.

Parents can tell their children what they believe without playing God. They can guide and instruct, listen and advise. Says one mother: "I believe in telling kids what you think is important, what you think can help them in their lives. You have to catch them at the right time, and you can never be sure when that is. You may have to say it a lot before they start taking it in. But they will remember it. They will say, 'My mother always used to tell me…'"

Here is how three people remember what their parents "used to say":

My mother always said, "Dare to be different. If people are painting themselves yellow and jumping in the pond, feel perfectly free to paint yourself green and walk backwards. Never mind what the rest of the world is doing; you are your own person." She also taught us that we were sacraments and our lives were a prayer.

When I was fifteen years old, I fell in a hole in the street and I broke my foot. We had a good case, and could have taken the town to the cleaners. My mother only wanted medical expenses covered, even though the lawyer thought she was nuts. Her philosophy was, "You only take what you earn." In my own life, I've done as my mother did. Now I try to pass on this same value to my daughter.

My father always emphasized that to help a friend in need was one of the best things you could do in life. This had always been a rewarding experience for him. It has been an equally rewarding experience for me when I have helped friends in need.

The lead article in the May 10, 1999 issue of *Newsweek* magazine was titled: "How Well Do You Know Your Kids?" While the article showed that American adolescents are highly privileged, affluent, well educated, and media savvy, there is:

…another dimension to this picture, and it's far more troubled. In survey after survey, many kids—even those on the honor roll—say they feel increasingly alone and alienated, unable to connect with their parents, teachers, and sometimes even classmates. They are desperate for guidance, and when they don't get it at home or at school, they cling to cliques or immerse themselves in a universe outside their parents' reach, a world defined by computer games, TV, and movies where brutality is so common it has become mundane.

The article goes on: "Half have lived through their parents' divorce. Sixty-three percent are in households where both parents work outside the home and many look after younger siblings in the afternoon. Still others are home by themselves after school...."

University of Chicago sociologist Barbara Schneider has been studying 7,000 teenagers for five years, and has found they spend an average of three and a half hours alone every day. Author Patricia Hersch profiled eight teens who live in an affluent area of northern Virginia for her 1998 book, *A Tribe Apart*. She says, "Every kid I talked to at length eventually came around to saying without my asking that they wished they had more adults in their lives, especially their parents." Kids are desperate for parents, for guidance, for an advocate, the Spirit of truth. They are often left to go into the world rudderless with no one to stand by them.

In the popular Generation X film, *Reality Bites*, the valedictorian, played by Winona Ryder, gives the commencement address at Houston's Rice University. Her address, like most commencement speeches, is full of challenges. As she moves to the climax of her address, the crescendo builds until she finally says with great passion: "And the answer is...." Then she loses her place in her notes and stumbles. Again: "And the answer is..." but once more she cannot find her next card. Finally, much subdued, she simply says, "And the answer is, I don't know."

Our children don't know because no one has told them. They are desperate for guidance. When it's given, consistently and repeatedly, you get someone like Michael Jordan. His father, as you might recall, was murdered in the summer of 1993. Before that happened, Michael said this to columnist Bob Greene:

My heroes are and were my parents....It wasn't that the rest of the world would necessarily think they were heroic. But they were the adults I saw constantly, and I admired what I saw. If you are lucky, you grow up in a house where you can learn what kind of person you should be from your parents. And on that count, I was very lucky. It may have been the luckiest thing that ever happened to me.

To Michael Jordan, good parents meant as much to him as his

incomparable basketball skill.

Does all this sound more like a lecture you might get at a PTA meeting, rather than a commentary on the gospel? Perhaps. But we have the words of Christ to put this homily in a context of faith: "If you love me, you will keep my commandments." "My Father will give you another advocate, the Spirit of truth." "I will not leave you orphaned."

Mothers and fathers and teachers and significant adults, engaged out there in the cultural wars, tell your children to keep your commandments, your teaching, your advice which has been repeated over and over again. Tell them to hold onto the Spirit of truth. Then especially, tell them, show them, what they most want to hear: "I will not leave you orphaned."

Remember, our children achingly want adults in their lives as they negotiate through the world, someone to teach them the way of righteousness. And there isn't a better day to begin to do this than on Mother's Day. Let us reach out in gratitude to our mothers, who were and are our advocates, those who with love stand by us.

31

FATHERS COUNT

MATTHEW 10:26–33

On this cheerful occasion of Father's Day, I want to share with you some rather dreary facts that were cited in a recent article in *USA Today*. For example, an estimated twenty-four million children live without their biological fathers. Further, there are nearly two million single fathers with children under the age of eighteen; twenty-six percent of absent fathers live in a different state than their children; and about forty percent of the children who live in fatherless households haven't seen their fathers in at least a year.

The article also quoted studies showing that children who live without their biological fathers are, on average, more likely to be poor; more likely to experience health, educational, emotional, and psychological problems; more likely to be victims of child abuse; and more likely to engage in criminal behavior as compared with their peers who live with their married, biological mother and father.

On the other hand, children whose fathers spend the most time with them and monitor their school progress are least likely to have behavior problems. Psychological research finds that children who grow up to exhibit the highest levels of moral virtue, as well as a healthy spirituality, learned to do so at their father's knee.

Why am I citing all these statistics? To underscore the fact that science shows what common sense has always known: fathers count. They are important to the health of a family. Further, the good dads outnumber the bad ones and are active in their families. The *USA Today* article also reports: "Fathers in intact, two-parent families have more than doubled their share of child care in the past twenty years." To put it in the words of today's gospel, a father is worth more than many sparrows and he teaches his children, that they, too, have worth.

I am happily finding more and more people like one man whom I spoke with recently. He wanted to be a better father to his three young children than his dad was to him. As we talked on the phone, this man said, "It wasn't that my dad was cruel to us. It was just that he was a shadow. He worked long hours and was active in the community. Everybody thought he was a great guy, but he was never home. And now I find myself struggling to make a connection with my own kids. I want to have the kind of relationship my wife has with them, but I'm not sure how to make that happen."

What I suggested to this man was that he try the three Ps. I'll share these with you now.

The first P stands for pastor. Just as a priest pastors a parish, so a father "pastors"—is shepherd to—his family. Scott Hahn, a father of six and a well known evangelical minister who became a Catholic, puts it well: "I give my family what my pastor gives his parishioners. [My pastor] provides us a home in the church, and spiritual sustenance in the Eucharist. He gives us a name in baptism. He forgives our sins in confession. He teaches, guides, and disciplines....Within the family, the father stands before God as pastor." That's a good image for fathers to adopt: pastor, shepherd to whom the flock of his family has been committed. A leader with a sense of honor and responsibility who provides, feeds, forgives, and disciplines.

The second P stands for prophet, here used in the original sense of "one who proclaims." A father proclaims in word, but more so in deed, by doing what is noble and good. These deeds provoke the "dad" stories that nurture children till the day they die. Here are a few of them. The first story is told by songwriter Cris Williamson:

> It was a great honor in our family to be chosen to place the Christmas angel at the very tip of the tree. Dad would hold the child high in the air and the angel would slip over the tip until

she shone high above the room.

That Christmas, as the afternoon gave way to gradual darkness, Mom cut my hair. My long braids had been shorn to shoulder length and the hair was all around me on the floor. I remember feeling sort of small and naked as I sat there on my hard chair in the kitchen. Dad came in out of the frosty cold with an armload of stove wood. He put it in the wooden box beside the stove and looked over at me sitting so pensively on my chair like a lamb that had just been shaved.

He knelt down beside me and picked up all the newly shorn hair from my head. The next thing I knew, he was calling me to the front room where the Christmas tree stood in all its shining splendor. I watched him as he carefully placed bits of my brown hair on the tree beside the tinsel and the glittering glass balls. He turned and smiled at me and said, "This year we will have real angel hair on the tree."

Prophet dads do and say things like that. Then there is this tribute found in a "Dear Abby" column:

A great man died today. He wasn't a world leader or a famous doctor or a war hero or sports figure. He was no business tycoon and you would never see his name in the financial pages. But he was one of the greatest men who ever lived. He was my father.

I guess you might say he was a person who was never interested in getting credit or receiving honors. He did corny things like pay his bills on time, go to church on Sunday, and serve as an officer in the PTA. He helped us kids with our homework; and drove our mom to do the grocery shopping on Thursday nights. He got a great kick out of hauling his teenagers and their friends around, to and from football games.

Dad enjoyed simple pastimes like picnics in the park and pitching horseshoes. Opera wasn't exactly his cup of tea. He liked country music, mowing the grass, and running with the dog. He didn't own a tuxedo, and I'm sure he never tasted caviar.

Tonight is my first night without him. I don't know what to do with myself, so I am writing to you. And I am sorry now for the times I didn't show him the proper respect. But I am grateful for a lot of other things. I am thankful that God let me have my father for fifteen years. And I am happy that I was able to let him know how much I loved him.

That wonderful man died with a smile on his face and fulfillment in his heart. He knew that he was a great success as a husband and a father, a brother, a son, and a friend. I wonder how many millionaires can say that.

Not all dads appear to be so sterling at first. A man tells of someone he knew named Al, who had lost a son. Then Al's wife left him, and he had to raise their other child, then six years old, alone. Unable to cope, he turned to alcohol. Eventually, Al lost everything, and died alone in a motel room. The man continues his story about Al:

"What a complete failure!" I thought. "What a totally wasted life!" As time went by, I began to re-evaluate my earlier harsh judgment. You see, I knew Al's now adult son, Ernie, one of the kindest, most caring, most loving men I have ever known. I watched Ernie with his children and saw the free flow of love between them. I knew that kindness and caring had to come from somewhere. I had not heard Ernie talk much about his father. It is so hard to defend an alcoholic.

One day I worked up my courage to ask him: "I'm really puzzled by something," I said. "I know your father was basically the only one to raise you. What on earth did he do that you became such a special person?" Ernie sat quietly and reflected for a few moments. Then he said, "From my earliest memories as a child until I left home at eighteen, my dad came into my room every night, gave me a kiss, and said, 'I love you, son.'"

Tears came to my eyes as I realized what a fool I had been to judge Al as a failure. He had not left any material possessions behind. But he had been a kind and loving father, and he left behind one of the finest, most giving men I have ever known.

You never know. Finally, not only is a father a pastor and prophet, he is, in his most basic role, a petitioner, one who prays. He petitions, he prays for many things, especially for his family, of course. But truth to tell, he prays mostly for himself, as well he should, because every father has too many experiences like this:

A little boy of five was left alone with his father at bedtime. It had never happened before. After some maneuvering and a lot of fun, the father finally got the little fellow into his night clothes, and was about to lift him into bed when the child said, "But Daddy, I have to say my prayers."

He knelt down beside his bed, joined his hands, raised his eyes to heaven, and prayed: "Now I lay me down to sleep, I pray the Lord my soul to keep; if I should die before I wake, I pray the Lord my soul to take." That was his usual prayer. But tonight he looked up at his dad, then raised his eyes to heaven and prayed, "Dear God, make me a great, big, good man like my daddy. Amen."

In a moment he was in bed, and in five minutes asleep. And then the father knelt by his son's bedside and prayed, "Dear Lord, make me a great, big, good man like my boy thinks I am."

That is what real fathers pray. Now, a quick ending. There is, I must confess, a fourth, postscript P to tack on to Dad's glorious role as pastor, prophet, and petitioner. It stands for progress; namely, that dads are always something of an unfinished product, always under construction, always pending, so to speak. And who helps in this ongoing formation of dad? This father tells it candidly:

After spending the entire dinner correcting my young son's table manners, I turned to my wife and said in exasperation, "Will the training never end?" "A boy's training never ends," my spouse said, "He just marries and his wife gets the job. And please stop talking with food in your mouth."

32

A TIME TO REMEMBER

Can you recognize yourself in any of these statements? You know you're getting older when you bend down to straighten out the wrinkles in your socks—only to discover that you're not wearing any. And, you also know you're getting old when you stroll through memory lane and get lost. Or, you find yourself before the open refrigerator door, asking yourself life's most profound theological question: "What am I here for?"

Memories are tricky. But perhaps the worst part about it, as Irving Berlin wrote in one of his memorable songs, is that we forget to remember. And so for us Christians and for us Americans, here are three things that I suggest we should never forget to remember.

The first is God's presence and love. At the Last Supper, Jesus commanded: "Do this in remembrance of me." We hear those words repeated each time we attend Mass. "Do this" means not only celebrating the Eucharist, but also breaking the bread of ourselves as Jesus has done. Wash feet as he has done. Serve one another as he has done. Remember the Eucharist and all it contains.

Jesus also said, "Remember all that I have taught you," and "Go make disciples of all nations." He also said, "Remember, I am with you always even to the end of the world." As disciples, we should remember we are called to worship around the altar table, to serve one another, to spread the gospel by our witness, and to know that we are never, ever alone. These are good and sustaining faith memories—for us, and for us to share with one another.

Next, we should remember the blessings of the past and the people who bestowed them on us. Let me share this story:

Robert Maynard, a writer for the *New York Daily News*, relates how he came to choose his vocation. As a boy, he was walking to school one day when he came upon an irresistible temptation. In front of him was a fresh piece of gray cement laid down to replace a broken piece of sidewalk. Maynard immediately stopped and began to scratch his name in the wet cement.

Suddenly, he became aware that the biggest mason he had ever seen was standing over him, holding a garbage-can lid as his choice of weapon for little boys that day! He tried to run, but the big man grabbed him and shouted: "Why are you trying to spoil my work?" Maynard remembers babbling something about just wanting to put his name on the ground. Then a remarkable thing happened.

The mason released his arms, his voice softened, and his eyes lost their fire. There was now a touch of warmth about the man. "What's your name, son?" the man asked. "Robert Maynard." "Well, Robert Maynard, the sidewalk is no place for your name. If you want your name on something, you go in that school over there. You work hard and you become a lawyer and you hang your shingle out for all the world to see."

Tears came to Maynard's eyes, but the mason was not finished yet. "What do you want to be when you grow up?" "A writer, I think," Maynard replied. This time the mason's voice burst forth in tones that could be heard all over the schoolyard. "A writer...well then, be a writer! Be a real writer! Have your name on books, not on this sidewalk."

As Robert Maynard walked away across the street, he paused and looked back. The mason was on his knees repairing the damage which Maynard's scratching had done. He looked up, saw the young boy watching, and repeated: "Be a writer."

Bless the masons in your life. Remember the people who have

made a difference to you. But also remember the difference you have made, and still make, in the lives of others. Here's another story.

> Bonnee Hoy was a gifted composer who died in the prime of her life. At her memorial service, a friend told of a mockingbird that used to sing regularly outside Bonnee's bedroom window on summer nights. Bonnee would stand at the window, peering into the darkness, listening intently, and marveling at the beautiful songs the mockingbird sang.
>
> Being a musician, Bonnee decided to respond musically. So she whistled the first four notes of Beethoven's fifth symphony. With amazing quickness, the mockingbird learned those four notes and sang them back to Bonnee. Then, for a time, the bird disappeared. But one night, toward the end of her life, when Bonnee was very sick, the bird returned and, in the midst of its serenade, several times sang the first four notes of Beethoven's fifth.
>
> The friend then said, "Think of that! Somewhere out there in this big wide world there is a mockingbird who sings Beethoven because of Bonnee."

And somewhere out there in this big wide world there are people singing because of you, people who are decent and honest and true to their word because of you; people who make a difference in the lives of others, because you made a difference in theirs. Your song lives on.

Finally, on this Memorial Day weekend, we must remember those who made it possible for us to be here and worship freely. Since the Civil War, more than 1,100,000 men and women have lost their lives in service to the United States.

Memorial Day, as you may know, was originally called Decoration Day. It was set aside as a day to remember those who died in the service of our nation, and was first observed on May 30, 1886, when flowers were placed on the graves of Union and Confederate soldiers. At first, people of the South refused to acknowledge Memorial Day, and honored their dead on a separate day. But since World War I, Memorial Day is observed on the last Monday of May in almost every state of the union.

Listen to this story of a high school girl who previously did not really know or care too much about wars and veterans—after all, she has never known war to this point in her comfortable lifetime. The girl had the opportunity to witness a memorial service in San Francisco, aboard the USS Pampanito, a submarine that was used in World War II and in Korea. At first, she was bored, but recalls:

> As our national anthem was played over the speaker system, I saw some of the veterans start to cry as they remembered all of their fallen comrades. I began to think about how many men and women had made the ultimate sacrifice of their lives so that we might all enjoy the freedom this country offers.
>
> As we began the Pledge of Allegiance, I saw on their faces a thoughtful, respectful look, a look of such sadness…suddenly, I started to cry myself with the realization of what it all meant. All those old sailors, my dad included, standing on the deck of an old submarine holding the flag with such pride and sadness.
>
> Then it was time for the speakers to give their speeches about their experiences and the meaning of Memorial Day. A World War II veteran talked about the hardships and struggles and the fact that he was lucky to be alive when so many of his brothers had fallen victim to the war. One talked about how it was up to the veterans to teach our children about the sacrifices made by so many. Another said that America will only be the land of the free so long as it is the home of the brave.
>
> I left the service with a renewed sense of appreciation. So many of the speakers spoke about America with so much pride that it was hard not to think about all the people who have no idea what this holiday is really about. While they go to their barbeques and beaches, there are some who keep up a tradition of pride in service to the United States of America. We too must remember all those who have fallen, and rejoice in the ones who still live and remember.

So, there are three memories to remember this weekend. First, we need to remember that Jesus is here present with us for all of our days. Second, we must bless and remember those who have made a difference in our lives, and remember that we have made a difference in the lives of others. Finally, we remember those who have died in the service of this country, so that we might live.

To forget to remember any or all of these is to die spiritually. To remember these things is to live—as disciples, as a people, as a nation.

33

FREEDOM, HUGS, AND NAPKINS

One of the persistent themes touted in the many patriotic speeches heard on this day is, as you might expect, freedom. And why not? Freedom and the people who made it possible are what we rightfully and proudly celebrate today. Gathered as we are today in church, however, we look at freedom through the lens of faith. Thus, we have a more subtle idea of freedom, and we should reflect on that.

For some people, freedom means doing whatever you want, however you want, whenever you want, regardless of other people. An obvious example is the kid with the blaring car radio who wakes up babies, upsets the elderly and ill, grates on everybody's nerves, and disturbs the serenity of the neighborhood. This type of person feels a sense of freedom in doing what he or she pleases—which is, in reality, a form of the deepest slavery; that is, the slavery to one's own ego.

Real freedom is different. Real freedom, genuine freedom, is the capacity to do what we should, not just what we want to do. Some of you might have read the wonderful book called *Tuesdays with Morrie*. Written by prize-winning sports journalist Mitch Albom, it recounts his weekly conversations with Morrie Schwartz, an old professor and friend whom Albom hadn't seen in years. At the time of the conversations, Schwartz is slowly dying from ALS, Lou Gehrig's disease.

As Albom tells in the book, after college he had gone on with his life, forgetting his beloved mentor. One night, while channel surfing, he accidentally happened to catch Ted Koppel interviewing, of all people, Morrie Schwartz! Koppel, it seems, had read about Morrie in an article in the *Boston Globe*, where Schwartz relayed that he was dying and that he had some wisdom to share.

So Albom watched, and heard Morrie say, "There are some mornings when I cry and mourn for myself. Some mornings, I'm so angry and bitter. But it doesn't last too long. Then I get up and say, 'I want to live.'" There he was on TV, his old friend, his old professor, his mentor, talking about life and death. Albom hadn't even known Morrie was ill, much less dying. Ashamed of his neglect, he decided to visit him. And that initial visit turned into regular weekly meetings until Morrie died. The conversations of those Tuesday meetings form the content of the book.

There is a poignant scene at the beginning of the book which I want to share with you because it deals with freedom. The scene depicts the first time Mitch Albom drives up to see Morrie, and it tells us a lot about slavery and freedom. Albom writes:

> As I turned the rental car onto Morrie's street in West Newton, a quiet suburb of Boston, I had a cup of coffee in one hand and a cellular phone between my ear and shoulder. I was talking to a TV producer about a piece we were doing. My eyes jumped from the digital clock—my return flight was in a few hours—to the mailbox numbers on the tree-lined suburban street. The car radio was on the all news station. This was how I operated, five things at once.
>
> "Roll back the tape," I said to the producer. "Let me hear that part again." "Okay," he said. "It's gonna take a second." Suddenly, I was upon the house. I pushed the brakes, spilling coffee in my lap. As the car stopped I caught a glimpse of a large Japanese maple tree and three figures sitting near it in the driveway, a young man and a middle-aged woman flanking a small old man in a wheelchair. Morrie.
>
> At the sight of my old professor, I froze. "Hello?" the producer said in my ear. "Did I lose you?"
>
> I had not seen him in sixteen years. His hair was thinner, nearly white, and his face was gaunt. I suddenly felt unprepared

for this reunion—for one thing, I was stuck on the phone—and I hoped that he hadn't noticed my arrival, so that I could drive around the block a few more times, finish my business, get mentally ready. But Morrie, this new, withered version of a man I had once known so well, was smiling at the car, hands folded in his lap, waiting for me to emerge.

"Hey," the producer said again. "Are you there?"

For all the time we'd spent together, for all the kindness and patience Morrie had shown me when I was young, I should have dropped the phone and jumped from the car, run and held him and kissed him hello. Instead, I killed the engine and sunk down off the seat, as if I were looking for something. "Yeah, yeah, I'm here," I whispered, and continued my conversation with the TV producer until we were finished.

I did what I had become best at doing: I tended to my work, even while my dying professor waited on his front lawn. I was not proud of this, but that is what I did....Now, five minutes later, Morrie was hugging me, his thinning hair rubbing against my cheek. I had told him I was searching for my keys, that's what had taken me so long in the car. He rocked against me not letting go.

I had forgotten how close we once were. I swallowed because I knew, deep down, that I was no longer the good, gift-bearing student he remembered. I only hoped that, for the next few hours, I could fool him.

Do you relate to Mitch Albom, who does five things at once? How free was he? How free are you, running all the time? "There's never enough time" has become our national motto. Busy, aren't we? So busy, in fact, with our careers that we subcontract our children out to others; we neglect our spouses and eventually divorce them, not for another woman or another man, but for work, power, profit, and the accumulation of things. We are addicted to what is called "the good life." But that's not freedom. No addiction is.

Albom confessed: "I did what I had become best at doing: I tended to my work, even while my dying professor waited on his front lawn." We confess: "I did what I had become best at doing: I tended to my work, even while my spouse, my child, my parents, my friends, my neighbors—dying for want of my love—waited on the front lawn." Where is the freedom in that?

And yet, more slavery: "For all the time we'd spent together, for all the kindness and patience Morrie had shown me when I was young, I should have dropped the phone and jumped from the car, run and held him and kissed him hello." But he did not. Mitch Albom was, as he discovered, not free. He was enslaved to his career, his producer, and his own self-importance at the expense of friendship and love. Is that us? You see, when you come right down to it, freedom lies in dropping the phone to do what we should do, not what we want to do.

And what is it that we should do to be truly free? In a later chapter, Albom unwittingly gives us the answer. There he reminisces about his old student days, about his macho pose to hide his insecurity, wearing an old gray sweatshirt, with an unlit cigarette in his mouth even though he didn't smoke. He, the student, meets Morrie, the professor, and they strike up a deep friendship. Albom writes:

> I begin to call Morrie "Coach," the way I used to address my high school track coach. Morrie likes the nickname. "Coach," he says. "All right, I'll be your coach. And you can be my player. You can play all the lovely parts of life that I'm too old for now."
>
> Sometimes we eat together in the cafeteria. Morrie, to my delight, is even more of a slob than I am. He talks instead of chewing, laughs with his mouth open, delivers a passionate thought through a mouthful of egg salad, the little yellow pieces spewing from his teeth. It cracks me up. The whole time I know him, I have two overwhelming desires: to hug him and to give him a napkin.

But later on, as we heard before, as he moved into the slavery of a job, a schedule, Albom did neither. He did not hug Morrie and he ministered to him less; eventually, he drifted away from this man who had made such a difference in his life. Mitch Albom became a summary and symbol for so many of our lives. Unintentionally, however, he left us a means of finding out what really counts, a practical definition of real freedom: that is, real freedom is the capacity to let go in order to give hugs and napkins. If you cannot do this or if you have no time to do this, if other things have become more important, then you are the most enslaved of persons.

True freedom lies in the ability to love and to serve, to be kind and compassionate. Really, giving hugs and napkins is just another way of expressing the two great commandments, to love God and our neighbor. It speaks of a commitment to putting people before things, of moving beyond the demands and wants of the ego and the enslavement of desires. Now *that* is true freedom; that is wisdom.

Jesus said, "The truth shall make you free." And so we ask on this Fourth of July, "What is the truth that makes us free?" The answer? Real freedom is giving hugs and napkins.

34

A LITTLE ROOM OF YOUR OWN

MATTHEW 10:37–42

A woman looked out her living room window one morning and was amazed to discover a dead mule on her lawn. She called the sanitation department and asked them to remove the carcass, but by the time the work crew arrived, she had changed her mind. She gave the men $10 each, and instructed them to carry the mule upstairs and deposit it in the bathtub.

After they had carried out her wish, one of the workers asked why she wanted the dead mule in her bathtub. "I'll tell you," she replied. "For thirty-five years, my husband has been coming home at night, taking off his coat, grabbing the newspaper, plopping into the easy chair, and asking, 'What's new?' So tonight, I'm going to tell him."

This is my way of introducing our reflection for today. If you recall, the first reading and the gospel carry the theme of hospitality. Normally, this theme would prompt a focus on caring for others. But because vacation time officially began this week, I want to shift the focus to ourselves.

Vacation is a time when people are supposed to change the pace a bit, alter their routines, and take a mental break from the everyday world of schedules and work. It's a time to do and say something different, the dead mule in the bathtub, so to speak. So we pack up our bags, corral the kids, and head for the mountains or Europe or the sandy dunes of the seashore.

Alas, of course, many people are addicted to the "stuff" of their lives, their routines, their work. A cartoon from the *New Yorker* comes to mind: a family of four on vacation is sitting on the beach. The father is working at his laptop, the mother is on the cell phone, the boy is playing a hand-held electronic game, and the girl is gyrating to the music coming in through her headphones. A modern-day family vacation, thanks to the marvels of the silicon chip. Four disconnected people who carry their world and its burdens with them, never taking the opportunity to break out into something challenging and new.

Be that as it may, I want to take the notion of vacation and expand it to a larger notion of time apart, of spiritual time apart. We can use the example of arranging a "little room" of hospitality, as the woman did for the prophet Elisha in today's first reading.

Like Elisha, we all need a little room to go to once in awhile, a place where we can step back from the rat race, refresh our vision, and perhaps tackle significant questions like these: what am I doing with my life? Am I growing, or just spinning my wheels? What is the quality of my relationships? How do I see others, treat others? What is my relationship to God? Am I happy with the way that I see life, see myself, see others? Am I aware of what I may no longer see because my life is on automatic pilot?

In an episode from the old TV series *All in the Family*, Edith and Archie are attending Edith's high school reunion. Edith encounters an old classmate named Buck who has allowed himself to become extremely obese. Edith and Buck have a delightful conversation about old times and the things they did together. Remarkably, though, Edith doesn't seem to notice how extremely heavy Buck has become.

Later, Edith and Archie are talking. She says, "Archie, ain't Buck a beautiful person?" Archie replies, "Edith, I'll never figure you out. You and I can look at the same guy, and you see a beautiful person and I see a blimp." And Edith replies, simply, "Yeah, ain't that too bad!" What is it that explains why Archie and Edith see the same person in a different way? It's the same thing that leads us to ask: am I content with my spiritual vision, the way I see? What do I want out of life, after all? What really matters? What is out of kilter in my life?

Let me share a minor incident that shows a need for spiritual renewal. This story is recounted by Max Lucado in his book, *And the Angels Were Silent*:

Some years ago, I was in the terminal of the Los Angeles airport, returning home after speaking at a religious education conference. As I walked through the terminal, a convert of an Eastern religious cult caught my attention. We would all recognize the type: beads, sandals, frozen smile, a backpack of books. "Sir," she said. "Sir, just a moment, please." Well, I had a moment. I was early and the plane was late, so what was the harm?

She said she was a teacher and that her school was celebrating an anniversary. In honor of the event, they were giving away a book which explained their philosophy. How generous, I thought. She placed a copy in my hand. It was a thick, hard-backed book with a picture on the cover of a guru-type guy, sitting cross-legged with his hands folded.

I thanked her for the book and began to walk away. "Sir?" I stopped. I knew what was coming. "Would you like to make a donation to our school?" "No," I responded, "but thanks for the book."

Once again, I began to walk away. She followed me and tapped me on the shoulder. "Sir, everyone so far has given a donation in appreciation of the gift." "That's good," I replied, "but I don't think I will. I do appreciate the gift, however." I turned and began to walk away. I hadn't even taken a step when she spoke again, and this time she was agitated.

"Sir," and she opened her purse so I could see her collection of dollars and coins. "If you were sincere in your gratitude you would give a donation in appreciation." That was low; it was sneaky and insulting. I'm not usually terse, but now I couldn't resist. "That may be true," I responded, "but if you were sincere, you wouldn't give me a gift and then ask me to pay for it." She reached for the book, but I tucked it under my arm and walked away.

Jesus taught that praying and giving were to be done in secret, where the Father sees—not in order to get a reward, or to get something back. "Freely you have received, so freely give," says the Lord. After all, this girl had not said, "I'll sell you this book," but "I give this to you as a gift." Yet then she wanted me to pay for it.

This incident made me think of my own self-serving gifts, how often I want something back and how far removed I am from the total giving of Jesus on Calvary. And so we ask ourselves: When we give a gift, is there a hook? Are we hospitable without expecting recompense, the "I'll have you over for dinner, and then you'll have to have me over for dinner" sort of thing? Can we be as generous as our heavenly Father, who makes it rain on both the just and the unjust?

Marley's ghost asked Ebenezer Scrooge if he saw his own chain, which link by link, Scrooge was forging every day. No, he did not. Scrooge needed a change of pace, a time apart to develop a new vision. He needed to have his eyes opened to what he had become and how he might become something else, that is, a human being with heart. Put in our terms, Scrooge needed to learn how to become Christlike.

And so all these ramblings have but one point. We rightly spend a great deal of effort to make plans to get away: to hire a dog sitter, find someone to collect the mail and watch the house, book plane or room reservations, and so on, in order to get a much-needed and well-deserved vacation.

My suggestion is that this year, you spend as much time and energy on planning a retreat for yourself as you do in planning a vacation. Make plans to get away for a few days of spiritual renewal and personal reassessment. Take a look at your life: who are you? What are you becoming? What is your relationship with Jesus Christ?

In a word, show some hospitality to yourself. Go away to that little room. The rewards will be great. In the first reading, recall what the prophet promised the lady: "This time next year you will be fondling a baby son." This is a symbolic way of saying that in return for your hospitality, for the time you have spent apart, you will find yourself embracing new life. And that is the best reward of all.

35

A WOMAN FOR ALL TIMES

REVELATION 11:19, 12:1–6, 10

The woman named Mary, whom we honor today and about whom we know so little, has intrigued us for twenty centuries. We don't know when she was born or when she died, but we can place her in history. Through Scripture, we know where she lived and who were some of her friends and family. But the question remains: why does Mary persist through the ages? What is her appeal? The answer is to be found in her human journey with God—which, in reality, is our journey too.

When we first meet her, Mary is the object of an ugly rumor: she is pregnant without a husband. According to the cultural norm for that time, her fiance, Joseph, is expected to deny her and anything about the pregnancy, and to put her at a distance. That she was innocent, invaded by the Spirit, was not believed. Thus, people down the ages who have suffered from false rumors, who have had their reputations soiled, who have been misunderstood and maligned, who are unwed mothers; all these people have identified with Mary.

Then, too, there was her very human anxiety and fear. What was this all about anyway, this "Mother of God" business? "How can this be?" she asked the angel incredulously. "What does God want? What about Joseph? How can this happen? How can I do this?" Confused and scared and full of questions, Mary is all those people who, throughout the ages, have cried out, "How can I tackle this challenge? How can I survive? What does God want of me? What's it all about, Alfie?"

When her son was born, shepherds and angels rejoiced, but the powerbrokers of that time seethed and conspired to kill her baby. They wanted his life, his spirit. And so, parents today and down the ages, faced with so many soul-assassins, have identified with Mary. They know well enough there are people out there—the drug pushers, the media which glamorizes uncommitted sex, the hawkers with cash registers for hearts, the preachers of false values—who are after their children in order to kill their spirits, trample their souls. Parents know what Mary knew and fear what she feared.

After Jesus' birth, Mary has to flee with her husband and child and become a refugee in a foreign land. And so she immediately joins the countless displaced persons, the homeless huddling in the world's doorways and sleeping on the nation's grates, and the twenty-seven million refugees walking the earth today. These lowly ones who need to be lifted up are cousins under the skin, and they can identify with Mary.

When Jesus is an adolescent, he becomes lost from her for a while in Jerusalem. Now Mary becomes every parent, every teacher, every mentor in history who can't communicate with a teenager, who loses someone to gangs or drugs, whose children have joined the small army of runaways roaming the streets, exploited by the sex trade, abused and beaten. Many can identify with Mary here.

At some point, this wife and mother became a widow. She buried her husband, and everyone who has lost a spouse cries Mary's tears, feels the gnawing void in his or her belly, and returns home to an empty bed. When her son is old enough he leaves home to begin his mission, while his widowed mother stays behind. Suddenly every mother and father who see their children grow up and leave them behind—especially those in nursing homes—know what Mary is feeling in her heart.

When she walks the streets now that she is alone, Mary has to give way to the rough Roman soldiers and leering men who pass by. She has to move quickly and live in the shadows. As a minority woman in an occupied territory, as a widow with no man around, she is always subject to sexual and physical exploitation and discrimination. Everyone with no rights, every minority figure who has had to swallow their pride, everyone ever called "nigger" or "wop" or "fag" can identify with Mary.

When she hears rumors that her son is preaching nearby, she goes with some relatives to see him but can't get near because of the crowds. She has to be content with sending word that she's out there on the fringe. The message arrives to Jesus that his mother and relatives want to see him and he, gesturing to the crowd, asks, "Who are my mother and brothers and sisters? Everyone who does the will of God is my mother and brother and sister."

It sounded like a putdown, a message telling his mother to go home. But Mary read his comment for what it was, an inclusive statement about the kingdom of God. Mary knew: her glory was not primarily that she was the biological mother of Jesus, but that she had always obeyed the will of God, even when she did not understand it. And every little person on the sideline, off-center, on the fringe, who doesn't understand what's going on but simply clings fast to God's will, can identity with Mary.

Then her son is caught, betrayed by one whom Mary had over to the house for dinner many a time. Her son was brought to a mock trial, beaten and humiliated and hanged on a public cross. Mary arrives in time to see him hanging there, every inch of her mind and body straining to go to him, but she is forced by the soldiers to keep her distance. And suddenly, every parent who has seen their child carted off to prison, every parent who wants more than anything else to help their grown children deal with alcoholism or other addictions, every parent whose children are living in sin or raising their children without having them baptized or going through a divorce— every parent who witnesses such "crucifixions" but who are told to keep their distance can identify with Mary as they pray and suffer in silence.

Finally, she cradles the dead and broken body of her only son in her arms, and sobs uncontrollably. There she is once more, every parent who has lost a child, any friend who has lost a friend, any classmate who has lost a classmate through overdose or gunshot can identify with the Mary of the Pietà.

This ageless woman, a pilgrim who savored the ups and downs of life, has been given to us as a legacy. "Son, behold thy mother." And so today we are beholden to her, for she experienced many of the same joys and sorrows as us, pilgrims on this journey of life. Yet although she was like us in so many ways, the church tends to romanticize Mary, on this occasion in particular. It clothes her with the sun, puts the moon beneath her feet, wraps her head with a halo of stars, dresses her in medieval robes, paints in winged cherubs to do her bidding, places her against a background of Italian villas, and has her whisked up into heaven to the sound of Handel's *Messiah*.

But we should understand that all this is metaphor, figures of speech, storytelling. What all this heavenly glamour means to say is that Mary—who is every woman, every man—is blessed now because she remained faithful to the will of God. In all of the unfairness of life, she clung to God. In virginity, in motherhood, in widowhood, at home, as a wanderer in a foreign land, with live child, with dead child; through it all she clung to God.

An so Mary becomes a woman for all ages; that is the secret of her enduring popularity and her appeal. Mary did not start out as great and travel a privileged path. She was a handmaid of the Lord and traveled the lowly path throughout her life. But then, God who is mighty has done great things for her. God has lifted her up when down, fed her when hungry, and because she responded to his loving invitation, God saw to it that all generations would call her blessed.

And that is what we are doing right now: calling this woman of flesh and blood, of our own experience, blessed. We are not honoring someone far away and high above us. No, we are calling blessed someone who is near and right with us at every human step. The message of this feast, this celebration of Mary being assumed into heaven, is a sign of hope for us. It is a preview of coming attractions for all who cling to God in perplexity and adversity. On this day the church tells us that what Mary is, so shall we be.

And who is Mary? She is promise fulfilled, humanity completed, faithfulness rewarded. Simply put, she is us when we finally come to the end of this journey called life. In the richness of her human experience as well as in her heavenly glory, Mary is indeed a woman for all times and all seasons.

THE PARABLES

36

IN THE DETAILS

LUKE 15:1-3, 11-32

The story of the prodigal son—or, more properly, the generous father, for he is the key figure—is probably the best known of all the parables of Christ. More than that, it is one of the most famous stories in the world. We have heard it so often that most of us take it for granted. And so we just might miss the details, and the power of the parable is in the details. So let us pull back from the story we know so well and see what the details offer.

First, notice this: the father divides his estate openly, so that before he dies his sons know exactly what is coming to them. The father doesn't have to do this; perhaps it's even foolish to do so, to fully reveal his assets, to be so transparent. But in this way, this point is made: the father is exceedingly generous and open. The sons now know what they can expect.

The elder son seems to take it all in stride. He can wait for his money. But the younger son cannot: "Give me my inheritance now," he says. Which roughly translates to this: I can't stand around here forever, waiting for you to die. Implicit in this, in fact, is the son's wish that his father would die. An implication like this from any son, much less a younger son, is a grave insult which must have hurt the father deeply. But he said nothing.

The next detail is this: the younger son, puffed up with his inheritance, blows it all on trying to buy friends. Of course, he soon finds himself out of money and therefore, out of his fair-weather friends. So now this lad, who by this time is in a far-off country, looks for a job, any kind of a job, to keep him from starving. He comes upon a man who sends him to feed the pigs—of all things!

The detail to remember here is that the son was a Jew for whom pork was unclean, forbidden. The pagans used pigs as sacrifice to their gods. And so the Jews considered these animals unclean, idolatrous, a symbol of everything a pious Jew detested, a sign of a culture alien and hateful to Yahweh. To be sent to tend the swine was to force the son into denying his tradition, his customs, his values. The moment that the son agrees to take on this job, he becomes an outcast from his people, from his father's house, one excommunicated from his religion. He couldn't have fallen any lower.

And so it is all the more poignant and marvelous that when his son returns—an outcast and renegade and apostate, with the smell of swine on his person—the father still runs to accept him as a son, not as an alien traitor. We should not overlook this critical detail.

Another detail: the father orders shoes for the boy's feet. In those days, being shoeless was a sign of slavery. Remember the old Negro spiritual, "All God's Chillun' Got Shoes"? Slaves wanted shoes that would show them as being free. And so in this parable, the father, realizing his son was a slave to every vice and degradation, orders sandals to be brought for his son. In so doing, he lifts him up out of slavery and sin, he returns him to the freedom of being a son.

Another interesting detail concerns the elder son. He refuses to enter the house upon the return of his brother. In the Middle Eastern tradition this is the greatest of insults. The father has every right to bristle and banish this elder son for refusing to enter the ancestral home. But he doesn't. Once more the father takes the initiative. He goes out to this son as well and tries to get him to join into the celebration for his brother.

What do we find in these details so far? We should note that in every situation where insult is implied—in the younger son's unspoken wish that the father would die, when the son betrayed his father's tradition, when the eldest son refused to come inside the house—the father moves beyond the insult. In all these details, Jesus subtly reveals what God the Father is like.

Yet there is another detail to ponder. Usually, we consider only three people in this story: the younger son, the older son, and the father. But there is a hidden character who may be the most sinister of all. He is the crafty and cunning man who offered the son the job of tending the swine. This unnamed man can plainly see that before him stands a Hebrew lad. He can also see what this young man is up against: no money, no friends, no place to call his own. This young man is obviously someone who is down and out, a stranger in a strange land. You can almost see the man smiling and rubbing his hands as he says, "OK, Hebrew boy, it's the pigs or nothing!"

In short, this wicked man took advantage of the son's plight and vulnerability to alienate him from his people, his culture, his tradition, his family, his religion, and his sense of decency. Do we have people like that in our society?

Sister Rose McGeady, of Covenant House in New York City, reminds us that in every large city you will find smiling people at the bus stations stalking the prodigal adolescents who get off the buses, knowing that very soon these teenagers will be desperate for food, clothing, and shelter. And these smiling, stalking people will say, "OK, boy, OK, girl; sell us your body and we'll give you something to eat. Give us your heritage, your culture, your religion, your values, all that you have been taught." This is just one example of the pigsty solicitation that goes on every day in our own time, our own culture.

This wholesale solicitation also occurs on television as the moral values of honesty, decency, pacifism, and chastity are sold down the river to sensationalism, the quick deal, violence, and freewheeling sex. It happens when the lure of materialism entices parents to the good life at the expense of their marriages, the well-being of their children, and their friendships. It happens when athletic scouts tempt high schoolers to forsake academics and share in the $10 billion sports market. It happens whenever anyone gives your child a drink or a snort of cocaine or solicits them over the Internet.

Oh yes, there are lots of people waiting to take advantage of our vulnerabilities, who ask for our heritage in exchange for a momentary high. The pigsty owner in today's parable is very much alive.

There is one more element of this story which we should not miss. The overall theme, the implications, come down to this: the younger son does not want a father, and the older son does not want a brother. And there you have it, the besetting sins of society.

The younger son represents all the people who want no father, no one to answer to, no limits, no restraint, no relationship, no responsibility, no judgment. They wish their father—God—dead. They want to be free to do their own destructive thing. The nightly newscasts are full of the stories of these people, full of their sound and their fury.

Then there are the people who say, "I have no brother. I have no concern for anyone else, and no one has a claim on me." Racism and discrimination and bias are "natural" to such people. The corporal and spiritual works of mercy make no sense to them. Only their own survival matters.

Well, there we are, an old story which we thought we knew so well—until we looked at the details. It is here that we find insights we probably never thought of.

Before we end, let me point out one final detail. As the son is returning home, still a long way off, the father—God—does what no parent in that time would ever consider doing: the father runs to greet his son. This action broke every rule of etiquette, propriety, and decency in a very rigid and proper society. No father in that culture would do such a thing: he would wait for the boy to come up to him, snivelling and falling at the father's feet. But here, in a most undignified manner, the father lifts up his tunic and runs, not walks, to his son.

Bad form, bad manners—good example. God will be God, and we must try to do likewise. And what is the bottom line to this story, this homily? As the architect Ludwig Mies van de Rohe once said: "God is in the details."

37

WHO IS MY NEIGHBOR?

LUKE 10:25-37

Let me tell you about Peter Godwin.

Peter was a bit of an oddity in the African village where he grew up. Though a British citizen, Peter and his family had moved to Rhodesia when he was just a child. His mother, a missionary doctor, was assigned to start a vaccination program. Under her supervision thousands of people were inoculated against tuberculosis, smallpox, and other diseases.

For some diseases, inoculation meant having a shot, but for others the vaccination was much more pleasant. A small dose of medicine was put on a sugar cube and fed to the patient. Little Peter was often enlisted to carry the tray of sugar cubes and to inspect the mouths of the children to make sure they had fully swallowed the cube.

In the 1970s, civil war in Rhodesia forced the Godwin family to return to England, where a now-grown Peter found work as a journalist. The *London Sunday Times* sent Peter back to South Africa in 1986 to cover the clash there between the Marxist government and armed rebels. While in Rhodesia, Peter decided to try and go to Mozambique, an area officially closed to foreign journalists. He managed to make it there, but was soon captured by a band of heavily armed rebels, who took him to their base camp.

When they arrived at the camp, Peter was hauled before the base commander. By chance, he heard the commander address his manservant in a dialect he recognized from his childhood in Rhodesia. Peter began speaking this language to the astonished commander, who demanded to know where Peter had learned the language.

Peter explained a little about his childhood in Africa, and when he mentioned that his family name was Godwin, the commander's previously harsh manner changed. The big man rolled up his shirt sleeve to expose a scar, the kind a vaccination shot usually leaves. Peter's mother had vaccinated this man when he was just a child, and the commander had received a medicine-coated sugar cube from Peter's own hand.

Only moments before, Peter Godwin had been treated like an enemy by the rebels; now he was a welcome guest among them. They returned him safely to the area where he had been captured, and even posed for a picture with Peter before they left.

Here is another story:

A fourteen-year-old girl from Cleveland, Ohio got so angry with her parents that she ran away to New York City. Cold, hungry, and friendless, she was shivering on a street corner when a cab pulled up. As some partygoers got out, a man in the group noticed the girl and, asking if she needed help, insisted that she join them for dinner in a nearby restaurant.

After hearing her story, the man took the teenager to the train station and bought her a ticket back to Cleveland. "Whatever your desire," he told her, "if you want it enough, you can make it happen." Then he gave her $20, along with his address and telephone number. If she ever needed anything, she was to call him.

The teenager returned to her family. Although she often thought of the man, she could not find the paper with his name and telephone number.

After high school, this teenager attended college and medical school and became a surgeon. She married another doctor, and they had two children. Soon her own daughter was fourteen, and asking for some vintage clothes and props for a high school program. As mother and daughter searched through trunks of old school things, the mother's lost paper from so many years ago fell out of a diary.

It took months of inquiries, but the mother finally located her benefactor. Twenty-five years after the two first met a kindly man named Ralph Burke received a letter and a check for $300. The woman asked that he accept it with the love and spirit in which it was sent. The idea, she said, wasn't to repay a "kindness that had no price"; rather, she hoped he would come meet her family.

Accepting the invitation, Burke was welcomed like a long-lost uncle. Today he insists that one should perform simple acts of kindness whenever one can. "Sometime, in some way," Burke says, "they always come back to you."

These stories bring us back to today's well-known gospel of the Good Samaritan. This parable raises two questions, the first of which is this: why did the priest pass by the fallen man? We can come up with some possible answers. One reason is that to touch what seemed to be a dead body would render a priest ritually unclean and so he would not have been able to perform his duties. Another reason is that frequently, robbers put out a decoy on the road, a man pretending to be hurt, and when someone went over to help the man, the robbers would jump him and rob him. And so these are two possible reasons why the priest passed on by.

So then the second question is, why did the Levite pass by the fallen man? We can take a few guesses here, too. Very likely, the Levite saw the priest up ahead walk by the fallen man, and decided to do the same. I say this because it fits in with a well known experiment performed some years ago.

In the experiment, an unsuspecting person was walking by an alley when from the darkness someone yelled for help—a woman who said she was being raped. Nearby were two other people who were part of the experiment. As instructed, these two ignored the woman's cries for help and kept right on walking. At first, the unsuspecting passerby hesitated; he did not know whether to respond to the pleas or not. But when he saw the other two people act as if nothing was wrong, he decided that the cries for help were insignificant and so he ignored them as well.

This experiment was repeated many times, with generally the same result. The studies led psychologists to conclude that our response to another person's plight is often determined by how other people respond. This gives us a clue about whether the situation merits our involvement. In other words, the most important person in any situation where compassion and courage are required is the first person to act. After one person acts, then others are prone to respond in like manner—but someone needs to step out from the crowd and go first.

So it was in the two stories we heard before. Peter Godwin and Ralph Burke set the wheels of mercy and compassion in motion: the priest in the parable did not. Need I say more? That is the lesson for today. In matters of the heart, in matters of the gospel, don't wait for someone else to go first. Like the prophet Nathan of old, the gospel points a finger at us and declares, "You are the one!"

And so, when the question is once again asked, "And who is my neighbor?" don't wait for someone else to answer.

38

A SIN OF OMISSION

LUKE 16:19–31

Because this parable is so familiar I will not spend time on the usual theme of the disparity between the rich and the poor.

I will just briefly mention what everyone already knows: that beginning in the 1970s right through the '80s and '90s, most of our economic growth has benefited the wealthiest Americans, and that, as a result, the richest 1% of us have nearly as much wealth as the entire bottom 95%; that the salary gap between our corporate executive officers and their workers is the greatest of any industrialized country, the ratio being about 225 to 1; that the 500 companies in the Standard & Poor's index increased profits by about 20% in the past four years and top CEO salaries have been rising about 13% a year, while at the same time as many as 2.5 million workers have lost their jobs in restructuring; and that workers' salaries have basically stagnated over the past few years, causing former Secretary of Labor Robert Reich to describe America as made up of the "overclass, the anxious class, and the underclass."

And in that same vein, I will briefly mention those horrifying pictures we see on TV or in magazines of the emaciated, bag-of-bones people in the Sudan or Rwanda or Bangladesh who are literally starving to death; that worldwide, 1.2 billion people live in absolute poverty; and that 800 million people—200 million of them children—are hungry all the time, malnourished or starving. We have all heard and seen pitiable Lazarus at our doorsteps, on our TV screens, many, many times before. His is an old story, one that brings guilt—which we quickly try to put out of mind.

And so, instead, I want to focus on two other issues in this thoroughly uncomfortable gospel. The first is a question: why did the rich man go to hell, "this place of torment," as he called it? We are not told that he acquired his wealth by foul means. We are not told that he is responsible for the poverty and misery of Lazarus. In fact, we are not even told that Lazarus begged from him and was refused. We are not told that the rich man committed any crime or evil deed. All we are told is that he feasted and dressed in fine clothing, as any successful person has a right to do. Why, then, did he go to hell?

The reason we have difficulty pinpointing why the rich man went to hell may have a lot to do with how we think of sin. We often think that we sin only through thoughts, words, and deeds. We forget that a fourth and very important way we can sin is through our omissions. At the beginning of the Mass, during the Confiteor ("we confess"), we announce these words: "I have sinned through my own fault, in my thoughts and in my words, in what I have done and in what I have failed to do." Yet how readily we forget this last criterion, the sin of omission. Today's parable reminds us this sin can send a person to hell. And this is what happened to the rich man.

The poor man, Lazarus, was lying at the gate, and the rich man simply couldn't care less. "Whatever happens to him there outside the gate is none of my concern," he probably said to himself. "I mind my own business; other people should mind theirs." The rich man probably called the police to report that a stranger was loitering outside his gate. In the meantime, dogs went and licked Lazarus' wounds. And the poor man died.

So someone from the town came and picked up his body and buried it in an unmarked grave. The rich man poured himself another cup of coffee. He had done nothing wrong against Lazarus, of course. But he did fail to do a good deed. He failed to reach out and share a little of his blessings with a poor man. And so the rich man committed a sin of omission, and for that he went to hell.

This brings us to the second question: why did Lazarus go to heaven? After all, we are not told that he ever performed a single good deed. So, what qualified him for heaven? The clue lies in his name. In biblical stories of this nature, names are significant because they often convey the basic character or personality of a person. And, in fact, this is the only parable of Jesus where the character in the story has a name. So the name must be significant for interpreting the parable, and thus understanding the reason why Lazarus went to heaven.

The name "Lazarus" is the Greek form of the Hebrew name "Eliezer," which means "God is my help." There is the clue. Lazarus is not just a poor person, but a poor person who believes and trusts in God: "God is my help." And so he found himself nestled in Abraham's bosom in paradise because of his faith and trust in God, not just because he was materially poor. Remember, poverty can just as easily turn a person bitter and angry and criminal.

And so, according to this parable, the gospel measurement for heaven or hell is in seeing. Spiritual blindness, spiritual indifference, condemns people. That's not new: we've heard this teaching of Jesus before, in Matthew 25: "Lord, when was it that we saw you hungry or thirsty or a stranger or naked or sick or in prison, and did not take care of you?" That is, when did we see you and yet not really see you? Then Jesus will answer them, "Truly I tell you, just as you did not do it for one of these, you did not do it for me. And these will go away into eternal punishment, but the righteous into eternal life."

The rich man saw Lazarus hungry, thirsty, a stranger, naked and sick—but he chose not to see him. He was spiritually blind and thus, he did not see. In not seeing, he did not act and in not acting, he omitted the compassion and sharing he should have given Lazarus. And so the rich man is condemned for his sin of omission.

It comes down to what we might call sensitivity. A Christlike sensitivity to those in need sees their need and responds to it. This parable confronts us not because we are wickedly rich and crass—hardly that—but because we so often fail to act in a compassionate manner. This parable challenges us to open our eyes and see, then to act on what we see. It prompts us to turn down the noise, pause from the rat race, put aside our own preoccupations—and notice Lazarus at the door.

Another element in this story is the question of the five brothers. Now here's some real drama! Hey, cried the rich man in hell, get a message to my five brothers to become sensitive. Tell them to open up their eyes and really see who's there, like Lazarus, so they won't come to this place of torment. Let me come back from the dead and appear before them and scare them into seeing, like Marley's ghost. But Abraham says, no can do. Moses and the prophets told everyone what they must do, and many just did not listen.

And in our time, Jesus came back from the dead; yet it hasn't made much of a difference to some. No, if you want to rescue your own five brothers—your children and grandchildren—you have to do it by example and leadership. Take an evening off every other week to go down to the homeless shelter and help distribute food. Say no to five TVs in the house and a stereo system in every room, and make regular donations to worthy causes. Bring a bag of groceries every month to the local food pantry, and bundle up your used clothing for the Salvation Army or the St. Vincent de Paul Society.

You must bring your children, so protected, so affluent, so brainwashed by consumerism, face to face with Lazarus at the door. Sponsor a needy child through an agency such as Save the Children or St. Jude's Mission. Encourage your teenagers to help out with Habitat for Humanity or volunteer at a hospital or spend some time working with the disabled. Ask your college-age children if they can give a year to the Jesuit volunteer program here or abroad.

None of us wish for our families to come to a place of torment. We want them not only to be successful people, but good and caring and sensitive human beings, people who have learned to see and to respond. Listen to this story:

> One bitter winter morning, Flo Whetley of Hop Bottom, Pennsylvania, took her son to Manhattan for a medical checkup. As she hurried through the cold she noticed many homeless people huddled in doorways. One stood out from the others because he was wrapped in a bright pink hand-knit afghan.
>
> Most of us have had similar encounters and felt helpless to do anything. No one of us alone can solve the staggering economic and social problems behind homelessness, so most of us just avert our eyes. But not Flo Whetley. As a nurse, she knew well the lethal potential of hypothermia and she could not stop thinking about that man and his handmade blanket.
>
> Back home that night, she took a pile of her children's castoff

clothing and some old bedspreads, and quickly assembled them into a simple sleeping bag. This first emergency sleeping bag was so gratefully received by a homeless person that she and her family continued to turn them out.

That first year, they made eight sleeping bags which she and her husband, Jim, distributed themselves. Soon Flo's neighbors began to notice this unusual activity. Once they saw the potential for saving lives with recycled discards they enthusiastically joined in. And so the project grew and acquired a name, My Brother's Keeper Quilt Group.

Today Flo Whetley is the dynamic leader behind a nation-wide movement of thousands of volunteers in dozens of cities and towns. As of 1996, Flo and Jim have had 49,000 Ugly Quilts (as these sleeping bags are sometimes called) pass through their own garage distribution center; thousands more are being made and given away by church groups, youth groups, and individuals around the country. The cost-free procedure that started on her kitchen table has grown into a nonprofit organization with a thirteen-member board of directors.

Flo's home has become command central for the project as she shares information and connects donors, volunteers, and distributors. Her front porch, barn, and garage have all acted as temporary clearinghouses for local donations, and her calendar is crowded with how-to pep talks for churches and civic organizations. Flo's basic message is simple: "Start here. Start now. Everyone can do something."

Some saw a homeless man huddled in a doorway. Flo saw more than meets the eye: not a man in a doorway but a doorway to a mission. Can you imagine the impact this has had on the Whetley kids? Their parents are teaching them how to see so they won't go to the place of torment—not for what they did but for what they didn't do.

39

STALKING GOD

LUKE 18:9-14

Today's parable is another familiar story whose theme—pride versus humility—we can all relate to in some way. So let me retell Jesus' story by using another famous story which is actually a variation on the same theme. The other story is called "The Bear," and it comes from William Faulkner. The story centers around a boy and a bear:

The boy, Ike McCaslin, is ten years old, and he has been invited for the first time to join the men as they go on a late fall hunting foray into the deep woods. They will shoot for quail and deer, but the ultimate goal of their quest is Old Ben, the legendary bear who roams an area one hundred miles square and who has, for years, terrorized the villages. The boy is, at one and the same time, frightened and fascinated at the prospect of facing it.

When he arrives at camp, deep in the forest, Ike enters into an experience not unlike that of a novice in a religious community. He is met by Sam Fathers, part Indian, part black, who will be his spiritual guide in the ways of the hunt. Ike soon becomes accustomed to the rude lifestyle of the hunter and to the damp and cold of the stands where he waits, through long hours, for the rush of deer through the woods. He soon learns that patience and humility are essential for survival in the forest, that the overeager or cocky hunter never lands a kill.

Well, one morning, during the second week of his novitiate, while he waits on his lonely hunting stand, Ike hears the unusually high-pitched yipping and barking of the dogs, and, with some trepidation, he readies his gun. Sam Fathers tells him, "It's Old Ben," and the boy stiffens in anticipation and excitement. The two listen carefully and watch until finally Sam knows that the bear has slipped back into the woods. "He do it every year," Sam explains. "He come to see who's here, who's new in camp this year, whether he can shoot or not, can stay or not."

The boy has been dreaming of the bear for years, reaching out to him in imagination and will, and now the bear has established contact with the boy, sizing him up and monitoring his readiness for a richer encounter, gazing mysteriously from the shadows of the woods, seeing without being seen. That's when Ike began to realize that the hunted is himself a hunter. (Those seeking God are long before sought by God.)

In time, Sam teaches the boy how to track the bear, and Ike manages to find a vestige of the beast, Old Ben's footprint in the mud, bigger and more fascinating than he had imagined. Then, sometime later, having moved deeper into the dark of the forest, stationed at another lonely stand, Ike listens carefully. He hears no baying of the dogs, only the solitary drumming of a woodpecker. When even that sound stops, he knows that the bear is, once again, looking at him. He has no idea whether the animal is before or behind him, whether he is far or near, and he stands still, the useless gun at his side, the taste of fear like brass in his mouth.

And then, just as abruptly, it is over, the bear is gone. When Sam emerges from the woods a few minutes later, the boy excitedly tells him of the encounter, but he adds, somewhat puzzled, "I didn't see him; I didn't, Sam." And the old man replies, "I know it; he done the looking."

The next June Ike returned to camp, this time with his own rifle. While the men hunted, Ike ranged out into the woods, using his compass as Sam had taught him, identifying landmarks, tracking animals, even finding, once more, Old Ben's crooked footprint. But the bear himself he did not encounter.

When he tells Sam Fathers of his exploits and of his frustration at not having seen the bear, the old man explains that the reason the bear has not come out into the open is the gun that the young man carries: "You will have to choose," Sam explains, between the safety the gun provides and the experience of seeing the bear close up.

The next morning, before light, the boy set out into the woods, consumed by the desire to commune with Old Ben. Purposely, he left behind his weapon and entered the woods armed only with a stick to ward off snakes and a compass to find his way back. By noon, he had wandered further into the forest than he had ever gone, and he knew that he would make it back to camp only after dark had fallen. Still, there was no sign of the bear.

He stopped to wipe his brow and to glance at the compass. Perhaps, he thought, the surrendering of the gun was not enough; perhaps the bear demanded that he leave behind everything, all weapons of defense and all instruments of direction. And so Ike hung the compass on a nearby bush and he leaned the simple snake stick against it, and, stripped of any of the signs of civilization, he entered deeper into the forest.

Before he knew it, he was lost, enveloped by the woods. Soon he saw the familiar crooked and enormous footprint, but this time it was not old; as he looked at it, it was still filling with water, proving that Old Ben had just been there. Frightened but fascinated, Ike followed the prints, though he knew the reckless decision to follow Old Ben into the trackless woods, hours from his home camp, would leave him either dead or hopelessly lost. Still he pressed on, deep, deep in the woodland.

And then he saw the bear.

It was just there, not as big as he had dreamed it but big as he had expected. Then the animal moved across the glade, pausing ever so briefly in the direct light of the sun and then, as it passed into the obscurity of the woods, it glanced once over its shoulder and spied the boy. Finally, it sank invisibly into the deep darkness of the forest.

Let's look at this tale through the interpretive lens of Jesus' parable. Like Ike, we are afraid of God (who makes demands, you know); at the same time, we are irresistibly drawn to God. And so, like Ike, we go out to meet the sacred. But just as there are disciplines and techniques that enable a person to survive in the trackless wood, so there are disciplines and techniques in the spiritual life, in the search for God.

We soon learn that though we are ravenously hungry for God, the divine is not One who responds to our demands and on our timetable. God appears when God appears, and for his own reasons—like Old Ben, who is a symbol for God. So we must be humble and docile in God's presence, ready to wait, if necessary, through long hours, days, and years, prepared to hear the rush of God through the woods when it comes. Moreover, God will not appear until the prideful ego has been liberated.

For Ike, the decisive moment of liberation is reached only when Sam Fathers, who is a Jesus figure, tells him of the choice he must make between the safety of the gun and the vision of the bear. Sam Fathers is saying that the bear will not show itself as long as Ike carries with him the instruments of guidance and violence, in other words, those things which contribute to his mastery of the situation.

This is the very point of today's parable. With his compass and rifle, you see, Ike is in control. He is doing the seeing, and he will determine the quality of his encounter with Old Ben. When the moment of truth arrives, the boy lets go of the compass, the stick, and the gun. With humility, he enters the deepest part of the woods. And it is there, in that place and in that state of soul, in emptiness, that he sees the bear. Caught in a glade, a small clearing in the forest, the bear is simply there.

Two men went up to the temple to pray. They both sought God, who had already seen them though they did not notice. One man had his compass, his stick, and his gun; in other words, his ego. The other man left it all behind. One man encountered God; the other did not.

So what is the point of both stories? God peeks at us in a thousand different ways. Only by letting go can we return the favor.

LESSONS *of* SCRIPTURE

40

THE BEST WINE SAVED

JOHN 2:1–12

Because the gospel we have just heard was written by John, we can expect many levels of meaning and much use of symbols. That's the way he wrote. So, for example, changing water into wine represents what happens to people who open themselves to the Spirit. They become something new. Or we can read this incident as the story of One who brings joy and defeats sadness, even the sadness of death.

Today, we will look at this gospel as a reference to Jesus who, when you come right down to it, is himself "the best wine saved till now." Certainly, that was the experience of many people in his time: sinners, outsiders, women, pagans. Jesus released these people from their fate; he accepted them as they were. Surely, for them, he was "the best wine saved till now."

This is the way it is at weddings—which is perhaps why this gospel is used so often at a wedding. The couple have met other people, may have dated other people; but now the one person who is at their side is "the best wine saved till now." There is no question in their mind. This is the way it is with lost souls: Paul, Augustine, Ignatius, Magdalene, Dorothy Day. Each one of them had gone down many roads, fleeing God, searching. And one day they encountered Jesus, and they knew he was "the best wine saved till now."

This, above all, is the way it is today. The "best wine" is often found in the small kindnesses of Christlike figures who pop in and out of everyday life, quietly fading away. But in their kindness we have savored something special and the taste remains with us. These people recognize our thirst and ultimately offer us "the best wine." Let me share an unexciting story of an ordinary teenage girl who accidentally sipped good wine. She tells her story so:

A warm spring breeze rustled the lace curtains at my bedroom window as I laid my head on the pillow. Friday night, and I had a date to the junior prom next week! This event was all we girls had talked about at school. I pictured myself gliding across the dance floor in my pale blue organza gown, its skirt billowing like my curtains when I twirled so lightly on my....And there my fantasy crashed.

I looked to the end of my bed, at the mound under the covers. Tomorrow I would have to search for a suitable pair of shoes. Matching my dress wasn't the problem; fitting the canoes attached to my legs was. My feet were too big. They were the most obvious thing about me. I tripped over them when I walked, and classmates teased me about the clodhoppers sticking out from under my desk. Who was I kidding, thinking I would actually dance at the prom? I rolled over, envisioning Cinderella's wicked stepsisters trying to jam their ugly feet into her dainty glass slipper.

I woke up early the next morning, rushed through breakfast, then dashed to the bus. I had made a list of the shoe stores in downtown Indianapolis, knowing I would probably have to visit every last one if I were to have any luck.

Starting out on fashionable Washington Street, I worked my way down the list. At a store near the bottom I asked again, "I'd like a pair of dressy pumps, please." "Of course," the salesman said. "What si...?" Looking down at my feet, he quickly corrected himself. "I'm sorry. We don't carry your size." I couldn't get out of there fast enough. What would I end up wearing, my brother's gym shoes? God, can't you help me out?

There was one more place: Stout's Factory Shoe Store over on Massachusetts Avenue. The musty establishment had been a fixture in Indianapolis for years. I doubted it carried anything I would be interested in. But I was desperate. Stout's yellowed window featured "sensible" styles: crepe-soled nurses' shoes, steel-toe work boots, white Keds, black patent leather Mary Janes.

A bell tinkled as I opened the door and went in. The worn hardwood floor creaked under my clumsy steps. The air reeked of shoe polish. I crinkled my nose. "Hello! Hello!" came a raspy welcome. The bright green parrot in a cage by the cash register had spied me. Great. I was about to bolt when a short elderly man appeared from the back of the store. Could I be of some service, young lady? How could this ancient man even imagine what a fifteen-year-old girl might need? "I don't suppose you have a pair of dressy pumps to fit me," I said, pointing ruefully at my feet.

The old man took me by the hand and led me to a chair. "Sit here," he said, bowing slightly, as if I were a princess. "I'll be back in a moment." What's he going to bring out? High but-toned granny shoes? The parrot squawked in the background. Finally, the salesman returned with a box. He sat on the sloped stool and deftly removed my saddle shoes.

Then he took a large pump from the box and slipped it onto my foot. "There now," he said. "Stand up and let's see about the fit." I rose and nearly fell out of the pump. The old man stead-ied me on my feet. He had misjudged my size. The shoe was too big—way too big. That had never happened before. My foot was swimming in the pump he had brought out! Suddenly, I felt giddy.

The gentleman's eyes sparkled. "Oh, dear," he said. "Obviously, these won't do. Let me get a smaller size." He scooped the reject back into the box and shuffled away. A small-er size, I thought. How do you like that? My elderly friend came back barely visible behind the double stack of shoe boxes he juggled in his arms. "Perhaps we have something for you here." I tried on pair after pair, in gold sateen, pink, bone, pearlized patent leather. The salesman sat on his perch surrounded by a sea of open boxes, gently dressing my feet as I decreed, "Yes, these are a definite possibility."

I told him about the prom, my date, my blue organza dress.

"Ahh," he said, "in that case, let's try these." He swept aside the clutter of boxes and opened one from the bottom of his stack. Carefully he unwrapped the prettiest shoes I had seen all day: royal blue satin pumps with decorative bows. I felt like Cinderella when he slipped them on my feet. A perfect fit! I wanted to get up and dance right there in the store. "I'll wrap them for you," he said, looking pleased.

While paying for my shoes I wondered about his initial misjudgment. Could this seasoned salesman honestly have been so wrong? Perhaps he knew more than just the business of shoes. As I left, the parrot squawked, "Good day." And it was, with a little help from a wise salesman in an old store, where my own two feet—and God—had taken me.

Well, as I said, this is not a spectacular story. But remember, grace is ordinary. And remember something else: all of us, like the nondescript, little old salesman, have wine to offer. And not just any old wine, but "the best wine saved till now."

Our comment, our gesture, our reaching out, our kindness to someone who is thirsting for affirmation, recognition, or help, can be the "best wine" they've had all day. Perhaps, even, in their whole life.

41

GATHER THE CHILDREN

JOHN 8:1–11

It no longer shocks us when celebrity stars announce they they are pregnant out of wedlock and then coyly tell no one who the father of the child is. The child of no marriage, a woman without a husband will join the fourth of American's children born fatherless. A fatherless culture joined to a divorce culture brings us to a cartoon I saw the other day when one kid is speaking to another and he says, "Yeah, my mom's boyfriend gave me a few pointers on commitment."

There was a report in the paper recently telling about a well-to-do married couple who didn't want the messiness of pregnancy. So they purchased a sperm from an anonymous donor and an egg from an anonymous donor, and had the baby concocted in a test tube. Then they hired a surrogate mother to gestate the baby. Before the birth, however, they divorced so the child has been legally declared to be parentless and will be "auctioned off" to the highest bidder. In this kind of moral environment, it is no wonder that there is alienation and fragility and non-commitment deep in the lives of so many young children.

Alienation because our pregnant starlet, for example, has made a terrible, long-range, self-serving decision for the unborn child; namely, "I hereby cut you off from one half of your heritage. I have decided that you will have no paternal grandparents, no cousins, no siblings, no extended family, no father. From the start, you are incomplete. My decision." Such children, then, with no father in place, will endure a series of intermittent boyfriends visiting mother. And so they will not learn much about commitment and responsibility.

Being very wealthy, of course, celebrities—along with those who are poorer, run-of-the mill mothers without fathers—will place their burdens where they always do, on the backs of other women, by subcontracting out their children either to paid strangers or unpaid family. Think of the vast number of grandparents throughout the land raising their children's children. Think of all the males, like the absent man in today's gospel, who get license to be irresponsible. Think of all the lonely children who live their lives without the presence of adults. A child whose parents are split by say, adultery, picks up certain assumptions about trust, security, and fidelity, doesn't he?

Add to this mix the culture of violence that is so omnipresent today. An average kid sees over 100,000 acts of violence a year, including some cartoon characters who are alarmingly vulgar and crude. And what about the violence we tolerate and even cheer on in sports? No wonder children believe that the world is unsafe, They have been desensitized to violence, sold on it. They are taught by the media that it is the best way to settle things. Only in real life, bullets kill and maim and cause immeasurable pain; in real life, there is no movie sequel to death. The four young girls and their teacher who were killed in Jonesboro, Arkansas a few years back don't get reruns.

No, there's blood on the playground for schools are now war zones. Psychologists, struggling to make sense of school killings, point to a combination of rampant violence, easy access to guns, and the absence of adult role models in children's lives as a major part of the problem.

A while back, *Time* magazine featured an article on talk show host Jerry Springer. His talk show is now number one, surpassing even Oprah Winfrey in the ratings. What makes his show so popular? In a word, nastiness. He lets people fight and brawl on his show, especially pregnant females. The closing paragraph of the article reads:

Which bring us back to those children-to-be [of these pregnant, unmarried females]. Time and again the women on the show are pregnant, sometimes several months along. But instead of being taken seriously, their condition is used to spice up the scandal: "Paternity result: I slept with two brothers!" The crowd roars when a pregnant woman socks somebody.

Meanwhile, the important questions are hardly ever asked, Who is going to support this baby? How is he or she going to survive the parents' bickering and entanglements? With his approach, Springer fosters a reckless (and vile) attitude toward having babies, and the children of his guests will suffer as a result. This is a joke?

Yes, the children who will see reruns of Mom socking someone will inherit violence. And who is in the crowd roaring approval? Who are the devotees of such degrading TV shows? Are you and your children among them? Are these the values you want them to absorb?

No one seems able to stem the tide of violence and divorce, along with the breakdown of family life. Certainly not the government, not with marriage being seen as merely one form of lifestyle and commitment. (It's hard to even say the word "commitment" with a straight face when so many politicians are publicly unfaithful.) Add to that the fact that cohabitation seems to be the "in" thing, even though research consistently shows that cohabitation arrangements are extremely fragile, far more so than marriage.

You take all these factors—a breakdown of the family, the abandonment of children in the interests of careers, widespread divorce (which is arguably the most common form of child abuse, even when it's necessary), a media culture whose aim is to desensitize, the prevalence of routine, casual violence, music and lyrics that preach anarchy, the lack of a common consensus about national values—and you have a climate hostile to the physical, mental, and moral health of children. It's time for other models, for healers. As Mary Pipher writes in her book, *The Shelter of Each Other: Rebuilding Our Families:*

> What made sense even thirty or forty years ago is counterintuitive today. For example, in the 1960s I admired the irreverence, rebelliousness, and wildness of the beat poets. Kerouac and Corso, Ginsberg and Orlovsky, were wonderful foils for sleepy, suburban citizens. They were a counterbalance to all the certainty, uniformity and smugness of the Eisenhower era.
>
> But today, Americans are a lost and uncertain people. While

some politicians boast they know the answers, in most families, smugness is in short supply. When the culture is having a nervous breakdown, wildness and chaos are less appealing. In the 1950s, America may have needed iconoclasts. Today we need healers, people who try to make broken things work.

Mary Pipher is right: it's time for healers. That's the theme of today's gospel. The woman caught in adultery was wrong. Jesus properly told her to avoid her sin. But he would not condemn her. Instead he offered her healing. And, what's more important, he offered her a future. Go, sin no more. Don't look back. Look ahead to a better life.

If there is any lesson to be learned from the recent spate of senseless killing by kids, it may be that these recurring, horrendous stories force us not to look back on those terrible tragedies, but to look ahead. There before us is the call to heal our relationships and put our priorities straight, a boldface directive to reclaim our families. Above all, now is the time to gather our children.

42

VIOLENCE

MATTHEW 21:33-43

What a mess this gospel is! The storyline is full of violence; people beating and killing and stoning servants, then killing a king's son, and then the king, wreaking vengeance by "putting those wretched men to a wretched death," as the gospel says. There is plenty of murder, revenge, and blood in this unsettling parable.

Today's gospel can be interpreted on many levels, but today I want to focus on the violence it contains. This is, as you sadly know, a timely topic. Violence forms the subtext of our daily lives. Nations, peoples, individuals of all ages—even kids—are routinely hurting, maiming, and killing one another. It has all become so commonplace that we hardly pay attention anymore.

What is behind this proliferation of violence in our world? I want to suggest that part of it is a shocking lack of empathy for other people, for the victims, an inability to feel what those who are hurt or dying are feeling. We lack empathy and we hurt and kill others because we have divided the world into "us" and "them"—a distinction, mind you, that is high on Jesus' list of what is horribly and terribly evil in the world.

For Jesus, there was no "us" and "them," no Hutus and Tutsis, no northern and southern Irish, no blacks and whites, no Crips and

Warlords, no gay and straight, no Jew and Samaritan. Jesus taught that our neighbor is everyone—especially everyone who is hurting. We must understand and appreciate his or her pain. In fact, it is not too far-fetched to say that empathy for victims is Christianity's cardinal virtue. Yet more and more, especially among the young, a sense of empathy is evaporating. With this loss comes an inability to be compassionate. And when there is no empathy and no compassion, there is easy violence.

Here's an example. I was listening to a therapist the other day, who was telling the story of a nun, a nursing sister, who had been in an accident. Two young teens had stolen a car and were weaving recklessly all over the road; at one point, they plowed straight into the sister's car. She was badly injured, and several bones were broken. She was in the hospital a long time; to this day, she still limps and suffers a great deal.

Since the two boys were underage, they were not charged with a crime. When the nun got out of the hospital she went to the police station and asked for the names of those two boys. Then she went to see them both. The nun spoke movingly and tearfully to them about her pain, her long hospital stay, and her inability to continue her work as a nurse. She was hoping for some sympathy, if not an apology. After she was done speaking, the kids simply looked at her and said "Look, lady, that's your problem." Then they laughed, got up, and left.

This story shows the measurable and growing lack of empathy among people: the inability to care, to feel for the victim, to show remorse, to enter into another's pain and humiliation. Psychopaths, sociopaths, deviants—indeed, more and more kids and adolescents and young adults—all have this in common: no empathy, no feeling, no conscience. It is a growing problem.

So, here is a question: where does this lack of empathy come from, people doing horrible things and not even batting an eye? Kids killing kids and wondering what the fuss is about, conscienceless killers? People cheering when someone is brutally hurt? Such moral deadness, such moral apathy, used to be confined to hit men. Now, even children experience this state. What happened? There are many reasons why this condition is so prevalent today: I'll mention two.

First, there is the pervasive philosophical vacuum in our society, which has its origin in the universities. The university professorate is largely agnostic, and so what is their message to students? That there is no truth. Nothing can be known. There are no objective standards, only culturally conditioned attitudes. All institutions, the places that used to mediate meaning, are corrupt. Religion is slavery.

In time, this type of reasoning leads to what we have today: a situation where, lacking any objective standards, the only way left to decide right and wrong is by one's own personal criteria. "If it feels good, do it. You do your thing, I do mine. Who is to say who is right? Don't impose your morality on me: we are all equally right." When truth is totally in the eye of the beholder, college kids become hesitant to condemn Hitler or to feel for his victims.

A well-publicized case in point is Professor Peter Singer, who was recently installed as professor of bioethics in Princeton. Singer teaches that it's all right to kill a handicapped infant. He has said that "Killing a disabled infant is not morally equivalent to killing a person....Very often it is not wrong at all." The belief that human life is sacred is, as he calls it, "speciesist"; humans are just one animal among many.

You would think, by the way, that his fellow Jews would be in an uproar over Singer's comments—like the president of Princeton, Harold Shapiro, who hired him—because it is well documented that this is exactly the way Hitler began. (Singer himself lost three of his grandparents in the Holocaust.) The first systematic attempt by the Nazis to eliminate a defined population group was directly at severely disabled children. Babies judged to be defective were routinely starved to death or killed by drugs or gas. Eventually, the philosophy that some lives were not worthy to be lived became ingrained in many of the people of Germany, and the Holocaust was able to become a reality.

If Singer's university students buy into his philosophy of abortion, infanticide, and euthanasia as acceptable practices, then a lack of empathy is given legitimization. If the students accept that human beings are just one animal among many, then killing other humans should cause no more concern than killing a rat.

The second reason for the lack of empathy today is because of the media, which is, as you know, a powerful influence on how kids develop empathy as a basis for morality. We see this most prominently in the message of most advertising: anything goes. And if anything goes, then nothing counts. We see this attitude everywhere; "whatever" is its common expression. We are only consuming animals going nowhere. Life is meaningless so grab your gusto as you go around. Look out for Number One.

The media celebrates being "cool." You are in control. You show power, have power. People move aside for you or fawn all over you. You don't show emotion when someone is riddled with bullets or the life blood is draining out of him or her. You're cool. In promoting this type of attitude, the media consistently and routinely promotes desensitization, the opposite of empathy. After the umpteenth murder, how much can you feel for the victim? It is estimated that the average child witnesses over 200,000 acts of violence on television by the time he or she is eighteen years old.

Here is something to attend to. Lieutenant Colonel Dave Grossman is an Army expert on the psychology of killing. Ironically, he's from Jonesboro, Arkansas, where, as you might recall, two boys, ages eleven and thirteen, killed four girls and a teacher and left ten others injured. In a talk given in Kansas recently, Grossman pointed out that violent crime is occurring at record levels here and elsewhere in the world. He told the audience that, "Although we should never downplay child abuse, poverty, or racism, there is only one new variable present [today which can promote violent behavior]: media violence presented as entertainment for children."

Throughout his Army career, Grossman's job was to condition soldiers how to kill. He said that killing is a learned skill because there is an innate resistance to it. Around the time of World War II, Army research showed that only fifteen to twenty percent of individual riflemen could bring themselves to fire at exposed enemy soldiers. To make soldiers more effective in battle, the Army had to fix this problem. And fix it they did. They were so successful that by the Korean War, fifty-five percent of the soldiers were willing to fire and kill; by Vietnam, that number had jumped to ninety percent.

How did they do it? Grossman outlined the process. In the first step, the men are brutalized at boot camp. Their heads are shaved and they are herded together, naked. Then they are all dressed alike. In this way, they begin to lose all individuality and become desensitized to violence. Grossman pointed out that the *Journal of the American*

Medical Association demonstrated the very same brutalization and desensitizing happened to children as they watched TV. There is a definite correlation, the study said, between watching violent TV and violent actions.

The second step used by the Army is classic conditioning. Remember Psychology 101, when you were taught about the dogs that learn to associate food with the ringing of a bell? Thereafter, the dogs could not hear the bell without drooling with pleasure in anticipation of food.

Grossman pointed out that our kids watch vivid pictures of human suffering and death. They see graphic depictions of stabbings, garroting, kicking in the groin and head, vomit, blood, and decapitations and they learn to associate all this with their favorite soft drink or candy bar which immediately pops up on the TV screen during the endless commercials. The success of this conditioning can be observed when you go to the movies. Listen to the young people laugh and cheer when there is bloody violence and someone is painfully hurt or gruesomely dying. They keep right on eating popcorn. Empathy, feeling for the victim, is a non-issue, a non-emotion. A mother adds her testimony:

> Recently, a thirteen-year-old in our community was raped by a group of teenage boys. Actually, the technical term was "sexual assault with a foreign object"—in fact, several foreign objects—but it still sounds like rape to me. It makes my thighs clap together and my guts shudder. But the comments I have since overheard by other teenagers—how she probably deserved it, how it's kind of funny (a cucumber, you heard? ha, ha, ha!), how they were just having some fun while their parents were out of town—make me queasy. They are chillingly nonchalant. They've seen it all before, anyway.

Desensitization negatively shapes the moral lives of children and opens the door to violence.

The third step in making soldiers killers is deploying what is called "operant conditioning." This means that one no longer shoots at a bullseye in a neutral round paper or straw target, but at realistic, human-shaped targets. Now think about this: in the video games, the kids do exactly the same thing and therefore get the same "operant conditioning." They shoot at lifelike figures.

Grossman commented, "It came as no surprise to me when I read that the two shooters in the Littleton massacre had allegedly been avid players of Doom and Quake, two popular computer games full of realistic violence in which players stalk their opponents through dungeon-like environments to kill them with high-powered weapons." One video game has the player kill children. The only way to exit this game is to put the simulated gun in your mouth and pull the trigger.

The fourth and last component in training killers is role models, that is, the drill sergeant who personifies violence and aggression. And who are the role models for our young people today? Clint Eastwood, Arnold Schwarzenegger, Bruce Willis, and Jean Claude van Damme.

We, as a culture, are conditioned to violence. Our children are conditioned to violence. We find it hard to feel for "the enemy," those nasty TV or video characters whom we dispatch as we pleasurably sip our soda. Empathy comes hard in a world made up of "us" and "them." Compassion comes not at all in a world made up of "us" and "them." Violence, the fruit of the absence of empathy and compassion, comes easy in a world made up of "us" and "them."

The answer to ending the violence present in the world today must come not only in turning away from a media which trains our minds to callous indifference. More positively, it must come from a return to Jesus' teaching: there is no "us" and "them." Put into the words of his disciple, St. Paul: "There is neither male or female, Gentile or Jew, slave or free. All are one in Christ." When we, like Mother Teresa, can look into the face of a victim and see Christ, violence will cease.

Bear with me as I close with the words of the great Russian poet, Yevgeny Yevtushenko:

> In 1941, Mama took me back to Moscow. There I saw our enemies for the first time. If my memory serves me right, nearly 20,000 German war prisoners were to be marched in a single column through the streets of Moscow. The pavement swarmed with onlookers, cordoned off by police and soldiers. The crowd was mostly women. Every one of them must have had a father or a husband, a brother or a son killed by the Germans. They gazed with hatred in the direction in which the column was to

appear. At last we saw it.

The generals marched at the head, massive chins stuck out, lips pursed disdainfully, their whole demeanor meant to show superiority over their plebeian victims. The women were clenching their fists. The soldiers and policemen had all they could do to hold them back....All at once something happened to them. They saw the German soldiers, thin, unshaven, wearing dirty, blood-stained bandages, hobbling on crutches or leaning on the shoulders of their comrades. The soldiers walked with their heads down. The street became dead silent. The only sound was the shuffling of boots, the thumping of crutches.

Then I saw an elderly woman in broken-down boots push herself forward and touch a policeman's shoulder saying, "Let me through." Something about her made him step aside. She went up to the column, took from inside her coat something wrapped in a colored handkerchief, and unfolded it. It was a crust of black bread. She pushed it awkwardly into the pocket of a soldier so exhausted that he was tottering on his feet. And now, suddenly from every side, women were running towards the soldiers, pushing into their hands bread, cigarettes, whatever they had. The soldiers were no longer enemies. They were people.

When the women saw the men hobbling through the streets, they were no longer the enemy; they were no longer those who killed their relatives. They were just victims, and the women felt for them. There was an outpouring of empathy and compassion. The violence they intended was no longer in their hearts.

Jesus Christ would approve.

43

TAKE UP THE CROSS

MATTHEW 16:21–27

"Whoever wishes to come after me must deny himself, take up his cross, and follow me." When Christianity comes up with these words of Jesus, we have a tendency to read them as an extreme statement. They seem to be an advertisement: "Come, join our faith and suffer!" And in a world where any kind of minor inconvenience is material for a lawsuit, the appeal of this "welcome" is not great.

Actually, Jesus is giving us the common sense wisdom of human life. If you want to follow a medical or engineering or legal career, you must deny too many nights out on the town, take up your cross of rigorous study, and follow the teacher. If you want to qualify for the Olympics, you have to deny yourself twenty scoops of chocolate ice cream a day, take up the cross of brutal exercise, and follow the coach. So it goes.

What Jesus is saying, therefore, is an insight into life itself: there are no free rides. No crosses mean no growth; no pain, no gain, as they say. But take note: Christianity goes further. It teaches that, as a mark of true discipleship, there are three types of crosses: the cross of inconvenience, the cross of witness, and the cross of martyrdom. Let's look at the first cross; a story will illustrate it.

An elderly nun went to see her spiritual director. She shared with him the story of a young nun who had just left their community. The elderly nun had very much liked this young nun and appreciated the spark and vigor she brought to the community. For a year, though, she had noticed that the young nun was obviously in distress, agonizing over whether or not she should leave the community and whether, indeed, the community even wanted her. So the elderly nun prayed for the young nun, prayed that she might stay, prayed that she might realize she was wanted and valued, prayed that God might give her the strength to see beyond her doubts. But she never went, at any time, and talked to the young nun. She never inconvenienced herself to tell her how much the community appreciated the gift that she, the young nun, was. Now she was upset that the young nun had left.

The spiritual director pointed out the older nun's mistake: she had prayed minus the cross of inconvenience. She never put herself out and tried to bring about what she was asking God to do. She never took up the cross; she left things up to God. But how was God to let the young nun know that she was appreciated inside the community when the community itself would never tell her that?

Let's put this on a more personal level. If my mother is sick and I pray that she gets better, but I have not inconvenienced myself to drive her to see the doctor, I have not prayed as a cross-bearing Christian. If I see a colleague or friend who looks depressed and pray for her, but do not go out of my way to speak to her, then I am not praying as a cross-bearing Christian. If I pray for a close friend today but do not inconvenience myself to go and send him a postcard to tell him I am thinking about him, how is that prayer supposed to touch him? If I pray for world peace, but do not openly forgive those who have hurt me, how can God bring about peace on this planet? Our prayer needs a level of inconvenience to back it up. It needs the cross to be fruitful.

The second cross deals with bearing witness under pressure. Everybody knows about this one, being different in a world of conformity. That is tough, very tough. Ask any teenage girl. Not having the right body and look sends them hurrying into diet mills and cosmetic surgery parlors. Not having well-chiseled chest muscles sends the teenage boys into steroids and gyms. Not having the right clothes on the opening day of school is to assign a student to the limbo of shame, social disgrace, and nerdiness. The point is, the tyrannies are there to force conformity—and they are also there, unfortunately, in the moral order.

And so the pressure of the cross increases. Many years ago, a friend of mine who visited me while I was in the seminary and who was in the service during World War II told me this story:

> I remember my brief stay at Fort Bragg boot camp: not one of the more uplifting experiences of my life....They dumped all of us college boys there in mid-June and tried to make soldiers out of us by the end of August. We were scared, trying to act big, wanting to fit the role, play the part. The first day was one of the worst, with physicals, haircuts, our first meeting with our sergeant. That night, when we at last were in bed and the yelling and the cursing had stopped and all was quiet, we heard, just a bunk or two beyond my own, someone speaking quietly. It was this guy. I still remember his name, Sweat; that was his name, Sweat. He was from Tennessee. Ran track for them, I think. He was saying his prayers.
>
> Well, need I tell you how this display of piety was greeted by his barrack mates? There were hoots, catcalls. "What the hell are you doing, Sweat?" they cried. "He wants his mama!" others shouted. He didn't move. He kept praying. When he finished, he got back in his bunk and went to sleep. Next night, after lights were out, there he was again. There were catcalls and comments again, but they were fewer. The next night, when Sweat said his prayers, only one person said anything and then very little. The night after, I heard someone else say "Amen," when Sweat finished.
>
> When boot camp was over at the end of August, our platoon voted Sweat the best cadet. He really wasn't that good a soldier. But he was what we might have liked to be.

Now, the question: would any of us have gotten down on our knees and joined Sweat? Not likely. Going against Paul's advice, "Do not conform yourself to this age," we would have conformed. The pressure increases, and the cross of witness gets heavier.

The third cross is martyrdom. Here we have two categories, if you will: "wet" martyrdom and "dry" martyrdom. The first, wet martyrdom, means shedding your blood for truth, for Jesus. We have a whole litany of people who did that. But then there's dry martyrdom—no bloodshed, but a wounding of the spirit. Perhaps this is harder in some ways, the martyrdom of surrendering your security for Jesus, the martyrdom of grace under pressure.

Harvard psychiatrist and author Robert Coles tells of interviewing a little black girl during the early years of the Civil Rights movement in the South. You've seen her picture many times: Norman Rockwell did a painting of her being escorted by two burly policeman to a newly segregated school.

The little girl was subjected to a great deal of harassment. Hate words were scrawled on nearby walls and fences along her street, and threats were made to her family. On her way to school each day she was subjected to catcalls and harsh stares and obscene gestures. At school, she was shunned by the white students. All of this amounted to a lot of pressure for anyone, much less a small child.

During a visit to her modest home, Coles asked the girl how she kept her composure. Good book Christian that she was, the little girl replied that she knew all the Bible stories of holding fast to God no matter what people did to you. She knew what they did to Jesus and how he held fast. And so she just put everything in the hands of Jesus, she said. He was her rock. Still, that didn't make the pressure any less.

People of honor like this student, whistle-blowers, those who sacrifice jobs and livelihood to hold onto principles—all bear the heavy cross of dry martyrdom.

So there we are, left with the haunting words of today's gospel: "Whoever wishes to come after me must deny himself, take up his cross—the cross of inconvenience, the cross of witness, the cross of martyrdom—and follow me." But remember, there is the promise which follows: "Whoever loses his life for my sake will find it."

The Christian path is as complex and as simple as that.

44

BURYING OL' BLUE EYES

ACTS 7:55–60

On May 14, 1998, as the whole world knows, Ol' Blue Eyes, the Chairman of the Board, the leader of the Rat Pack, Francis Albert Sinatra, died.

For fifty years he was a star. No one could wrap himself around a song like Sinatra, the master of intimate popular singing. He was, as Frank Rich of the *New York Times* wrote, "one of the greatest artists of any kind this country has produced." Just listen to his 1955 master-piece, "In the Wee Small Hours," and you'll know why. But as Frank Rich continues: "In death, though, it's abundantly clear that Sinatra creates a national problem for American sensibilities...[for] as a human being, he not infrequently resembled a thug."

We all know what happened in Sinatra's life. He went from being the skinny singer in the bow tie to the hard-drinking sophisticate who personified the new modern mood which was, according to critic Stephen Holden, "the golden age of bad behavior without conse-quences." He hung around with mobsters from Lucky Luciano to Sam Giancana, and bedded and abused women by the score. He had those he disliked beat up or he did it himself. He was vindictive and insult-ing, calling Barbara Walters "the ugliest broad on television," and get-ting one of his critics, the famed musicologist Jonathan Schwartz, fired from his job.

Committing public adultery with Ava Gardner while married to his first wife, Nancy, then marrying Ava as well as two more women after her, Francis Albert Sinatra can hardly be called an exemplary Catholic—even though his first marriage was annulled, his second and third marriages were declared invalid, and his fourth marriage was validated in a private ceremony at St. Patrick's Cathedral in 1979.

Yes, he was a Catholic, for he met the sole minimal requirement for that position: he was baptized in the same church as the pope. When he died, people came from all over to view his body, including the Catholic Cardinal Archbishop of Los Angeles. And he was given a Catholic burial following a Catholic Mass.

Some sneer at this. They say, "Money talks." How can they—"they" meaning the Cardinal, the church as a whole—give a Catholic Mass to an obvious public sinner, who was in his lifetime and in his conduct no more "Catholic" than the man in the moon? Let it turn out, for example, that Sinatra leaves the archdiocese a couple of million dollars (although I doubt it), and the sneering will broaden.

These cynics have a point. And here is where we must rise above the knee-jerk reactions and tabloid thinking, and pause as a Catholic community to ask, "Why?" Listen now, for your own personal spiritual benefit, to two reasons why Francis Albert Sinatra was given a Catholic burial—and should have been.

The first reason can be found in the parish policy from our own parish manual. It reads: "With few extraordinary exceptions, everyone shall receive a Christian burial. No one, no matter how poor or indifferent a Catholic, no matter how evil or how a person died, whether naturally or by his own hand or another's, will be denied a Christian burial.

"The gospel imperative is that when a person is dead, all is over and the only final obligation the Christian community has in charity is to pray for the deceased and to demonstrate by its liturgy that wideness and kindness which Christ himself showed. For a Christian community to deny its ritual of prayer and worship to even a public sinner is not to imitate our Master, who prayed for those who crucified him."

What this policy is saying is that the focus is never on the deceased—whether saint or sinner—but on the faith community, which takes to heart these words of Jesus:

> You have heard that it was said, "You shall love your neighbor and hate your enemy." But I say to you, Love your enemies and pray for those who persecute you, so that you may be children of your Father in heaven; for he makes his sun rise on the evil and on the good, and sends rain on the righteous and on the unrighteous. For if you love those who love you, what reward do you have? Do not even the tax collectors do the same? And if you greet only your brothers and sisters, what more are you doing than others? Do not even the Gentiles do the same? Be perfect, therefore, as your heavenly Father is perfect.

"Love your enemies and pray for those who persecute you." Frank Sinatra—as well as other people, both known and unknown, who are Catholic yet live apart from the values of their faith—are "enemies" in that they do not practice or uphold or exemplify Catholic life. In fact, they embarrass and shame us; they have persecuted us by their lifestyles and scandals. There is no denying that.

But remember this: *they* are not the point. *We* are. Under the imperative imposed by Jesus in the words we just heard, we are to pray for those who persecute us. Therefore, giving Christian burial and a Mass to the unworthy and scandalous says nothing about them but everything about us and our obedience to Christ's words. Giving Christian burial to the unworthy does not endorse their life. It endorses ours.

Do you see what is at stake here? Oh, I know that in this imperfect world money and celebrity talk and both the famous and infamous get what they want, even in death. But, once more, the point is this: how seriously do we want to be disciples, even to practicing the hard sayings of Jesus?

So, how come Frank Sinatra got a Catholic burial and Mass? Is it because money and fame talk loudly? As I said, some will say that. They always do. But now you know better. Sinatra got a Catholic burial and Mass because, as much as we might like to, we will not hate the enemy. We will not love only those who love us; we will not greet only our brothers and sisters in the practice of the faith. But we will try hard to love our enemies and, in our public liturgy, pray for those of our own who have persecuted us by their behavior. We refuse to let them determine who we are.

The Catholic burial and Mass, you see, lets Jesus determine who we are; that is, his followers who show public love to the "enemy" and who go beyond the pagan rejection of them. Offering a Catholic burial Mass for the scandalous is one way the faith community lives out the gospel. It has, I repeat, nothing to do with the scandalous or their status as public sinners. It has everything to do with us and our status as public disciples.

There is, as I said before, a second reason for giving a Catholic burial to those who might be deemed unworthy. And this is that we dare not confine the Spirit or define the limits of what the Spirit can do— or give any kind of public notice that we do. We dare not pronounce on the compassion and grace and the action of God. We are in no position to make a final judgment on anyone's soul. Allowing a ritual Catholic burial to be performed leaves open the question of God's mercy.

In the Acts of the Apostles we find the story of Stephen, the first martyr. He is stoned to death, a painful and horrible way to die. Another young man named Saul is there, approving and holding the coats of the stone-throwers to make their dreadful task easier.

Imagine that Stephen's mother has heard about the commotion and comes upon the scene. Sobbing, she runs over and cradles the broken body of her son in her arms. She rocks him back and forth as if trying to return life to that dead body. Finally, she senses the other young man standing there. She looks up with anguish and hatred, and screams at him: "Damn you! May your soul rot in hell for this!" and she collapses in grief.

Who would not sympathize with her? Who would not say the same, wish the same? Saul and Nazi torturers and Saddam Hussein— may they all rot in hell for what they did, and do. But after the understandable anger and hurt and pain, something else must remain for the disciple of Jesus. Because we know that Jesus never closed the final door, never said no forever. That damned young man, Saul, became St. Paul. Stephen's mother may have written him off—we can understand that—but not God. The Spirit went beyond the limits of her grief in a way she could never have imagined—or he.

On Calvary, a despicable young man who admitted to terrible deeds and accepted his punishment as fair was promised paradise at the last minute. His was a deathbed conversion known only to him and Jesus—a conversion that may well have been the result of years and years of his parents' tears and prayers.

The publican, the prodigal son, the woman caught in adultery, Peter, the Samaritan woman at the well, Zacchaeus, Augustine, Ignatius, Malcolm Muggeridge, Thomas Merton, and Dorothy Day: all are testimony to the fact that we never have the last word, but God does. Granting a Catholic burial Mass to one seemingly unworthy says that we don't know what happens within the secrets of the heart at the last moment.

We are in no position to judge. We have no right to weigh what went on between the divine God and the human heart of a wretched sinner. The Mass of Christian Burial for the public sinner simply proclaims the faith community's humility before this issue and its refusal either to dictate to or second-guess the Spirit. In other words, the Catholic service proclaims the sovereignty of God, the everlasting possibility of a mercy we are not privy to.

So there we are. People like Francis Albert Sinatra—many before him and many to come after him—will, with few exceptions, be given a Christian burial in the Catholic Church. This is not because of their position, but because of ours, a position derived from Jesus himself: our obligation to publicly pray for our very own who have persecuted us, our obligation to allow the good thief scenario its full play.

As I said before, we must rise above the knee-jerk reaction of cynicism and tabloid gossip and the accusations of church politics. Rather, we must look to ourselves as serious Christians who try hard to practice the teachings of Jesus. Thus, we must realize that the question, for believers, is never about Frank Sinatra—or any of the scandalous, the sinners, the seemingly unworthy. The question, remind your interrogators, is always this: what are we all about?

45

ON THIS SHAKY ROCK

MATTHEW 16:21–27

"And I say to you, you are Peter and on this rock I will build my church." Some rock. Swamp might be more accurate for this man who walked on the water and then sank in doubt, who went to watch in the garden to be a comfort but who fell asleep, who boasted fidelity but wound up with denial, who promised presence and fled leaving his master to die alone. This was a man who clearly did not have the charisma of John the Baptist, the connections of Joseph of Arimethea or the loyalty of Mary Magdalene.

Yet…he was chosen as a rock on which to build. Why? Perhaps for two reasons. First, there was his fundamental humility which led him to exclaim, "Depart from me, Lord, for I am a sinful man!" He knew he was a sinner and could never claim credit for whatever the Lord would do, and that counted for something. And secondly, as a sinner, he is an object lesson for ages to come. Which is to say, God will always build on fragile, sinful people—even us.

Let me translate what I mean with a true story. Listen with patience as a woman, a broken woman, writes:

Mom's voice on the phone was urgent, "Can you take a few days off to come to see me? We have to talk." "Sure, Mom. But why

215

wait? Let's talk now." "Not over the phone, Sharon. Come and see me soon. Please." I was fifty-five at the time and living in California, and my mother and I had always been close. I dropped everything and flew to Arizona.

As soon as I saw Mom I could tell that her health was getting worse. She and I sat on the couch. "There's something I've never told you," she said, her frail hands shaking as she put a packet in my lap. Puzzled, I opened the large brown envelope and pulled out a stack of yellowed newspaper clippings. "Mystery still surrounds the 'Hatbox Baby' found abandoned in the desert on Christmas Eve, 1931." What was this all about?

I kept on reading. "The finding of the six-day-old infant not only touched off a mystery; it was considered almost miraculous....She was swaddled in old cotton wrappings...a hatbox was her crib...investigators said it was surely a miracle that she had not been devoured by prowling coyotes or died in the cold." I was starting to feel very strange. "Mom?" My mother took both my hands in hers, her eyes full of tears. "It's you, Sharon. You were that baby." I stared at her in disbelief. Until this moment I had no idea that I was adopted. Over the next few hours, Mom told me the incredible story.

At sundown on Christmas Eve, 1931, an Arizona couple was driving home across a barren stretch of desert some forty miles out of Mesa when they developed car trouble. While the husband worked to repair a broken fuel line, the wife walked away from the road, wandering under the glittering stars. Then she caught sight of something in a clump of bushes. It was a round, black hatbox, its top not tightly closed.

The woman called her husband, who prodded the box gently with his foot. They heard a cry and opened the lid. Inside was a baby—a baby with red hair and blue eyes. The astonished couple took the baby into town to the Mesa police station and gave her to the deputy sheriff on duty; he took the baby to a maternity home run by a midwife named Ma Dana. The next morning, investigators returned to the desert to search for anything that might identify the infant. There was nothing.

Word of the "hatbox baby" spread rapidly. "I heard the news on the radio that Christmas morning," Mom said, "I'd always longed for a baby, but had never been able to carry one to term. So I shut off the oven without a thought of the turkey cooking inside and we rushed to get our names on the list to adopt you." As the paper said, "Found in the desert a week ago, the baby must depend on the law to give her a mother and father to succeed those who deserted her to die in a cheap hatbox."

Mom stroked my red hair. "By the time the court date came two months later," she said, "more than 200 couples had signed up to adopt you. I figured we didn't stand much of a chance, but I prayed and prayed. The night before the hearing it rained so hard that the bridge into town washed out, and most of the streets were flooded. Only one other couple was able to get to the courthouse, and since they already had an adopted child, the judge awarded you to us."

"I'm so glad you were the ones who got me," I whispered, clinging to my mother the way I had as a child when something was wrong. I loved her dearly and I always would. But now I was an adult, and once again something was wrong, involving deep emotions I wasn't yet ready to examine.

I took the packet of clippings with me when I left that night. I tried not to think about them. But Mom's failing health concerned me. She was alone, as my stepfather had died several years ago. I was divorced, so I decided to retire from my job and move back to Mesa to be with Mom.

Eight months later she died. Her death filled me with grief. But one night as I stared out at the desert hills, I began to be haunted by other thoughts. I opened that packet again and read the newspaper clippings. "It is surely a miracle that the baby had not been devoured by prowling coyotes or wolves, and that she didn't die of cold." I put the clipping down. Had my birth mother really left me to die? Was I so unacceptable that she'd reject me completely, discarding me without a thought in such a barren, lonely place?

My rational mind said, "You're an adult now; it doesn't matter." But on some deeper level it mattered terribly. Had my real mother not cared whether I lived or died? Please, God, I prayed, send some word to comfort me.

Then, with the help of Orphan Voyage, an organization that

tries to reunite adopted children with their birth parents, I searched for more information. I learned that Ma Dana was now dead, and the couple that had found me in the desert had long ago left the area. But what about the deputy sheriff on duty the night I was found? His name was in the old articles—Joe Maier. Was he alive? And still somewhere in the area?

I could hardly believe it when I found a listing for Joe B. Maier in the phone book. I was shaking as I walked up to a frame house and rang the bell. Joe Maier was a friendly, big man with white hair and a keen gaze, and he took my hand in a warm grasp. Now in his nineties, he lived with his daughter. And he remembered the night in 1931 very well.

"Mesa was a small town then, and the people here all fell in love with you," Joe said. "They showered you with gifts." On Christmas Day at Ma Dana's, he told me, folks from miles around brought shawls and dresses and booties, and a jeweler sent a ring and a locket. Joe's kind eyes twinkled as he talked. "You were a gift to all of us."

I struggled to tell him how I felt. "It's been really hard for me," I said, "to think I was just…dumped in the desert to die." Joe Maier shook his head. "No way," he said firmly. "You were clean, in a tidy flowered sleeper, with a blanket around you. You were in good shape, you'd been well cared for, and it was clear that you couldn't have been in the desert for long."

He leaned forward, "There's a lot of questions about where you came from that night, questions that may never be answered. God knows, a lot of folks had theories about what did and what didn't happen." His steady gaze never wavered. "Was somebody hiding in the sagebrush watching to make sure you'd be found? Was that goodhearted couple who brought you in telling us the whole story? Nobody knows for sure. But this much I am certain of: the baby put into my hands was clean and well-cared for and was meant to be found and given a good home."

I said goodbye to Joe with a sense of peace I had not had for months. That night I reread a letter my adopted mom had written me before she died, describing the first time she saw me: "A little redheaded mite, so perfect and so perfectly adorable."

Mom said she felt that maybe women like her, who loved children so much but couldn't give birth, were created to care for those babies who didn't have mothers.

This is a moving, true story. Now think about it. There are three flawed people in it: the adoptive mother who was unable to bear children, the adopted divorced daughter left in a desert, and the birth mother who, for whatever reason, was unable to raise her baby. None of them expected the blessing they received: the childless mother a baby, the abandoned baby a home, the birth mother an answer. None on them could expect to be a rock on which human redemption was built. All, in fact, were like Peter and could well have cried his cry: "Depart from me, for I am sinful person O Lord." Yet the Lord chose to build on them as the foundation for a human drama of grace.

So let's go back to the gospel. Beyond what you think of the papal claims touted in this familiar passage, it carries a deeper spiritual meaning that is quite clear. All of us spiritual redheads, all of us childless mothers, all of us birth mothers unable to cope, all of us hidden in a hatbox, all of us in the desert of our lives, all of us who fall on our knees exclaiming how unworthy and sinful we are; the truth is, we are all, like flawed Peter, the special objects of God's calling and God's desire to build his kingdom on the likes of us.

It is not for us to ask why, not for us to protest our unworthiness, not for us to parade our sins. No, we have only one choice: to humbly receive the keys of the kingdom and open up the doors of grace to as many people as we can.

46

EVANGELIZATION

LUKE 10:1–12, 17–20

What a strange gospel we have just heard. Jesus is talking about evangelization. He sends out disciples to prepare the way but his instructions are puzzling: take no staff or traveling bag, and greet no one along the way.

What kind of send off is that? No comb or toothbrush? Greet no one? How can you influence people if you don't even say "good morning" to them? And then Jesus tells the disciples that if the people won't receive them, they are to shake the dust from their feet knowing that such people will be punished worse than Sodom. You won't hear this kind of technique taught by a good promotional sales trainer! But wait: it all makes sense if you add just one factor.

The people in the time of the gospel all believed that the end of the world was very near. Therefore, there was a necessary urgency and haste about the whole business of evangelization. That was the reason for taking no luggage nor pausing to greet anyone. Time was running out and any evangelization needed be fast and quick. It's a lot like the evangelical fundamentalists today who think the world will end in the year 2000, and so they must get as many people as possible to profess Jesus in their hearts so that they will be raptured into heaven before Armageddon strikes.

In one sense, the time for evangelization is always urgent, especially in our troubled and God-seeking times. Most of us think that evangelization is the province of missionary priests and nuns. We also cling to the "romantic" notion that evangelization means bringing the gospel to the pagans "out there," the unchurched, those who have fallen away, people in foreign lands. We envision someone like Isaac Jogues, who left his native France to evangelize the North American Indians.

The truth is we are all called through baptism to share the faith, to evangelize, to announce the Good News of Jesus—but we resist that notion. Let others do it. Besides, we don't want to impose our faith on others. Our mistaken ideas about evangelization, about mission, keep us from doing the work that rightfully belongs to all baptized in Christ. But there are two other obstacles to sharing the faith which we must consider. Let me tell you about both of these by way of a story:

Most of you are familiar with the name "Harriet Tubman" from our early American history. She knew how precious freedom is. You see, Harriet's grandparents were members of the Ashanti people of Ghana. Her grandparents were kidnapped from their land in 1725 and sold into slavery.

Harriet was the third generation in her family to live as slaves. But Harriet Tubman became a link to freedom, not just for her family, but for hundreds of other slave families as well. She was consigned into history as the most famous conductor on what has come to be called the Underground Railroad.

Harriet's flight from slavery was sparked by rumors that there were plans to sell her and two of her brothers to a chain gang. As if the back-breaking labors of the chain gangs weren't enough, they would probably never see their family again. So Harriet decided to escape. She wandered by her parents' cottage that night, plaintively singing a gospel tune about being "bound for the Promised Land." It was a secret code many slaves used to signal that they were planning to leave.

Harriet Tubman's escape that night was successful. She traveled mostly by night and hid in fields and barns during the day. There were designated stops along her multi-state trek at the homes of those sympathetic to the cause of freedom. Her destination was the Northern states, or even Canada, where many escaped slaves made their homes. Her life depended on every step she took.

The fact that this lone woman successfully traveled to freedom is remarkable enough in itself. The fact that she chose to return to slave country hundreds of times to lead others to freedom on the Underground Railroad is astounding. She risked recapture, beatings, jail time, and even death to help others out of slavery.

Harriet and her charges must have suffered from hunger, fear, lack of sleep, extremes of weather, and exhaustion—but they still traveled on. Surely there were times when they all wanted to turn back. It was at these times that Harriet counseled, "Children, if you are tired, keep going; if you are scared, keep going; if you are hungry, keep going." And Harriet Tubman herself kept going, risking her life to lead thousands of slaves to freedom. That's her story.

The March 1997 issue of *Ebony* magazine contains a telling quote from Harriet Tubman, one we should consider in the context of evangelization. She once said, "I freed thousands of slaves. I could have freed thousands more, if they had known they were slaves." That is the first obstacle to evangelization: we think evangelization means bringing the good news of Jesus to the foreigners or to unchurched Americans. But no, first and foremost, evangelization means bringing the good news to our fellow Catholics—and perhaps even to ourselves.

"I could have freed thousands more, if they had known they were slaves." Too many Catholics don't know they are slaves. A *New York Times* survey taken a few years ago showed that the views of Catholics, like most mainline Protestants, were indistinguishable from any other American on issues such as the death penalty, euthanasia, nuclear weapons, welfare, education, housing, job training, assisted suicide, divorce, premarital sex—you name it. If there is no measurable difference from any other American in the way we look at such critical issues, then we are slaves to the culture, accepting and living by its values. Evangelization means looking into our lives and lifestyles and those of our fellow Catholics, and announcing the good news that there is more to life than what we currently embrace.

The second obstacle is related to the first: even when we do recognize our slavery to the culture, we hedge and fudge and change the script to suit ourselves. Listen to this true story from a reflective man:

During my senior year in high school, I had a small part in the senior play. Truthfully, it wasn't actually a part in the play—I was far too shy for that. It was a part offstage; I was the sound effects person. When the script called for knocking at the door, I rapped two sticks together. When the phone was supposed to ring, I touched the wires together on the battery operated bell, watching carefully so that I would stop just as the actor picked up the receiver.

We worked hard on that play. The director was a young woman who taught English at school, a new addition to the faculty, and she poured herself into us and into the play. In the afternoons when school was out, she carefully coached all the actors on their lines and helped them get their timing right. She would then dash to get some fast food, returning to the school in the evenings for rehearsals. Afterwards, she would often stay late at night, working with us on the props and pitching in on the painting of the sets. Unselfishly, she gave herself to this moment in our lives.

Night after night we rehearsed, and on opening night we were ready; we had the play down perfectly. The curtains opened; the house was packed with our families and friends; electricity was in the air. The first act was a dream. The play was a comedy, and every funny line evoked rich laughter from the audience. They were enjoying themselves, and we were, too. But in the second act, an actor forgot his lines. You could see on his face that he knew it was his turn to speak, but he could not find the words. The audience did not sense it yet, but the other actors and those of us offstage did. What to do?

Everybody was paralyzed as this unfortunate classmate squirmed and tried to remember what he was supposed to say. I was standing in the wings, next to the young teacher who was the director. She was leaning toward the stage, every ounce of energy aimed encouragingly toward the struggling kid on stage. The script in her hand, she was just about to whisper his line out to him, when suddenly he spoke. It was not the line in the script—in his anxiety, he just made something up—but he spoke. Not only that, what he said happened to be funny, and the audience roared with laughter.

Everybody on stage relaxed; they had gotten through a bad spot and could now work past it. Unfortunately, though, the forgetful actor heard the laughter of the audience and liked it, so he made up another line. This, too, was funny...not as funny as the first line, but the audience chuckled. So, the actor made up another line, and another, and still another. The other actors were trying to respond to him, but they couldn't. He was out of control now, spinning off whatever came into his head. The play was disintegrating, lost.

The audience had now figured it out, and what little laughter was left was nervous and mocking. I don't remember how we got out of it, how we finished the play, or even if we did. The memory that sticks in my mind is looking up to see the director, the young woman who had given night after night of her time to work with us and make us ready, this woman who had poured herself into this play for our benefit, standing in the wings, watching and crying.

We, too, have been given our parts to play in the drama of God's redemption. "Seek first the kingdom of God, pray without ceasing, repay no one evil for evil, feed my lambs, bear one another's burdens, be kind to one another, forgive one another, love your enemies, be merciful, even as your Father is merciful." Even now the tempter whispers in our ears, "Change the script, make up your own lines." But everything is at stake, and the one who has poured his life into preparing us is watching.

The beginning of evangelization lies in recognizing our own slavery and our own need of deliverance. It means living fully the script handed to us by Jesus, not changing it to suit our own vanities or fears or consciences. The time for evangelization is as urgent now as it was back in the time of Jesus. For the reign of God is at hand.

47

ABRAHAM AND THE PLEADING

GENESIS 18:20–32

The episode about Abraham that we just heard in the first reading is at once comical, cunning, and challenging. It's comical because here you have a mere human being going one-on-one with God, a man-to-man face off, like an old-time merchant and his would-be customer arguing each other down under the canopy of the town bazaar. Traditional haggling is going on, and it's comical because the two antagonists are unequal, to say the least: the puny, earthly creature and the Lord God Almighty of heaven and earth, Don Knotts arm-wrestling with Arnold Schwarzenegger.

But the reading is also cunning because there is more going on than meets the eye. Biblical scholars of late believe that Abraham was not bartering for souls but rather, feeling God out; he is seeking to understand this God who stands before him in the guise of a man. What is God like? What is the nature of God's justice, God's values? How does God operate?

And so Abraham tests God by citing the decreasing number of just people in the wicked cities, pushing the number lower and lower each time to see if this sways God. In this sense, Abraham is not trying to save the cities through bold bargaining; rather, he wants to know if God distinguishes between the just and the unjust who inhabit them.

Abraham gets the answer he wants. By agreeing to save the wicked cities if finally, only ten just people are found there, God lets Abraham—and us—know that in fact God does discriminate between those who seek the way of holiness and those who choose to serve the forces of destruction. This God is a God of justice and consideration. Abraham's ruse worked. He found out what he wanted to know about this God disguised in human form. He found out that God is merciful and compassionate.

You couldn't go to the cities of Sodom or Gomorrah today because they lie under water, under the Dead Sea. The valley floor sank many centuries ago, and water gradually engulfed them. By the time of Jesus these two cities were long gone. In fact, it all happened so long ago that Bible scholars and geographers are not really sure of the exact locations of those ancient places. But their names live on even today as twin symbols of licentiousness and wickedness.

Perhaps it is best that these cities no longer exist, that in time the course of nature put them out of business. But in their day they must have been the wildest and vilest of places. At least that was their reputation, and hence the reason for the outcry against them that apparently reached to heaven itself.

The interesting idea emerging from this story is that, as a result, the Lord himself came down to investigate the matter. While he was doing so, God met Abraham on the road. At this point, the Lord was considering drastic action against Sodom and Gomorrah. And why not? Most people probably would have cheered the Lord on, hoping that sinful Sodom and Gomorrah would simply be destroyed.

But not Abraham. And here is where we get a twist in the story. Abraham did not want mass destruction. Perhaps that is because most of the others thought only of those wicked cities as places, thought only of the moral pollution that spilled out from them. But Abraham, he was different. He first thought of the people, especially the innocent people. And perhaps he also thought of the not-so-innocent ones.

Yes, of course, God could solve the problem of the wickedness of Sodom and Gomorrah by destroying them in one heavenly bolt. That would be so simple, so final. But the lesson in this colorful episode may well be that the seemingly simplest solutions are not usually the best; our judgments based upon what is most apparent are not always the wisest.

How many times we have heard people say "just nuke them"— whoever "them" implies at the moment? Wage total war against the enemy of the moment, the whole darn country, whether it be the North Koreans, the Vietnamese, the Iraqis, or the Bosnians. How often have you heard it said, "We should have just gone in there and finished the job. Cleaned it up. Destroyed the whole blasted country and been done with it."

Some of you may recall the incident at My Lai, which occurred during the Vietnam War. Here American soldiers, on the orders of their officer, massacred more than four hundred people—mostly old men, women, and even little children—in that small Vietnamese village. Recently, a memorial was dedicated to those who died in that incident. At the same time, there was a recognition of what we might call two Abraham figures: the pilot and the gunner of an American helicopter who bravely inserted themselves between the soldiers and the few remaining peasants and said, no this is wrong. The pilot and the gunner managed to save about a dozen of the villagers from those who had come to destroy that village.

Listen to Abraham's impassioned plea: "Will you sweep the innocent with the guilty?" Suppose there were fifty innocent people in My Lai; would you wipe out the place rather than spare it for the sake of the fifty innocent ones? Should not the judge of all the world act with justice? And Abraham goes on, perhaps presumptuously. What if there are fewer than fifty? What if there are only forty? How about thirty, or twenty? And in each case the Lord answers, "Even for that many I will not destroy it." Then Abraham plays his last card. "How about ten?" "For the sake of those ten," the Lord answered, "I will not destroy it."

Abraham takes sides for the innocent, however few there may be. And he is a passionate advocate for them, even though he feels there is some risk in doing so. There are always too few advocates for the innocent, and for those trapped in wicked and sinful situations. The image found in the Genesis reading is of one man, alone, pleading for mercy in justice. Abraham, the patriarch, the man of God, is not overcome by vindictiveness but moved by compassion. Truly great leaders of the world, when you think of it, are honored not so much for power or the enforcement of justice, but for compassion.

It is interesting to note that George C. Marshall, who was the Chief of Staff in the Second World War, is remembered not so much for the important role of head of all armed forces. He is primarily remembered as the architect of what came to be known as the Marshall Plan, a monumental effort to feed and clothe and heal the very people that a short time before had been our bitterest enemies. Some were opposed to this heroic effort and spoke out against it. But Marshall's cause was championed by President Roosevelt, and so this great humanitarian program went on to save lives, turn enemies into friends, and have an impact on the course of history. Perhaps we can believe that there was something of Abraham in General Marshall's approach: do not destroy, but redeem.

Many would have rejoiced in the destruction of the sinful cities of Sodom and Gomorrah, and all their people. But Abraham sought to save them. And so it was that centuries and centuries later, there stood in Jerusalem amid the people one of Abraham's descendants, and this man gave a teaching. As he opened his mouth to speak, I am sure that in his mind he hearkened back to the ancient patriarch, his ancestor, who opted for compassion.

This is what the descendant of Abraham said, carefully, powerfully, beautifully, and deliberately: "For God so loved the world that he gave his only Son so that everyone who believes in him may not perish but may have eternal life." Indeed, God did not send the Son into the world to condemn it, but in order that the world might be saved through him.

48

GREED

LUKE 12:13–21

So there's this man who goes to a tailor to buy a suit of clothes. He tries it on in front of the mirror and notices the suit coat is a little uneven at the bottom. "It needs a hand adjustment," the tailor suggests. "Just pull it down with your hand."

The man does this, looks in the mirror and notices that the lapel has popped up. He is told it needs a chin adjustment. So he puts his chin on the popped-up lapel to keep it down. Finally, the pants are too tight in the crotch and have to be pulled down by a hand adjustment. Although he is bent over and crippled by the many "alterations," the man buys the suit.

The next day he is walking through the park wearing his new suit. He passes two old men sitting on a bench. The first comments on how crippled the poor man is. The second one says, "Yes…but I wonder where he got such a nice suit?"

There's a little bite to that story, isn't there? It gives us a good idea of what greed is about, the theme of today's gospel. For the sake of pride or style or one-upmanship, people walk around crippled in spirit just so others may comment on their possessions.

Greed is one of the seven capital sins. Capital sins, as you might recall, are so called because they are a "font," or capital, from which others sins flow. There are two mortal evils that flow from greed. The first is that it skews spiritual vision; greed is blinding.

Once there was a man who dreamed of nothing but gold. He was obsessed with it. Morning, noon, and night he dreamt of gold. One day he got up from his desk and ran to the market-place. He ran through the crowd to the table where a man was selling gold coins. He swept them all into his little bag and ran away.

A policeman was standing right next to the table, and he nabbed the man. He took him to the police station and as he was locking him up he said to the man, "I can't understand it. There you are, with me right next to the merchant's table and at least 100 witnesses, and you steal something right in front of us all!" The man replied, "I never saw anyone. I only saw the gold."

Greed blinds. It keeps us from seeing rightly, from seeing not only what we are doing but who we are becoming. Notice how the man in the gospel is all personal pronouns: I have no place to store my harvest...I will build larger barns...I will say to myself...enjoy yourself!

The use of I, me, mine are overwhelming, clouding the man's vision of how poor he really is, how poverty-stricken is his life, his soul. He is blind to the needs of others. Notice too, only the rich man is speaking in the parable—and he is speaking to himself. When you are this rich, you don't have to consult anyone, even God. Greed is that blind.

There is a story in Jewish tradition about Elijah, who is not only a prophet of biblical legend but also a bit of a trickster and magician.

Elijah is walking through a town when he hears the sounds of a party coming from a very large and beautiful house. He twirls around and instantly, he is clothed in the rags of a beggar. He knocks on the door, and the host answers. He takes one look at Elijah's miserable clothing and slams the door in his face.

Elijah twirls around a second time and is instantly clothed in the fine garments of a gentleman. He knocks on the door, and the host answers. He takes one look at Elijah's splendid attire and ushers him in.

At the feast, there is a long table of food. Elijah goes to it immediately and begins stuffing food into his pockets. The guests step back to watch this strange sight. Then he pushes more food inside his shirt and pours wine over his shoulders and down the front of his fine attire. The host is irritated and asks Elijah what he thinks he is doing. Elijah replies, "I came to your door dressed in rags and you did not invite me in. Then I came to your door—the same person—dressed in fine garments and you welcomed me to your feast. I could only conclude that it was not me that you invited but my clothes. So I fed them with your food and drink."

The story goes on to say that the people were ashamed. They looked down. When they looked up, Elijah was gone.

The loss of spiritual sensitivity, vision, and human priorities are the usual effects of greed. Unfortunately, it usually takes a tragedy to put things in perspective. We watch, for example, as people's homes and lives are devastated by floods and tornados and mudslides. Some of these folks appeared in a recent television documentary about people who had experienced some trauma or calamity which resulted in severe loss.

In this documentary, one woman looked on helplessly as her home was swallowed up by a mudslide and tumbled down the cliff into the bay below. An elderly couple had survived the tornado that ripped the roof off their home and flung all of its contents into the air. Another person had returned from a trip to find his home and business in ashes. Yet another told of losing all he owned in a faulty investment. When asked how they had coped with their losses and what they had learned, every person interviewed shared a similar insight. "Yes, we have lost everything," someone said, "but that is precisely the point...we have lost things. What matters is that we are alive!"

Each person emerged from their experience of loss having learned the same lesson Jesus wished to impart to his disciples. Each had gained a keener appreciation of their authentic needs and wants, and a newfound freedom from useless and transitory wants. Each resolved to live life more carefully and wisely, aware that this day is God's gift and that tomorrow may never come. They see that now. But it was not always that way, for greed skews spiritual vision.

The second mortal evil that flows from greed is displacement.

When you fill a glass with water, you displace the air. Greed is like that. It displaces other values. And so the fundamental question to ask of greed is, "What is it keeping me from?"

First, greed keeps us from self-knowledge. All the energy and time spent in acquiring things, all the time spent bowing to wants and declaring them needs, all the effort to turn luxuries into necessities, eventually leads us to believe that we are only what we have. Yet in fact, faith tells us that we are always more than we have.

Comedian Mort Sahl used to say that if you ask a Californian who he is he would point to his car. This identification of ourselves with our possessions and this lack of self-knowledge makes us ever more pliable to the incessant advertisers who are in the business of creating needs, then selling their products to satisfy them. Soon we have no center. We have become the marketer's dream: an eternal, shop-'til-you-drop consumer. Greed doesn't allow us the time to find out that we are more than that—until it's too late.

Secondly, greed keeps us from making connections. It displaces the only thing in life that ever really matters, relationships. Ben Stein captures this when he says, "No corporate title can replace the times when your son leans his head on your chest and falls asleep. No limousine or private jet makes up for being there when your son is growing from a child into a young man. Time spent with your child isn't a distraction from the main event. It is the main event."

Greed puts children and spouses at the bottom of the list for time and attention. Parents subcontract their kids out while they go off and "build for their future," storing up luxuries—when the only luxury the children really want is the parents themselves. Greed builds walls. Every added room, every additional car, every extra television set separates.

True enough, people need a certain amount of material goods and money to live a decent life and provide for the future. But the question is: when does a legitimate desire to meet present needs exceed reasonable limits? Greed is present in the desire to accumulate more even when one already has what is sufficient and reasonable. With that accumulation comes separation, separation from the very ones we profess to love.

A rich tycoon had not yet made a contribution to the local hospital fund drive. The chairman of the drive paid him a personal visit saying, "Our records show you've not yet donated to our drive."

The tycoon said, "And do your records show my mother died penniless? Do they show that my only brother is disabled? Do they show that my sister was abandoned and left to support four kids?"

The chairman felt ashamed of his approach. He apologized, "No, they don't. I'm sorry."

"Well," said the tycoon, "if I didn't help my own family, why should I help you?"

This funny little story prompts us to look at our own version of greed. How has it kept us so busy acquiring, working, making money, and building egos through possessions that we no longer really care for or know our family and friends? Many of us no longer even eat together, no longer spend time together, no longer are there when tears need to be dried and bodies hugged. Why? Because we are too busy building for a "better life" down the road instead of capturing the irretrievable, never-to-be repeated moments of closeness and love, here and now. Greed separates.

Listen to this prayer written by a very senior citizen:

When I was poor I prayed to be rich. I learned that my true riches were in family and friends, in my faith and in my values.

When I was sick I prayed to be well. It did not happen soon, not without suffering. But I learned that in sickness I needed others, and that health was a gift I should use well when it was given back to me.

When I was older, I prayed for understanding. Not for youth, because it was gone. No, I prayed for wisdom to understand that all life, in every moment, is a gift. It is much too short to hold grievances. And it is much too abundant not to look around and to enjoy.

And so you have the two mortal evils, the seriously wrong behaviors, that flow from greed. First, greed clouds our vision of self, neighbor, and God. Second, greed displaces relationships. No wonder it's considered one of the seven deadly sins.

49

PLANTING THE UNSEEN FUTURE

HEBREWS 11:1-2, 8-19

What is the biggest heartache, the greatest sorrow of a parent? It is that as much as they want to, as much as they try, they cannot keep their children from pain. No parent can sufficiently warn their children about the dangers of life—nor can they hope to be understood even if they try. Nor can a parent suffer for their child.

Naturally, parents do warn their children of many things, but they cannot fully prepare them for their inevitable encounter with the limitations and follies of the human condition. These run the gamut from illness, aging, and mortality through tangled emotional involvements, broken relationships, and everyday hurts. And, of course, sin. The pain of being human cuts across the board and no one, not anyone's child, is safe from it.

So what can parents do? They can do the best they can. They can give their children the tools to cope with the inevitable "slings and arrows of outrageous fortune" found in life. This seldom, if ever, means external things, for nothing external can prevent temptation and evil. Rather, parents can try to give their children internal values and strengths, in the hope that their children will grow strong at broken places.

Our interest today, however, is not the children or the grandchildren, but the parents, the adults. The question is, what sustains them as they watch anxiously from the sidelines, savoring every victory and dying with every defeat? The answer, for all good people, is in the stories of their religious tradition. And we have one such story today, about Abraham and Sarah.

According to the second reading, Abraham and Sarah went forth. Went forth into what? Into an unknown land and an unknown future. Indeed, as Scripture says, Abraham was "looking forward to the city with foundations." And Sarah? She looked forward to the grandchildren she never expected and in fact would never see. In a word, people like Abraham and Sarah were asked to have faith enough to plan for a future they would not enjoy, scatter hope which they would not see realized in their lifetimes, and freely give love that might not be immediately returned. They were asked to trust God at every turn. They were asked for faith, not fatalism.

Fatalism resigns us to the here and now. Faith, on the other hand, looks to the future in spite of the here and now. It is faith, for example, that enables us to work faithfully at teaching a Sunday school class to a group of children, not knowing how the Christian faith will take root in their lives. It is faith that leads us to volunteer each week in an inner-city school, teaching a child to read yet not being able to see the results of our efforts. It is faith that says, although we will not be here for the harvest, there will be a harvest.

The other day I ran into some friends from high school. We got to reminiscing about old times, and we remembered a teacher, Miss Rotand, who taught us English. Miss Rotand combined both threat and love in her teaching, and we all agreed that she accomplished much. Years later, each of us still vividly remembered her classes. Yet none of us had had any contact with Miss Rotand since our graduation. None of us had ever taken the time to thank her or to tell her how much she had meant to us. In fact, we agreed that many of us did not know how much her teaching had meant to us until years after we had left high school.

I think Miss Rotand taught us what faith was all about by giving her life to the classroom. She had her eyes set on a site, not immediately available but one which she knew would be there in the future, a future she would never see. We were testimonials to the validity of her faith. And yet, she never knew.

Fatalism kills us. It requires a great deal of faith to take a long view, to work on projects that will not be fulfilled in the near future. I well remember interviewing a candidate for director of continuing education for teachers. She said to me, "A good teacher has got to be in love with the process of planting the seed, but cannot need to be around for the harvest." I like that. A good teacher must constantly be sowing seeds among the students, while knowing that he or she might not be present for the harvest. Many other occupations require the same attitude, including parenting.

During the last century, the United States planned, financed, and built the Panama Canal, a project that took over ten years to complete. And so many legislators from the House of Representatives who voted for the expenditure of funds for the canal were not in office when the canal was completed. It took four or five congressional terms to complete the canal. It's hard to imagine a politician today taking such a long view, risking his or her career on a project from which they would never reap a benefit.

In pushing for funds for elementary education in the state of Mississippi, the governor there told a story about his father, who was then eighty years old. A short time before, his father had planted about a thousand trees on his farm. These trees were of a kind that take forty years to reach maturity. Of course, the father will never live to see those trees grow to maturity, and yet he planted these trees.

Some of us would have trouble with that. Raised in a time of instant gratification, able to have whatever we want almost immediately, without too much effort, we become hooked on the here and now. We do not take the long view. Rather, we insist on instant, immediate gratification. We want a payoff for our efforts now. This is why we are so addicted to the casinos and state lotteries. These promise instant gratification without any long-term effort.

Scripture, on the other hand, talks about faith in the future, the long view. It tells us that having children in these dangerously uncertain times is an act of faith; creating beauty in vulgar times in an act of faith; going to church in a faithless time is an act of faith; teaching, guiding, and living the moral life in a cynical time is an act of faith; praying for your wayward children or grandchildren in a rootless time is an act of faith; holding onto values in a valueless time is an act of faith.

All these acts of faith say that, in spite of it all, you are seeding the future. Just as late in life, Abraham became the father of many nations; and old Sarah, past the age of childbearing, rocked her son, Isaac, on her knee; so we too plant faith, hope, and love for another day. We may not see that day; nevertheless, God will make it fruitful.

It has always been my conviction that the only reason the thief who hung alongside Jesus became good was because his parents prayed for him without ceasing. Most likely, they never knew what became of the son who had disgraced them, whether he was dead or alive. They only knew that the last time they heard, he was living a life of sin and crime. But still, staring into a blank future, they had faith. One day they would know what became of him.

So take heart from today's second reading. Whatever is fractured or difficult or contentious in your life, whatever is broken or sour or unfair, whatever is blank or barren or hopeless, have trust in God like Abraham and Sarah. Remain faithful even when it's hard to do so, loyal even when you're mocked for being so. Seed the future with your compassion, your fidelity, and your prayer. Remember, after all, that we are all but instruments in God's hands, servants to his will, and glorious co-creators in his kingdom. God is in charge.

Let us end with this powerful prayer from John Cardinal Newman:

God has created me to do him some definite service. He has committed some work to me which he has not committed to another: I have my mission.

I may never know it in this life, but I shall be told it in the next. I am a link in a chain, a bond of connection between persons. He has not created me for naught; I shall do good—I shall do his work; I shall be an angel of peace, a preacher of truth in my own place while not intending it if I do but keep his commandments.

Therefore I will trust him. Whatever I am, I can never be thrown away. If I am in sickness, my sickness may serve him; in perplexity, my perplexity may serve him. If I am in sorrow, my sorrow may serve him.

He does nothing in vain. He knows what he is about. He may take away my friends, he may throw me among strangers, he may make me feel desolate, make my spirits sink, hide my future from me—still he knows what he is about.

50

THE LORD OF DIVISION

LUKE 12:49–53

Once upon a time, the Devil and a friend went for a walk. They saw a man ahead of them stoop down and pick up something from the road. "What did the man find?" asked the friend. "A piece of truth," said the Devil. "Doesn't that disturb you?" asked the friend. "No, it does not," the Devil said. "I shall allow him to make a religious belief out of it."

I'd like to suggest that the Devil has been particularly successful in giving us one piece of truth from which we have made a religious belief: that is, the portrait of a benign, sweet, marshmallow Jesus. We Christians have focused on passages like, "Learn of me for I am meek and humble of heart," and ignored counterbalancing passages such as, "I have come to bring, not peace, but division." In today's gospel we have just such a Christ, a demanding figure, the very Lord of division.

The fact of the matter is that Jesus Christ generated hostility. We find the sentence, "They were seeking to kill him," more than once in the gospels. You were either for or against Jesus. You either shouted "Alleluia!" or you shouted "Crucify him!" Jesus demanded that he not be treated with indifference. And the logical fact of the matter is that true disciples of Jesus also generate hostility. Casting their lot with Jesus, they also create divisions in their families, as well as within their nations. Let me share with you the stories of three lives who stood with Jesus, the Lord of division.

On August 9, 1943, the Nazis executed an Austrian peasant farmer. He was not a spy. He was not a saboteur. He was not part of any scheme to assassinate Hitler. He was, in fact, a young man of quite limited education. A nobody. He was a devout Catholic who served as a sacristan in the village church. He was married and had three small children. His name was Franz Jagerstatter.

How did this very ordinary man become a threat to the state? How did he become a man of division? It was simple: he opposed the Nazis because he thought they were wrong. He voted "no" in the nearly unanimous plebiscite in 1938 that ratified the Nazi takeover of Austria. That made him different and noticed.

He refused to contribute to Nazi-sponsored collections. He refused to take any assistance from the now Nazi-controlled government. When inducted into military service during World War II, he refused to serve as a soldier in Hitler's army, knowing that the penalty for such a refusal was death. He was arrested, held in prison for a few months, and then beheaded.

During the time of his resistance, divisions were rife. His pastor advised him to think of his duty to his country and, above all, to his family. His bishop felt that, though sincere, Franz was in error. Later on, when the war was over, the bishop refused to publish articles about Franz in the diocesan newspaper on the grounds that such articles might create confusion and disturb conscience. People in his own hometown were divided in their feelings about him. Franz stood alone in his opposition to the Nazis. Even today, if you go to his village, you will find a war memorial dedicated to the fifty-six Catholics who died fighting in World War II on the Nazi side, but nothing for Franz.

There was only one silent witness to his heroism. There was a Catholic chaplain in the Brandenburg prison on the same day Franz was executed at 4:00 in the afternoon. That evening, the priest spoke with some Austrian nuns who were working in

Berlin. He told them that he would never forget the joy shining in this man's eyes and the confidence with which he lived his final hours.

The priest concluded by telling the sisters, "I can only congratulate you on this countryman of yours who lived as a saint and has now died a hero. I say with certainty that this simple man is the only saint that I have ever met in my lifetime."

Let's move ahead to some twenty years later, same month, August:

The place is not Austria but England, and the year is 1961. A man, an ordinary man, a lawyer, is reading the morning newspaper. His eye catches a news item from Portugal about two students who had just been sentenced to seven years imprisonment for what was called a crime against the state. And what was that crime? They had raised their glasses in a toast to freedom.

The lawyer, whose name was Peter Benenson, was familiar with the fights of political prisoners. He had defended some of them in countries like South Africa, Spain, and Hungary. Somehow, this item sparked something different in him. He decided then and there to form an organization of citizens who would unite their efforts on behalf of political prisoners throughout the world.

Benenson announced his intent in an article that appeared in hundreds of newspapers in both London and in Paris. Within a month, he received a thousand offers to help. Thus he began the organization now known throughout the world as Amnesty International. In 1977, the group was awarded the Nobel Peace Prize. Today, it has over 250,000 members in 134 countries.

When you read about this group it may seem that they do little more than write letters. But the thousands of letters, along with the publicity and pressure on governments, actually do bring about the release of many victims of injustice. How many victims? More than 25,000 of them in more than 100 countries since Peter Benenson read his newspaper that morning and made his decision. As you might imagine, his decision caused a lot of division, especially from oppressive governments.

Again, twenty years forward, to August, 1983. A widow, Coretta

Scott King, is speaking. Commenting on the election of a black mayor in Philadelphia, she said:

> I thought of the 1965 Selma to Montgomery march led by my husband...and how that campaign created a groundswell of public support leading eventually to the passage of the Voting Rights Act of 1965. I remembered how proud I was to march at Martin's side. His concern for my safety and our children's welfare had always made it difficult for me to persuade Martin to let me join him....
>
> I also thought of those courageous individuals who gave their lives in the voting rights struggle from 1964 to 1965...of our white brothers and sisters [who lost their lives in that struggle]....There were many other whites who exchanged the privileges afforded their race for a "season of suffering" to make democracy a reality for millions of black Americans.

Talk about a time of division! A minister of the church following Christ's declaration that the ones who do the will of his Father are his mother, brother, and sister—whoever they are, whatever their color.

Jagerstatter, Benenson, King: people angry at injustice. When one shares that anger and does something about it, you have a prophet. Being a prophet means taking a stand. Taking a stand means causing division. You were either for or against Jagerstatter. You were either for or against Benenson. You were either for or against Martin Luther King, Jr. You are either for or against Jesus Christ, the Lord of division.

In a way, if we have never caused division in our lives or the lives of others, it may suggest a low level of Christianity. If we have not suffered for the truth—turning down a bribe, rejecting smut, refusing to one-up our neighbors—we may very well have only a small piece of the truth, a very small piece, at that. From our small piece, we have erected a whole religious belief.

51

THE NARROW DOOR

LUKE 13:22-30

To the question, "Lord, will only a few be saved?" Jesus replied, "Try to come in through the narrow door, for many, I tell you, will try to enter and be unable."

The narrow door is a strange figure of speech. What does it mean? Is it literally built to smaller specifications, so downsized that only slim people can get into heaven? Could there actually be such a double whammy: you fight the flab on earth but are still excluded from heaven for being too fat? Or is something else implied? Yes, there is. The adjective "narrow" does not refer to the door as such. The door, in fact, is perfectly normal. The point is, it's narrow only for those with too many extensions to get through.

A few years ago, I saw a Charlie Brown cartoon which showed him going skiing. He put on his bulky clothes, his fur hat, large shoes, and heavy gloves. He then strapped on his snowshoes across his front and crisscrossed his skies and poles across his back. He hung his camera and his first aid kit over his coat. Finally, he was all ready; the only problem was, with all that "stuff" on him, he could not get through the door. And that is the meaning of the narrow door.

Don't worry. I won't focus on the usual admonitions that go along with this gospel: we have too many possessions, too many toys, too many sins, and all of these will prevent us from entering through the narrow door. So repent! I don't want to emphasize how our vices will keep us from entering through the door, although that will indeed be the case. Rather, I want to emphasize something more serious and less obvious. It is our virtues that will keep us from entering through the narrow door.

Let me explain this by sharing some real life stories. Listen first to Paula D'Arcy, who lost her husband and her baby in a car crash:

> The obvious persons to question about life passages are those who have gone ahead of us. Our grandparents, great-grandparents, the elders. I never knew my paternal grandfather, and my paternal grandmother spoke no English. My maternal grandfather was said to be as fine a person as anyone knew. But he died when I was barely four years old, and all my memories of him are sketchy. It is only my maternal grandmother whom I remember, and with whom we even lived for the first four years of my life.
>
> Throughout my childhood she visited us often, and I have vivid memories of seeing her at her place of work. She ran a small city tea room at a time when women hardly worked at all, let alone managed a business. She was spitfire, and I admired her initiative.
>
> But when she died in her eighty-third year and the family met to capture her essence for the minister's benefit, I was stunned with an awareness that we barely knew her at all. We knew, of course, names, dates, and places. We knew amusing anecdotes and significant moments. But we didn't know her. She hadn't let us in. She died with her story. No one could say what her true feelings, needs, and loves were.
>
> That impacted me like a blow to my person. To have lived and died and to never have been deeply known. To have always been proper and right, but to never have shared your dreams, hopes, and hurts. Your acquired wisdom.

There was wisdom to be shared, stories to be told, spiritual gifts to be given—but this lady gave none of those things away. She will have a hard time getting through the door with all the gifts that were not given, all the virtues not shared, all the stories untold. All these things will still be with her, making her too bulky to enter the narrow door.

So we ask, is that us standing before the door? Are we unable to get through, not because we're loaded down with sins, but because we're loaded down with dreams, hopes, hurts, and acquired wisdom that was never shared, shackled with all the virtues that should have been scattered?

Some years ago, Ann Wells wrote a widely circulated article about her sister who had recently died:

> My brother-in-law opened the bottom drawer of my sister's bureau and lifted out a tissue-wrapped package. "This," he said, "is not a slip. This is lingerie." He discarded the tissue and handed me the slip. It was exquisite: silk, handmade, and trimmed with a cobweb of lace. The price tag with an astronomical figure on it was still attached. "Jan bought this the first time we went to New York, at least eight or nine years ago. She never wore it. She was saving it for a special occasion. Well, I guess this is the occasion."
>
> He took the slip from me and put it on the bed with the other clothes we were taking to the mortician. His hands lingered on the soft material for a moment, then he slammed the drawer shut and turned to me. "Don't ever save anything for a special occasion. Every day you're alive is a special occasion." .
>
> I remembered those words through the funeral and the days that followed when I helped him and my niece attend to all the sad chores that follow an unexpected death. I thought about them on the plane returning to California from the Midwestern town where my sister's family lives. I thought about all the things that she hadn't seen or heard or done. I thought about the things that she had done without realizing that they were special.
>
> I'm still thinking about his words, and they've changed my life. I'm reading more and dusting less. I'm sitting on the deck and admiring the view without fussing about the weeds in the garden. I'm spending more time with my family and friends and less time in committee meetings.
>
> Whenever possible, life should be a pattern of experiences to savor, not endure. I'm trying to recognize these moments now and cherish them. I'm not "saving" anything; we use our good

china and crystal for every special event, such as losing a pound, getting the sink unstopped, or the first camellia blossom. I wear my good blazer to the market if I feel like it. My theory is if I look prosperous, I can shell out $28.49 for one small bag of groceries without wincing.

I'm not saving my good perfume for special parties; clerks in hardware stores and tellers in banks have noses that function as well as my partygoing friends. "Someday" and "one of these days" are losing their grip on my vocabulary. If it's worth seeing or hearing or doing, I want to see and hear and do it now.

I'm not sure what my sister would have done had she known that she wouldn't be here for the tomorrow we all take for granted. I think she would have called family members and a few close friends. She might have called a few former friends to apologize and mend fences for past squabbles. I like to think she would have gone out for a Chinese dinner, her favorite food. I'm guessing—I'll never know.

It's those little things left undone that would make me angry if I knew that my hours were limited. Angry because I put off seeing good friends whom I was going to get in touch with—someday. Angry because I hadn't written certain letters that I intended to write—one of these days. Angry and sorry that I didn't tell my husband and daughter often enough how much I truly love them.

I'm trying very hard not to put off, hold back, or save anything that would add laughter and luster to our lives. And every morning when I open my eyes, I tell myself that it is special. Every day, every minute, every breath truly is a gift from God.

Here we are again: standing before the door with unwritten letters, unseen sunsets, unloved children, unspoken compliments, uncelebrated friendships, unappreciated people, unwrapped joys. All those accumulated gifts of life all unused, all being saved for "someday." Like Charlie Brown's ski equipment, they make quite an encumbrance, which will keep us from entering the kingdom.

This story, which was first told by Kathi Littlejohn of the Eastern Cherokee, captures the same thought:

In the days when people and animals spoke the same language, there was a bird called Meadowlark, whose feet grew so big that he was ashamed of them. While the other birds flew through the air and sang in the treetops, Meadowlark hid himself in the tall grass where no one could see him. He spent all his time staring down at his big feet and worrying about them.

"Provider must have made a terrible mistake," thought Meadowlark, turning his feet this way and that. No matter how he looked at them, all Meadowlark could see was how big his feet were. "Perhaps Creator thought this would be a funny joke to play," said Meadowlark. "I'm sure anyone who saw my big feet would laugh at them, but I do not think this is funny at all." And so Meadowlark continued to hide himself away in the tall grass.

One day Grasshopper was going about his business, making his way through the tall grass, when he bumped smack into Meadowlark, sitting on the ground and staring sadly at his feet.

"What are you doing here?" asked Grasshopper. "You are not one of those birds who live on the ground! You should be in the treetops with the other birds. Why do you not fly and sing as they do?" "I am ashamed," answered Meadowlark. "These feet that Provider gave me are so big and ugly that I am afraid everyone will laugh at me!" Grasshopper looked down at Meadowlark's feet, and his eyes grew big with amazement. It was true; Meadowlark's feet were huge! Grasshopper did his best not to smile; he did not want to hurt Meadowlark's feelings.

Finally he said, "Well, it is true that your feet are perhaps a bit larger than those of other birds your size. But Creator does not make mistakes. If your feet are big, you may be sure that they will be useful to you someday. Big feet will not keep you from flying. Big feet will not stop you from singing. You are a bird and you should act like one!" And Grasshopper went on about his business.

After Grasshopper had gone on his way, Meadowlark sat and thought about his words. "Perhaps he is right," said Meadowlark. "The size of my feet cannot change the sound of my voice or the power of my wings. I should use the gifts Creator gave me." And so Meadowlark took Grasshopper's advice and flew out to sing. He landed in the top of a tree, threw back his head, and let his song pour from his throat.

Meadowlark could really sing! Piercingly sweet and beautiful, the liquid notes of Meadowlark's song spread through the forest. One by one, the animal people stopped what they were doing and gathered to listen to Meadowlark's voice. Raccoon, Possum, and Skunk; Deer, Bear, and Wolf; even Rabbit paused in his scurrying about to listen in wonder to this marvelous singer. The other birds flocked around Meadowlark, listening. Even Mockingbird fell silent, entranced by the melody that Meadowlark sang.

When Meadowlark began to sing, he forgot everything else, even his big feet. He closed his eyes and lost himself in the joyful song Creator had given him. When at last he finished his song and looked around, there were all the other birds and animals, staring at him. With a rush of shame, Meadowlark remembered his feet. Thinking that the others were staring at him because he was so ugly, Meadowlark flew back down to the tall grass and hid. And this time he would not come out.

Not very far from the tall grass where Meadowlark hid, there was a wheat field planted by the Human Beings. Now there was a Quail who had made her nest and laid her eggs in the middle of this wheat field. Every day she sat on her nest and waited for her eggs to hatch. As the wheat grew ripe and her eggs had still not hatched, Quail began to worry. Sure enough, one afternoon she heard the people talking about how they were going to come out and cut the wheat the very next day. Quail knew that her nest would be trampled and her eggs crushed, and she began to cry.

Now Grasshopper heard Quail crying, and he came to see what was wrong. "The men are coming to cut the wheat," Quail cried, "and my family will die!" Suddenly, Grasshopper had an idea. "Wait here," he told Quail. "I think I know someone who can help." Grasshopper hurried to find Meadowlark. "Quail needs help to move her family," said Grasshopper, "and I think your big feet are the answer."

When Meadowlark heard of Quail's trouble, he agreed at once to try to help. He flew to Quail's nest. There he found that his big feet were just the right size to pick up Quail's eggs. Very carefully, Meadowlark lifted Quail's eggs and flew with them to the safety of the tall grass. There Quail built a new nest, and it was not long before the eggs hatched. As Meadowlark watched Quail tending her beautiful babies, he thought to himself, "My feet may be big and ugly, but they did a good thing. I should not be ashamed of them!"

And so Meadowlark flew out of the tall grass, back to the tree-tops where he began to sing. He is singing to this day, and his song is still so beautiful that everyone stops to listen.

Are we the Meadowlark? Do we have lovely, haunting, beautiful and melodious songs left unsung, stuck in our throats, never sent forth, because we are so self-absorbed with our defects? Are our gifts left silent inside us, the gifts that will keep us from getting through the narrow door?

Not shared dreams, hopes, and stories; unwritten letters, unmade calls, unhugged children, unspoken love, unused gifts; all of these beautiful things, these wondrous virtues, these "somedays" and "one of these days" alas, still intact.

Well, I think you get the point—Jesus' point. "Try to come in through the narrow door. Many, I tell you, will try to enter and be unable." And we will ask, "Why, Lord? Because of their wicked vices?" The Lord will shake his head sadly and reply, "No; because of their unused virtues."

52

SELF-ESTEEM

LUKE 14:1, 7-14

There are two characters into today's gospel story: the host and the guests. Both come under criticism, the host because he invited only the Beautiful People and the guests because they jockeyed for favored places.

Actually, in one sense, neither can really be blamed. They were both doing what is part of human nature, what is natural to all of us. They were pumping up their self-esteem. When you come right down to it, self-esteem is based on the drive to exist and to be significant. Look at me: I count! I'm somebody! I am. These are basic human drives and needs. So in this regard, the host and the guests were "doing what comes naturally."

In this story, then, Jesus does not tell us to ignore our self-esteem. Rather, he asks us to consider what criteria we use to make ourselves feel important, significant. The criteria for both the host and guests were all wrong. They were based on competition and external status—fragile measurements, I might add.

Jesus says that genuine self-esteem is based within. Let me share with you the five major categories which social scientists have found are used by most people to measure self-esteem. They are significance to others, competence in terms of performance, power to influence people, body image, and possessions. Most people have developed their self-esteem around one or more of these five criteria. Let's take a look at each one of them.

Significance to others. As we grow from childhood and adolescence, we really do not have "self"-esteem but "other"-esteem; that is, what others think about us ultimately leads us to think the same thing about ourselves. Moving into adulthood, we still need to be in relationship with others. But now the question is, to whom have I given control over my sense of self-esteem?

Here's where the trouble lies. If our self-esteem is based on what someone else thinks about us, what happens if that person is no longer in our lives? Fearful of being measured badly by others, we will always work to please them in a kind of ongoing co-dependency; our true self never emerges, that is, who we are and what we stand for. So basing our self-esteem solely on what others think is very risky business—and, ultimately, a false criterion. For in this way one can never learn to be one's own person.

Competency. If my self-esteem is based on what I do—and do well—then my self-esteem will always be fragile. Why? Because when work and ability falter—and sooner or later they will—self-esteem falters as well, especially in our capitalistic culture which values people for what they can do, not for who they are. We see this with the elderly, who, because they are useless for production and reproduction, are not respected. Nor are those who are retired.

Priests, CEOs, managers, and the like are often praised for their competency, but never praised simply for who they are. And there comes a time when being praised for competency is just not enough. Suspicions arise in all of us that when I lose my competency I will lose respect, I will lose value, and I will lose the esteem of other people. I will even lose my identity.

A retired man, the founding genius of the company, went back after several years to visit the plant. The young receptionist did not have a clue who he was. When he mentioned that he had worked there for many years, she asked, "Oh? And who did you used to be?"

Power over other people. This works for a while as a source of self-esteem. But often, people begin to grow, they need to get out from under your power. And then what happens? Who are you without the power to influence others?

Body image. In our time of slick commercialism, when inner virtue and character are considered negligible and external imagery is everything, there exists a whole industry of spin doctors to create illusions. And so, body image becomes crucial for a sense of self-esteem. Pick up any women's magazine and you'll note right away that obsessions with weight, skin, hair, and clothes are a national pastime and have spawned a multi-billion-dollar market.

Products abound that will "cure" whatever is wrong with our appearance. Bulimia and anorexia thrive as the dark side of this culture of body image. To have the right currently acceptable image, to be "in," people will suppress what is more noble in the human spirit. The kids, raised on media imagery and not inner character, are the prime victims of this market madness. God forbid you have the wrong "look" on the first day of school! You'll be dubbed as a nerd forever.

Possessions. These are some people's criteria for self-esteem. The more possessions, the louder the applause or greater the envy, and the bigger the boost to self-esteem. I recently saw this headline on the front page of the *New York Times:* "Millionaire's Mega-Mansion Shocks Even the Hamptons." The article that followed told us this:

> Ira Rennert's dream house in the Hamptons will have 29 bedrooms, 39 bathrooms, a 164-seat theater and a restaurant-sized kitchen with five refrigerators, 6 sinks, and a 1,500 gallon grease trap. Its outbuildings will include a sports pavilion with 2 tennis courts, 2 bowling alleys, and a basketball court; a garage sufficient for 200 cars, and a power plant with 4 huge water tanks, a 2.5-million BTU furnace, and a maze of underground tunnels.
>
> The 63-acre, 5-building spread at the rim of the Atlantic Ocean will dwarf the White House, San Simeon, and Bill Gates's mega-mansion. All told, the structures will occupy 110,000 square feet, 72,000 in the house, making Fair Field, as it is known, the largest home in America. (The average home is about 1600 to 2000 square feet).
>
> Mr. Rennert's grandiose plans have produced protest and speculation among the Masters of the Universe who summer here, where private tennis courts are commonplace, squadrons of gardeners tend manicured lawns, and the neighborhood market sells lobster salad for $40 a pound.

Because this house is not our topic, we won't even mention that the cost, the labor, the raw materials, the maintenance, the resources, and the enormous amounts of energy used to build this mega-house complex for a handful of people would keep almost all the third world countries in South America functioning well above the poverty line for an entire year.

Nor will we mention that such gross conspicuous consumption of the planet's resources is part of the reason why third and fourth world countries look with deep suspicion on Western plans for population control, urging them to have fewer children so they won't use up the world's resources. They, the majority poor, suspect that such policies exist only so that the minority rich can have even more resources to use on themselves. I'd wager that the poor of the world would be more convinced to voluntarily have fewer children if those in industrialized nations would, for example, voluntarily have fewer cars. And there's not much chance of that happening, is there?

Anyway, back to our point: people who base their self-esteem on their possessions live by the rule that the less sense of inner worth one has, the more one must display grandiose outer worth. But let the market crash, and people who identified themselves with their possessions also crash. They jump off buildings.

These five criteria for determining self-esteem—significance to others, competency, power, body image, and possessions—are all so fragile, so false, so empty. In the end, all these criteria will do is betray us; they will let us down. That is the point behind the gospel story. The host invited only the Beautiful People, and the Beautiful People jockeyed for status and betrayed an inverted sense of self-value.

And so the gospel teaches that self-esteem, self-worth, is centered elsewhere. It is centered in being a child of God, being beloved by God, therefore, in doing the Godlike things of our nature such as telling the truth, keeping your word, giving to those who cannot repay, and taking the lowest seat. Self-esteem is what we used to call character. It is an inner anchoring in truth, a sense of the "deep within," an awareness of our core identity as beings made in the image and likeness of God.

There is a reward for those who strive for an inner character that reflects God's image; there are words for those who learn that using external criteria as a basis for self-esteem will ultimately betray them: "My friend, come up higher."

53

TOUCHED BY AN ANGEL

LUKE 17:11–19

"Keeping their distance, they called out, saying, 'Jesus, Master, have pity on us!'"

Each year on October 2, the Catholic Church celebrates the feast of the Guardian Angels. Twenty-five years ago, the sophisticates, the yuppies, the over-educated, snickered at this quaint Catholic superstition: angels and spirits and all that hilarious religious jazz. Theirs was the age of therapy, do-it-yourself everything, no rules, and no religion—especially no organized religion. They felt they were free of all authority. All that mattered was the self.

The self measured everything. Theirs was the freedom of the sexual revolution, approved greed, freewheeling drugs, ongoing Club Med vacations, and nonstop consumerism. They had achieved the American dream: two cars, two TV sets, two computers, two or three consecutive spouses. And, most of all—what gave permission for all of this, as it were—God was dead. Dostoyevsky wrote: "If there is no God, everything is allowed," and everything was allowed.

So why weren't these people happy? Why were they, underneath it all, so dissatisfied, so self-destructive? Why were their relationships so fragile? Why did they have a gnawing emptiness inside? Whatever the reasons were, little by little, they began to sense the vacuum. Little by little, they began to open up to the harrowing recognition that there had to be something more to life. No, make that "someone," with a capital S. There had to be Someone more. And so the hunger for God began to take hold.

But there was a problem, a vast problem. By the time most of the yuppies realized their need for God, they had broken the link to the past, the link that would enable them to find God once more. Even their modern parents, who no longer went to church, had memories of the Mass and processions and novenas and ember days and parish missions and confession and catechism study—even if they had discarded all these practices. But the children had been cut off from learning about all these church practices and traditions. All that was required was attendance at weekly religious education classes so that the children could, with parental approval, officially graduate from religion when they had finally received the sacrament of confirmation.

And so the yuppies, with the link to tradition broken, had no religious resources. All they had was the very thing that formed their lives from the beginning. They had the mass media, especially television. So they embraced the fuzziness of the New Age with its hodgepodge blendings of Eastern religious techniques and humanistic pop psychology. Because they had not learned about the God of revelation— or perhaps God proved to be too much for them—they embraced New Age charlatans and prophets. And ironically, coming full circle, they discovered angels!

Suddenly, the spirit world was in. Angel calendars and angel stories and angel songs and angel pins and angel books were literally and figuratively flying off the shelves. The Catholic angels whom the educated once snickered at became their personal genies. They were indeed, touched by an angel. Their angels, of course, were not those of the Scripture—scriptural angels were far too demanding—but of their own construct, designed to help them be productive or change their tires on wintery nights.

Nevertheless, the return to angels signaled something important: if the generation of twenty-five years ago proclaimed that God is dead, this generation declares that God is very much alive. If the generation of twenty-five years ago was an unbelieving one, this generation is besotted with God. They are desperate for God and are willing to

---

search for the divine, even if often they look in the wrong places. This generation is very religious even if they disdain "organized" religion.

That is part of the reason why young Catholics—sociologically considered to be between the ages of eighteen and thirty-nine—are, as you have noticed, largely absent from church. These young people, your children and grandchildren, are not irreligious. On the contrary, they just don't buy into organized religion. They are "good" people—defensive parents are quick to tell me that. But being "good" or ethical is not the same as being religious. Being ethical without the context of a pattern of belief leaves you no foundation for why you are moral; it cuts you off from the wisdom and tradition of the larger community. For Catholics, not participating in a parish cuts you off from the Eucharist, the heart and center of our communal faith.

Relevant to all this are the findings of a current, in-depth study concerning young Catholic adults. You might be interested in some of the findings. Dean Hoge, his associate, William Dinges, and their colleagues have come up with a list that identifies, in descending order of importance from one to nineteen, the way young Catholics define Catholic identity and the importance of Catholic teachings. Here are some of the rankings: first in importance are the sacraments, seen across the board as an essential sign of Catholic identity. Third is the teaching of Christ present in the Eucharist. Mary, the Blessed Mother, is fourth on the list.

Further down, seventh on the list, is the necessity of a pope. Comments William Dinges: "[This finding] does point to a kind of lessened institutional sense of being Catholic." Translation: Catholic identity is weak. As for whether or not the papacy is a necessity, disagreeing with or disliking a particular pope is a far cry from dismissing the office altogether, since it is surely one of the basic foundational elements of Catholicism. It would be like dismissing the office of president as irrelevant and non-essential to our democratic system because we do not like or agree with the particular person currently holding that office.

Back to the list: twelfth is the importance of the saints. Saints are just not that big with young adults—except, of course, media-made saints like Princess Di. Confession to a priest is way down on the list of importance, while fifteenth are the reasons why abortion is wrong. Sixteenth is the need for a celibate priesthood, while seventeenth in importance are the reasons for being against the death penalty. Eighteenth is the need for only male priests. You can see the wide disparity between official church teaching and the beliefs held by young Catholic adults.

More comments from Dinges:

> There is [also] a sizable part of the young adult Catholic population that have a very denominational sense of Catholic identity, by which I mean they see Catholicism as by and large another form of religious preference and it isn't necessarily more true or more valid than any other kind of denominational religious preference….They also tend to mimic the larger cultural trend, that is, the tendency on the part of many people to simply reduce religion to ethics, to being a good person.

Again, the argument here is that it really doesn't matter whether you're a Methodist or Catholic or Episcopalian. What matters is whether or not you are a good person.

Several things were heartening for me, as a priest, to read in these findings. I was pleased to see that young adults see Mary as an essential identifying mark of Catholicism. More than that, service and works of charity as defining religion were ranked second in importance, right behind the sacraments as an identifying mark of a Catholic. That is heartening.

The other thing about young Catholic adults which comes across in this survey is that their faith is as strong as their high religious ideals. The reason most of them just don't resonate with a parish is because they say, correctly I think, that the parish has lots of things for parents and children and teenagers and senior citizens, but nothing for young adults. They are like the lepers in the gospel who kept their distance, crying out, "Jesus, Master, have pity on us!" Those who have distanced themselves from the church, from the eucharistic community, from their family still cry out, "Jesus, Master, have pity on us."

There is a deep hunger for God out there. People, especially young adults, need the encouragement of your witness, your prayer, your fidelity, your words. They need to see your example of reaching out in charity to others, like Jesus did, as they negotiate their journey toward wholeness.

Let's go back to the words we heard in the second reading last week, from Paul's second letter to Timothy: "Do not be ashamed, then, of the testimony about our Lord....Hold to the standard of sound teaching that you have heard from me, in the faith and love that are in Christ Jesus. Guard the good treasure entrusted to you, with the help of the Holy Spirit living in us."

Don't be ashamed of being Catholic. People, especially young adults, need the encouragement of your witness and your words. Like St. Paul, be a model of sound teaching. Guard the good treasure of faith, but above all, share it. In doing so, our young adults will be touched by an angel: you.

54

SLOTH

2 THESSALONIANS 2:16—3:5

In today's second reading, St. Paul prays for his readers, that God may "comfort your hearts and strengthen them for every good work and word." Clearly, Paul envisions an interested, active congregation, disciples of Jesus who must be about "every good work and word." There must be no indifference for these people, no "let the other guy do it," no laid-back gospel truth. In a word, they were to avoid what we would call sloth.

For most of us, the word "sloth" conjures up an image of people sitting on their couches dropping bons-bons into their mouths. It suggests laziness. Thus, we do not relate to sloth since our lives are exhaustingly active as we add our anguished voices to the nationwide cry: "there's never enough time!" Sloth in the spiritual sense is not physical laziness, but a laziness of the spirit and intellect. This kind of sloth is called *acedia,* or apathy, in the old religious manuals. Apathy was always considered by the mystics to be the worst of sins.

Today, we might describe this spiritual sloth or apathy as the "whatever" syndrome:

"Do you want coffee or juice to drink with your breakfast?" Whatever.

"Do you want thick crust, thin crust, stuffed crust, or no crust on that pizza?" Whatever.

"I'm leaving you for someone else." Whatever.

Scandals abound in high public figures. Whatever.

Every night in the United States a million children go to bed homeless and hungry. Whatever.

Soft money continues to corrupt our political system. Whatever.

Apathy is the indifference we display to things of the moment. We don't know and we don't care to know. We play it cool, and to be cool is the height of hip. Perhaps this is partly the result of the society in which we live, where we are constantly hit with tons and tons of information. Saturated, we easily slip into overload and shut down for protection. Dumbed down, we become immune to shock TV and shock radio; we normalize pathology. Jerry Springer, Howard Stern, whatever. Another child killed a child? Whatever.

This is spiritual sloth. We are "whatever-ing" our lives away. This spiritual sloth keeps us uninvolved, isolated. It says, go away. Don't disturb my little world. Perhaps the quintessential example of apathy is the young man with a baseball cap on backwards, driving his car with the windows open and the radio blasting hard rock music you can hear for ten blocks away. Never mind the stress this noise gives others; never mind that it might wake a sleeping baby; never mind that the elderly might be resting; never mind that it might upset the sick. Nobody else matters to this young man besides himself. Sensitivity to others is simply not in his vocabulary: he is a living "whatever." Apathy is his name.

We need to be aware of this kind of sloth and move on. Writer Jonathan Kozol speaks of his own journey out of academic detachment and apathy, and toward belief:

Well, I had a religious upbringing. I'm Jewish, and my mom and grandma were religious, but, as happens to many people who go on to places like Harvard College, that got washed out of me very quickly. At Harvard, you didn't talk about religion. Even if you believed in God, you didn't mention it, because people would make fun of you.

I went on from Harvard to Oxford, where I had a Rhodes

scholarship. And then after a few years I came back to the States, in 1964, to Boston, my hometown. I probably would have done something normal like go to medical school or law school if it hadn't been for the civil rights movement. In the summer of '64, you'll remember, those three young men were killed in Mississippi—two white, one black. One of them happened to be Jewish, from New York. And I identified with him.

One day I just got on the subway. The end of the line was Harvard Square. I went to the other end, which was the ghetto of Boston, and signed up and became a teacher of little kids— black kids in a segregated school. And, in a sense, that was my formative decision. I didn't think of it that way. But, in a sense, that twenty-minute ride took me to a place from which I've never returned.

Reading the gospels and the lives of the saints will help dispel the "whatever" soul sickness. Prayer will keep you open to the Spirit. Dag Hammarskjöld, who was an author as well as a much-respected Secretary General of the United Nations, writes:

I don't know who—or what—put the question. I don't know when it was put. I don't even remember answering. But at some moment I did answer yes to Someone—or Something—and from that hour I was certain that existence was meaningful and that, therefore, my life in self-surrender had a goal. From that moment I have known what it means not to look back and to take no thought for the morrow.

Finally, intellectual sloth is apathy toward that which makes life worth living. It is a spiritual dryness, a deadness of the soul, intellectual laziness. This is at least partly due to the philosophy of relativism that dominates our educational system.

A year or two ago, the *Chronicle of Higher Education* had several articles by professors alarmed at the attitude of students toward the Holocaust. The students agreed that Hitler was a nasty man but could not bring themselves to condemn him. After all, in his time and place, who is to say he was wrong? Everything is relative. One era's vices are another era's virtues, and vice versa. People construct their own morality. Whatever.

The result? As Jesuit professor Joseph Linehard says:

A generation of college students has been so anesthetized by relativism that they cannot say that Shakespeare was the greatest master of the English language for fear of offending someone who thinks Danielle Steel is. But if they can never say, "You are wrong" they can never say, "I am right," either. So we take no stands, bear no witness, flee evangelization, and dub heroism as pathological and useless, for nothing really matters anyway.

It's a good thing the signers of the Declaration of Independence didn't suffer from apathy. Have you ever wondered what happened to them?

Five signers were captured by the British as traitors and tortured before they died. Twelve had their homes ransacked and burned. Two lost their sons in the Revolutionary Army, another had two sons captured. Nine of the fifty-six fought and died from wounds or the hardships of the Revolutionary War.

What kind of men were they? Twenty-four were lawyers and jurists. Eleven were merchants, nine were farmers and large plantation owners, men of means, well educated. But they signed the Declaration of Independence knowing full well that the penalty would be death if they were captured. They signed and they pledged their lives, their fortunes, and their sacred honor.

Carter Braxton of Virginia, a wealthy planter and trader, saw his ships swept from the seas by the British navy. He sold his home and properties to pay his debts and died in rags. Thomas McKeam was so hounded by the British that he was forced to move his family almost constantly. He served in the Congress without pay, and his family was kept in hiding. His possessions were taken from him, and poverty was his reward. Vandals or soldiers or both looted the properties of Ellery, Clymer, Hall, Walton, Gwinnett, Heyward, Rutledge and Middleton.

At the Battle of Yorktown, Thomas Nelson, Jr. noted that the British general Cornwallis had taken over the Nelson home for his headquarters. The owner quietly urged General George Washington to open fire, which was done. The home was destroyed, and Nelson died bankrupt. Francis Lewis had his home and properties destroyed. The enemy jailed his wife, and she died within a few months.

John Hart was driven from his wife's bedside as she was dying. Their thirteen children fled for their lives. His fields and his grist mill were laid waste. For more than a year he lived in forests and caves, returning home after to find his wife dead, his children vanished. A few weeks later he died from exhaustion and a broken heart. Lewis Morris and Philip Livingston suffered similar fates.

Such were the stories and sacrifices of the American Revolution. These were not wild-eyed rabble-rousing ruffians. They were soft-spoken men of means and education. Standing tall, straight, and unwavering, they pledged: "For the support of this declaration, with a firm reliance on the protection of the Divine Providence, we mutually pledge to each other our lives, our fortunes, and our sacred honor."

Sloth was not part of the vocabulary of the signers of the Declaration of Independence.

If we want a sign of intellectual sloth in our lives, look at our magazine racks, the newspapers, the magazines we read, and the TV shows we watch, all commercial enterprises, filled with celebrities and ways to consume. Do we read good Catholic magazines that challenge us and give us a gospel perspective, gospel values to live by and get excited over?

Sloth, with its spinoff, apathy, is one of the deadliest of sins today. Moral, spiritual, and intellectual sloth run rampant. But a life of prayer and reflection, pious devotions and spiritual reading, can liberate us. Going back to the words of St. Paul, these practices can help restore our hearts, our minds, and our souls so that we may pledge "our lives, our fortunes, our sacred honor." These practices will "comfort your hearts and strengthen them for every good work and word."

55

BETRAYAL

LUKE 21:5–19

"You will be betrayed even by parents and brothers, by relatives and friends...." Delivered up by your own? Betrayed by your own? Betrayal is a terrible thing. But we must distinguish between two types of betrayal, the first of which has its origin in evil, the other in weakness. As for the first, it was a sad, frustrating, and frighteningly familiar story. Two young men were arrested for making arrangements with a big-time drug trafficker to import cocaine into their community. The twenty-two-year-olds would become the main dealers, selling coke to any and all of the teenagers whom they could interest in, then addict to, that potent pleasure drug.

Because this deal crossed state lines, it was the FBI who finally moved in and made the arrests, breaking up the alliance between the locals and their out-of-state supplier, and cutting off the drug supply to the teens of that community.

What about this otherwise all-too-common story made it so shocking? What brought this report about a drug bust into prominent play on network news? It was because this particular case took place in Lancaster County, Pennsylvania. The two young men arrested were members of the Amish community. The teenaged customers cut off from their drug supply were young Amish boys.

The parents of all these young people were like every parent: stunned to think such a thing could happen in their community, shocked that such a drug tragedy could involve their own children. If the lure and danger of drugs could infiltrate the cloistered, close-knit community that the Amish have intentionally built up as a bulwark against the sins and seductions of the world, what chance do any of the rest of us have at keeping our own families, schools, and communities safe?

Perhaps the most disturbing and insidious part of this story for the Amish community was that this betrayal came at the hands of two of their own. It was not outsiders but insiders who jeopardized the safety of their youth and compromised the moral standards of their tradition.

The Amish community traditionally schedules events known as "hoedowns" in order to offer young men between the ages of sixteen and twenty-four time off from the strict rules and regulations of the community. At these unchaperoned events the young people can carouse a bit, sowing a few behavioral wild oats, before they are baptized as adults, all the while remaining within the supposedly safe confines of their community. It was during these hoedowns, when nobody was watching and the community was trusting, that the betrayal occurred.

Betrayal by an intimate—one of the themes in today's gospel—has always been considered the gravest of crimes and hurts. There is no hurt like the one reserved for a spouse who has violated the vows and broken the covenant of marriage. How many divorced individuals speak fondly of an ex-spouse who left them for another? There is no revulsion like that reserved for men or women who sexually abuse their own children. The child molester is seen as the lowest of the low even in prison. There is no repugnance like that shown traitors who betray their country.

Dante reserved the lowest part of hell for betrayers. Satan, frozen in ice, has Brutus who betrayed Caesar in one hand and Judas in another. This type of betrayal is rooted in evil, aided by pride and self-gain. As more and more people put both God and morality aside, we can expect this kind of betrayal to increase.

But there is another kind of betrayal, one that is rooted in weakness. These are the daily betrayals rendered by those who are near to us, as well as the ones that we ourselves give. Such daily betrayals need daily forgiveness. But, above all, we need to learn how to control our tendency to betray one another, for this tendency is there in everyone from the very beginning of our lives. To illustrate, here is my favorite Bill Cosby monologue, called "The First Parent."

> Whenever your kids are out of control, you can take comfort from the thought that even God's omnipotence did not extend to his kids.
>
> After creating heaven and earth, God created Adam and Eve. And the first thing he said to them was: "Don't."
>
> "Don't what?" Adam replied.
>
> "Don't eat the forbidden fruit."
>
> "Forbidden fruit? Really? Where is it?"
>
> "It's over there," said God, wondering why he hadn't stopped after making the elephants.
>
> A few minutes later, God saw the kids having an apple break, and God was angry.
>
> "Didn't I tell you not to eat that fruit?" the First Parent asked.
>
> "Uh huh," Adam replied.
>
> "Then why did you?"
>
> "I dunno," Adam answered.
>
> God's punishment for this disobedience was that Adam and Eve should have children of their own.

Children betray out of weakness—call it original sin, if you will—but as I said, they must be lifted beyond their natural self-centeredness to learn fidelity to family, friends, spouses, country, God. In short, the answer to curbing the tendency to betray is by training children to be responsible. But in today's climate, we run into obstacles because the words "healthy" and "sick" have replaced "good" and "evil." This brief story will illustrate:

> Dennis Prager was playing one day in the park with his two-year-old son. A five-year-old boy walked over to his son, threw him violently onto the concrete, and hurt him. The five-year-old's mother rushed over to her son and demanded: "Honey, what's troubling you?"
>
> Prager wondered, where is the reprimand? Where is the sense that it is wrong to throw another human being to the ground

and hurt him? The mother, oblivious to the crying two-year-old, gave her five-year-old a life lesson: that he is not responsible for his behavior, only troubled.

What will this boy be like at twenty-five? He might be selling cocaine to the Amish. And later, through the prison bars, his mother will ask, "Honey, what's troubling you?"

Self-esteem is now deemed more important to teach our children than self-control. In a recent book called *Inside Human Cruelty and Violence*, Roy Baumeister has found four root characteristics of the most violent criminals. One of them is "high" self-esteem, which translates into "I am the center of the world." This kind of attitude is in complete opposition to the gospel, which tells us, "your life is not your own."

Practicing compassion as opposed to indifference, loyalty as opposed to self-fulfillment, fidelity as opposed to betrayal, comes only after long years of training and example. Simply put, learning to be noble takes time, time we don't always give. We spend a great deal of time on our children's intellectual progress: we send them to the best schools, give them every advantage, show them how to be popular. And there's no problem with that—except, often, we do not give equivalent time to training our children in the moral life. We take that for granted and so, in effect, we let the TV do the job.

In ancient China, the people wanted security against the barbaric hordes to the north, so they built the Great Wall. It was so high they believed no one could climb over it and so thought nothing could break it down. They settled back to enjoy their security. During the first hundred years of the wall's existence, China was invaded three times. Not once did the barbaric hordes break down the wall or climb over it. Each time, they simply bribed a gatekeeper and then marched right through the gates.

The moral? The Chinese were so busy relying on walls of stone they forgot to teach integrity to their children. Are they any different from some parents today?

Closer to our time, consider this powerful scene from Robert Bolt's play, *A Man for All Seasons*. Here Richard Rich, a promising and ambitious young man, petitions the saintly Thomas More for a position among the glitterati at the court of Henry VIII. More tells Rich that he can offer him a position not as a courtier, but as a simple teacher. The young man is crestfallen, and More tries to cheer him up: "You'd be a good teacher."

Rich fires back, "And if I were, who would know it?"

The patient More explains, "Yourself, your friends, your pupils, God; pretty good public, that!"

More is saying that the only audience worth playing for in the end is the divine audience; the only drama worth acting in—even in the smallest role—is God's.

Interestingly, Rich's life takes a terrible turn when he refuses to accept More's offer. Instead, he compromises, schemes, and worms his way into political prominence at court. To obtain the position of Collector of Revenues for Wales, he perjures himself and betrays Thomas More (there it is again!). As Rich passes the condemned man on the way out of court, More sees the insignia of office around his neck and then remarks devastatingly, "You know, Rich, it profits a man nothing to give his soul for the whole world…but for Wales?"

It profits you or your children nothing to become successful—maybe even a celebrity—at the cost of betraying your own soul, your own integrity. In that there is so much concern for the head, and so little concern for the spirit. Let me end with one of my favorite quotes, which I use whenever I speak at PTA meetings. It is from Chaim Potok's book, *The Chosen*. A man is crying out to his friend, Reuven, about his son:

Reuven, the Master of the Universe blessed me with a brilliant son. And he cursed me with all the problems of raising him. Ah, what it is to have a brilliant son! Not a smart son, Reuven, but a brilliant son, Daniel, a boy with a mind like a jewel. Ah, what a curse it is to have a Daniel whose mind is like a pearl, like a sun. Reuven, when my Daniel was four years old, I saw him reading a story. He swallowed it as one swallows food or water. There was no soul in my four-year-old Daniel, there was only his mind. He was a mind in a body without a soul.

It was a story in Yiddish about a poor Jew and his struggle to get to Israel before he died. Ah, how that man suffered! And my Daniel enjoyed the story, he enjoyed the last terrible page, because when he finished it, he realized for the first time what a memory he had. He looked at me proudly and told me back the story from memory and I cried inside my heart. I went away and cried to the Master of the Universe, "What have you done to me? A mind like this I need for a son? A heart I need for a son, a soul I need for a son, compassion I want from my son, righteousness, mercy, strength to suffer and carry pain: that I want from my son, not a mind without a soul!"

56

TRUE TREASURE

MATTHEW 13:44–52

Given at the time of John F. Kennedy, Jr.'s death.

The deaths of three young people is bad enough, bad enough to make a minor headline on the inside pages of a local newspaper. Unfortunately, it happens routinely at prom time. But if the three are celebrities, then the whole nation—the whole world—is stirred. Then the media can't dish out enough information about the tragedy because, as it says, that's what the public wants. And so every detail, every person who even remotely knew the people, carried their luggage, opened the door for them, filled their gas tank—no one, past or present, is absent from the ever present microphone and video camera for as long as the traffic will bear it.

What is it, our fascination with celebrities, with the too sad death of John F. Kennedy Jr. and others like him? It is that celebrities—people famous for being famous, as Daniel Boorstin put it—become projections of our aspirations and needs. We filter out the bad parts, like sexual predation or drug use or infidelity or alcoholism. Thus, people like Elvis Presley, John F. Kennedy, Sr., and Princess Di remain in the pantheon of idols long after their deaths. We, the public, focus only on the glamour, the grandiose lifestyles, the power, the kindly and tender parts of their lives.

Celebrities appear to have it all, so we dearly want to believe. Video star wannabes seek the fame and adulation and popularity that their idols seemingly possess. We follow their every move, buy every record, dress like they dress, talk like they talk, wait hour after hour, sometimes days, to catch a glimpse of them. They set the pace and we follow. Why? Because our own lives seem so ordinary, so humdrum, so gray in comparison; their lives are technicolor. Our problems appear so pressing and confining; they are so free. We are overlooked, and they are looked for everywhere.

Celebrities are a modern media invention. In the past, there were instead quiet heroes and heroines, like the people featured in *The Greatest Generation*, a recent book by Tom Brokaw. Before that, there were saints, and people made pilgrimages to their shrines and sought their relics. Such saints were noted for charity, kind and heroic deeds, miracles of grace and valor. They embodied—we're almost embarrassed to use this word today—virtues like dying for the faith, embracing the leper, giving away all their possessions, feeding the hungry, teaching the poor, courage, and a thirst for justice.

But Francis of Assisi, Ignatius, and Teresa of Avila have given way to Jerry Springer, Eddie Murphy, Madonna, Leonardo DiCaprio, and Dennis Rodman. The relics have given way to items sold at auction, like a pearl necklace that belonged to Jackie Onassis, sold for a quarter of a million dollars at Sotheby's; shrines have given way to Graceland. Our ideals have changed.

Mother Teresa's simple sari is quaint—if you are a little, wrinkled old woman; we really envy Liberace's nine-hundred-suit wardrobe and Imelda Marcos's thousands of pairs of shoes. The hermit's hut is cute, but we'll take Bill Gates's mansion, thank you very much. External possessions and the image they create are how we judge success; not by the inner qualities of people. Personality has triumphed over character.

A decision made by the Kennedy family may help move us in a different direction and turn us toward today's gospel. Their decision to have John, Jr. cremated and his ashes tossed into the sea was sensible and prophetic. They specifically and deliberately did this in order to avoid turning him into a celebrity in death, something which he tried to avoid in life. They did not want people trampling over his gravesite, making endless pilgrimages to his burial plot, taking endless photographs of his resting place, and hawking souvenirs at his monument. A quiet man of quiet virtue, they wanted John, Jr. to be remembered and valued as he was and not to become one more vulgar media commodity.

And this brings us to today's gospel. "The kingdom of heaven is like a treasure buried in a field for which a person sells all he has and buys that field." Suppose you see the field through the eyes of Jesus. Initially, he sees what everyone else sees: dirt, weeds, brown soil. But he knows that beneath the grime and dirt there lies a treasure: you. And so he goes and sells all he has, that is, his divinity—"being in the form of God, he emptied himself and took the form of a slave" is the way St. Paul puts it—and purchases this treasure at the price of his blood.

And therein lies our true celebrityhood. As we indulge our natural instinct to venerate our ideals, as we wait in line to catch sight of our idols, as we imitate our celluloid dreams and desire our media heroes, we must not forget the foundation of our own worth and fame. We are made in the image and likeness of God, not in some advertising agency's notion of what we are. We are deeply loved by Jesus who sees in us, everywhere and at all times, a treasure which he ardently desires and for which he has literally given everything, even his life, to possess.

Each of us is a child of God, gifted by the Spirit, given a task to do in this life, a task which will make us genuine celebrities forever. That task is to feed the hungry, give drink to the thirsty, visit the imprisoned, care for the sick, be chaste and honest and tell the truth. This is the stuff of true celebrity—and it will last for more than fifteen minutes.

This is the treasure Jesus sees in us. This is the treasure we are, and we ought to tend to that treasure. To idolize celebrities from afar is all right to a degree, as long as you don't overlook your own celebrity. To acknowledge the treasure you are; to know that Jesus sees you as a treasure, one he fully desires; to know you are beloved of God, armed with a mission in life—well, that is reality, not shadow; that is substance, not image; that is gospel, not hype.

So go ahead and join the parade of people who worship the celebrities—it's hard to resist. But remember that it's all fleeing image; deep down, where it really counts, the only true celebrity is you. Who made you so? Who told you so? Who has such great expectations of you? Who is your biggest fan? Jesus.

57

SO(W) WE MUST

MATTHEW 13:1-23

"A sower went out to sow...." Yes, indeed. But, according to the parable, not very carefully. He tosses the seed wildly, helter skelter, all over the place. It falls on exposed soil—an obvious bird feeder—shallow rocky soil, thorn-choked soil and, almost by accident, rich soil. And even there, the yield—thirty, sixty, a hundredfold—is uneven to say the least.

We shake our heads not only at the inefficiency of the sower's efforts, but at the whole issue of extravagance and waste which this parable symbolizes. Life is like that, isn't it? So much effort, so little results; so much spent energy, so little return. In everyday life, countless things are wasted, people are wasted, lives are wasted, good deeds are wasted, honorable intentions are wasted. Why bother? In all of the senseless losses of life, in all of the senseless extravagances of nature, we are faced with mystery.

Jesus himself, it seems, is no exception to life's rule. He is born and hundreds of little innocent boys are slaughtered because of him. It just doesn't seem right. He lives in a land of poverty, and magi bring him costly gifts. Great crowds follow him, but only twelve join him. Jesus even preaches wasteful sowing: you know, the nonsense about a herdsman who leaves ninety-nine sheep to search for one easily replaceable lamb; the Samaritan who gives all his goods to a stranger. And then there is the terrible waste of his own life on a cross, right after a woman had wasted precious ointment in perfuming his feet.

In our own ways, we resonate with Jesus and we resonate with the sower, don't we? We sow a perfect wedding and sprout divorce. We scatter the seeds of our parenting and the birds of drugs and a secular media come and peck away daily at our efforts. We plant an honest day's work and are downsized. We cultivate decency and virtue and the so-called lifestyles touted by some celebrities choke our hopes for those dearest to us.

We freely toss out the seeds of teaching and instruction and they seem to fall on shallow ground. We breed a firm faith and wind up with non-practicing children. We nurture liberty and produce license. We are passionate about fairness and justice and look around to see the haves and the have-nots and tyranny.

Like the sower in Jesus' story, we have extravagantly and liberally sown the seeds of our lives. But so often we find that the weeds have taken over. The other side seems to be winning. How do we handle this mystery of disappointment and waste which we see all around us? Does today's parable give us a direction, if not an answer? Yes. Perhaps this true story will illustrate:

> Several years ago a baby boy was born in a Milwaukee hospital. The baby was blind, mentally retarded, and had cerebral palsy. He was little more than a vegetable who didn't respond to sound or touch. His parents had abandoned him. The hospital didn't know what to do with the baby.
>
> Then someone remembered May Lempke, a fifty-two-year-old nurse who lived nearby. She had raised five children of her own. She would know how to care for such a baby. They asked May to take the infant, saying, "He'll probably die young." May responded, "If I take the baby, he won't die young; and I'll be happy to take him."
>
> May called the baby Leslie. It was not easy to care for him. Every day she massaged the baby's entire body. She prayed over him; she cried over him; she placed his hands in her tears. One day someone said to her, "Why don't you put that child in an institution? You're wasting your life." As Leslie grew, so did May's problems. She had to keep him tied in a chair to keep him

from falling over.

The years passed: five, ten, fifteen. It wasn't until Leslie was sixteen years old that May was able to teach him to stand alone. All this time he didn't respond to her. But all this time May, wastefully so to speak, continued to love him and to pray over him. She even told him stories of Jesus, though he didn't seem to hear her.

Then one day May noticed Leslie's finger plucking a taut string on a package. She wondered what this meant. Was it possible Leslie was sensitive to music? May began to surround Leslie with music. She played every type of music imaginable, hoping that one type might appeal to him. Eventually May and her husband bought an old second-hand piano. They put it in Leslie's bedroom. May took Leslie's fingers in hers and showed him how to push the keys down, but he didn't seem to understand.

Then one winter night, May awoke to the sound of someone playing Tchaikovsky's Piano Concerto no. 1. She shook her husband, woke him up, and asked him if he had left the radio on. He said he didn't think so, but they decided they'd better check. What they discovered was beyond their wildest dreams.

Leslie was sitting at the piano. He was smiling and playing it by ear. It was too remarkable to be true. Leslie had never gotten out of bed alone before. He'd never seated himself at the piano before. He'd never struck a piano key on his own. Now he was playing beautifully. May dropped to her knees and said, "Thank you, dear God. You didn't forget Leslie." Soon Leslie began to live at the piano. He played classical, country western, ragtime, gospel, and even rock. It was absolutely incredible. All the music May had played for him was stored in his brain and was now flowing out through his hands into the piano.

Doctors describe Leslie as an autistic savant, a person who is mentally retarded from brain damage, but extremely talented. They can't explain this unusual phenomenon, although they have known about it for nearly 200 years.

Leslie's story figures in our parable. Remember, May Lempke extravagantly sowed and sowed the seeds of her love and her prayers for years with no return. It took her sixteen years just to get mute

---

Leslie to stand. But in the end she saw a harvest. Not, true enough, a hundredfold one or even a sixtyfold harvest—Leslie is still mentally retarded—but a thirtyfold one of musical genius.

The point of her story—and our story—is that she was bound to try, for if she did not there would be less beautiful music in the world and God's splendor would be hidden. And there, I think, is the direction the parable gives us: namely, whatever the success or failure or partiality of our efforts—thirty, sixty, a hundredfold—we are compelled as God's sowers to scatter our seeds of faith, hope, and love wherever and to whomever we can, for without us there would be less of God's splendor in the world. And when that splendor disappears, it will be the end of the world.

An old Hebrew legend says that as long as there are thirty just people in the world, God will not destroy it. There's where we are: the "thirty just ones" called by God, given a commission to sow his truth, never knowing why so much of our sowing will wind up on exposed, rocky, or prickly soil. It is a mystery.

But we do know that we Christians, like our Master, are a people who must do our best, try our hardest, live in hope, and keep God alive in the world because we believe that somehow, someday, we can and will make a difference. Many of us will, in fact, see the wonderful outcome of our sowing in our children, friends, or students.

Someday, we are assured, there will be a harvest. At that time God will make all things right and new because of the seeds we have sown. Therefore, we are part of God's plan. And so we continue to play music for the spiritually damaged in the hope that there might be a concerto some day. We may never hear it, but there will be music in the world and there will be a harvest when it is all over.

God has spoken. I recall here a woman, a teacher of teachers, who once said to me, "A good teacher has got to be in love with the process of planting the seed, but cannot need to be around for the harvest." That is the lesson for today. Be in love with the sowing. Leave the rest to God.

58

ALL WE HAVE IS ENOUGH

MATTHEW 14:13-21

"'Give them some food yourselves.' They protested, 'Five loaves and two fishes are all we have here.' And he said, 'Bring them to me.'" There are two life-lessons for us in this familiar story. The first is found in Jesus' direction to his disciples when they were faced with an overwhelming situation: "Give them some food yourselves." Somewhat embarrassed, they hold up a few loaves and fishes before him and shrug their shoulders. Jesus takes the food and blesses the little they have to offer. But then, rather than hand out the loaves and fishes himself, he returns them to the disciples who are told to distribute them to the crowd.

There we are. This first lesson is clear. God depends on us to take part in the aid and redemption of the world. Our poor, limited, small talents, taken and blessed by him, are returned to our hands to share with others. If we fail to do so, both our gifts and his blessing go wanting. And how simple it all is, as we learn from this man:

I could tell from the bus driver's greeting when the blind lady climbed aboard that she must be a very frequent passenger. She sat down directly behind him and they carried on an animated conversation as he drove.

When we reached the woman's stop, the driver got out and

escorted her through heavy traffic to the other side of the street. When he returned to his seat, I noticed the woman still standing where he had left her. "She won't budge till she knows I got back safely," he explained. He honked his horn three times, the woman waved, and off we drove.

Here you have it: a blind lady and a lowly bus driver, two insignificant people on the world stage. Hardly five loaves and two fishes between them, if you will. Yet Christ blessed what they had, so to speak, and handed it back to them. Each then made a contribution from what little they had. They could, of course, have complained that they had so little and withheld their meager gifts. But instead, they fed each other from their small store of compassion and love. And that was enough. It is enough to teach us that our small talents have been blessed and returned to us, and so we too must feed the crowd from what we have, however few, however paltry our gifts.

A little sparrow is lying on his back with his feet up in the air. A rooster comes along and asks what he is doing. The little sparrow replies, "Chicken Little said the sky in falling and I'm trying to hold it up." "What?" exclaimed the rooster. "Do you think a little twerp like you can hold back the sky?" The sparrow replied, "One does what one can."

With what we have, no matter how few our loaves and fishes, we do what we can because Jesus has asked us.

The second lesson is to be found in Jesus' words, "Bring them—bring that insignificant five loaves and two fishes—to me and don't back off. Don't say, but it's so little, what can we do? I know the problems are great and your resources are tiny, but don't give up. Bring them to me to be blessed."

That "what-can-we do?" with our "so little" is a cry that might be the response of the parents worried about their children. The children have so many peers who exert so much pressure, and their child is with those peers at school and at play far more than he or she is with the parents. In their young lives there are so many influences, so much crude and rude talk, so much violent action on TV and in the movies, so much drug use around, so many temptations to face. Parents, beside themselves, hungry for answers, ask, "What are we to do? We have nothing here but five loaves and two fishes."

That might also be the response of someone trying to make an honest living, but the pressures to cut corners, the "everyone-is-doing-it" philosophy, cutthroat competition, and dirty office politics sap his energy and his spirit. He is hungry for answers about how he can be a Christian in the workplace. "They" have all the power. He has nothing but "five loaves and two fishes."

That might be the response of the spouse who is desperately trying to make a go of a troubled marriage, and who has grown weary of being the only partner working at the relationship. Her husband is still around but not too often. And when he is home, his mind is clearly somewhere else. Hungry for a rekindling of passion, for companionship, she is left with saying sadly, "There is nothing here in this marriage but five loaves and two fishes."

That might be the response of our young people, who have so much and yet so little. I was intrigued by a letter to Ann Landers from an adolescent. It was written in response to a letter sent by someone who lived through the Depression, who had described how hard it was to be a teenager in the 1930s. His message was that kids today have an easy time of it compared to teens in his day. Here's what the young respondent wrote:

> Let me ask your generation a few questions:
>
> Are your parents divorced? Almost every one of my friends comes from a broken home.
>
> Were you thinking about suicide when you were twelve?
>
> Did you have an ulcer when you were sixteen?
>
> Did your best friend lose her virginity to a guy she went out with twice?
>
> You may have had to worry about VD, but did you have to worry about AIDS?
>
> Did your classmates carry guns and knives?
>
> How many kids in your class came to school regularly drunk, stoned, or high on drugs?
>
> Did any of your friends have their brains fried from using PCP? What percentage of your graduating class also graduated from a drug and alcohol rehabilitation center?
>
> Did your school have armed security guards in the halls?
>
> Did you ever live in a neighborhood where the sound of gunfire at night was "normal?"
>
> You talk a lot about being dirt poor and having no money. Since

when does money mean happiness? The kids at school who have the expensive cars and designer clothes are the most miserable.

When I am your age, I won't do much looking back, I'll just thank God that I survived.

So, what are we to do these days? Young people are understandably overwhelmed. They cry, "Lord, we have nothing here but five loaves and two fishes. Perhaps not even that. What is that when you are drowning in so many cares and anxieties and sorrows? What are we to do?"

Certainly, as we saw, that was the response of the disciples when five thousand plus followed Jesus into the desert. Jesus' reply to them was: "You give them something to eat." And the disciples protested, "How? We have nothing here but five loaves and two fishes." Then Jesus said softly: "Bring them here to me." He looked up to heaven, and blessed and broke the loaves and gave them to the disciples, and the disciples gave them to the crowds.

I think the second lesson, then, for those at their wit's end, those stuck with a mere five loaves and two fishes in the face of over-whelming hunger, is to realize that they have a friend who whispers: "Bring them to me. Bring them to me—your skills and weaknesses, your strengths and fears, your children and their futures, what little you have. Bring them to me, and I will make you adequate for the task at hand. Bring them to me—your hopes, your dreams, your convictions. Bring them to me—your burdens, your challenges, your responsibilities, your hurts."

You see, when life gets the best of us, perhaps it is often because we focus too much on how little we can do and too little on how much Christ can do. In any case, know that he will have the last word any-way. When all the anxieties have passed, the worries gone and the crosses disappeared, one thing will remain: God's love. As Robert Louis Stevenson wrote:

The stars shine over the mountains,
The stars shine over the sea,
The stars look up to the mighty God,
The stars look down on me.

The stars shall last for a million years,
A million and a day
But God and I will live and love
When the stars have passed away.

59

THE TROUBLES I'VE SEEN

1 KINGS 19:9, 11-13

"At the mountain of God, Horeb, Elijah came to a cave where he took shelter." With these words, the story of the first reading—part of the fascinating cycle of Elijah tales of the Old Testament—begins. To catch the real drama of the story told here today, however, we have to see what Elijah was doing hiding out in a mountain cave, like some runaway criminal, to begin with.

The answer is, he was a runaway criminal. A chapter or so before our account he had just crossed swords with the reigning ruler, Queen Jezebel. He had mocked her pagan prophets, ridiculed them publicly, and proven their gods and hers were frauds. Queen Jezebel did not take kindly to this humiliation so she declared Elijah an outlaw and sent her soldiers to fetch him for execution.

And so here he is, out of breath, a fugitive from justice, hiding in a cave for fear of his life, despondent and rapidly losing faith with no divine help in sight. He was God's prophet and God had let him down. Where was God now? Did it pay to put his life on the line, to live and preach the truth? Crime doesn't pay? You couldn't prove it by him. Crime paid handsomely in his time: Jezebel was queen. She had all the power. And in our time too. Crime pays: celebrity, big cars, high living, fawning hangers-on, money, sex, power. So Elijah is suffering from the age-old question of faithful people: does it pay to be virtuous? Why do bad things happen to good people? Where is God?

As he sat in the mouth of the cave feeling depressed and abandoned, a strong wind drove by, loosening the rocks and sending them cascading down the mountain with a mighty roar. Ah, Elijah thought, God must be there. He will finally reveal himself in such tremor. But God was not there. Next there was a shattering earthquake opening up dangerous fissures, scaring Elijah out of his wits so that when he opened his eyes he thought he surely would see Yahweh. But God was not there. Then came a raging fire and the prophet felt that surely the flames would twist and configure into the burning presence of God just as he once appeared to Moses in the burning bush. But God was not there.

Then nature quieted down and there was an eerie silence as the smoke and dust and clouds disappeared and the sky appeared once more. All was still. Dreadfully quiet. A strange calm. Then he heard it. Not much, but it was there. A kind of whispering sound in the recesses of his own heart. And he knew God was there.

Let me tell you the story of someone of our own time who, like Elijah would know in a unique way the absence of God, the awesomeness of nature and the stillpoint of God's presence which spoke to him.

He was fifteen years old at the time. He and his father were driving past a tiny airport in a small town in Ohio. Suddenly a low-flying plane spun out of control and nose-dived into the runway. The boy yelled, "Dad! Dad! Stop the car!" Minutes later the boy was pulling the pilot out of the plane. It was a twenty-year-old student flier, who had been practicing takeoffs and landings. The young man died in the boy's arms. It was a traumatic thing, for the boy knew the man who was killed.

When he got home, he threw his arms around his mother and cried, "Mom, he was my friend! He was only twenty!" That night the boy was still too shocked to eat supper. He went to his room (to his cave, so to speak), closed the door, and in the silence and darkness lay on his bed wondering where God was.

You see, the boy had been working part-time in a drugstore, and every penny he made he spent on flying lessons. His goal was to get his pilot's license when he turned sixteen. The boy's parents now wondered what effect the tragedy would have on their son. Would he stop taking lessons, or would he continue? They agreed that the decision would have to be his.

Two days later the boy's mother brought some freshly baked cookies to her son's room. On his dresser she saw an open notebook. It was one he had kept from childhood. Across the top of the page was written, in big letters, "The Character of Jesus." Beneath was listed a series of qualities: "Jesus was sinless; he was humble; he championed the poor; he was unselfish; he was close to God."

The mother nodded to herself. She saw that in her son's hour of decision he was turning to Jesus for guidance. She was happy for that. Then she turned to her son and said, "What have you decided about flying?" The boy looked into his mother's eyes and said, "Mom, I hope you and Dad will understand but with God's help, I must continue to fly."

The boy was like Elijah. He had to shut down the noise: the wind, the earthquake, the fire and turn to the quiet of solitude of his room where he heard the still whispering of Jesus. Like Elijah who was tempted to give up prophesying, the lad was tempted to give up his dream. But, like Elijah, he didn't.

And so, on July 20, 1969, Neil Armstrong became the first human being to walk on the moon. Few people who watched that historic event on television knew that one of the reasons that he was walking on the moon was Jesus. They didn't know it was from Jesus that he drew strength and guidance to make a crucial teenage decision which was now responsible for his historic feat.

The spiritual journey is perilous. You are here this morning because you want to walk it. You have your dreams. You want to be a disciple of Jesus. You want to be a good Catholic.

But Queen Jezebel is so influential, so threatening. She wears the face of sickness and disappointment, of foul talk, of loose morals, of false promises. She lies, cheats, makes crude TV shows and movies, mocks religion, and makes us feel like nerds for trying to live the life Jesus showed us. And there she is: popular, rich, applauded, sought-after. She persecutes the hell out of us, but she has all the power. And so we sit at the door of the cave and wonder when God will rescue us from all this.

Because of our culture, so loud and psychedelic, so hostile to the life of the spirit, we think we'll find God in special effects: wind, earthquake, fire, Jurassic Park, Woodstock. But we won't. God is in the quiet.

God is in the time Jesus spent apart in prayer, the time we spend apart in prayer…the time spent with nature, on a retreat…the time reading a spiritual book. Any time spent turning down the noise of the cell phone, incessant rock music, the ubiquitous commercials and traffic noise that we have learned to take for granted is a gift to self and to God, who often can't be heard above the din. Then you will know once more that God is present and you are his prophet.

I would like to end here—and doubtless you wish the same—but I must honestly tell you that there is this one further truth to face. Knowing that God is present in the quiet of your prayer and the depth of your being won't make life easier, only full of meaning. Let me end with the story of a couple of prophets to show what I mean.

The great African writer, Alan Paton, tells the story of Robert Mansfield, a white man in South Africa. Mansfield was the headmaster of a white school who took his athletic teams to play cricket and hockey against the black schools until the department of education forbade him to do it any more, and so he resigned in protest. Paton continues about Mansfield:

> Shortly thereafter, Emmanuel Nene, a leader in the black community, came to meet him. He said, "I've come to see a man who resigns his job because he doesn't wish to obey an order that will prevent children from playing with one another."
>
> Mansfield said, "I resigned because I think it is time to go out and fight everything that separates people from one another. Do I look like a knight in shining armor?"
>
> "Yes, you look like a knight in shining armor," Nene replied, "but you are going to get wounded. Do you know that?"
>
> "I expect that may happen," Mansfield shrugged.
>
> "Well, you expect correctly. People don't like what you are doing, but I am thinking of joining with you in the battle."
>
> "You are going to wear the shining armor, too?"
>
> "Yes, and I'm going to get wounded, too. Not only by the government, but also by my own people as well."
>
> "Aren't you worried about the wounds?" Mansfield asked.

"I don't worry about the wounds," Nene said. "When I get up there, which is my intention, the Big Judge will say to me, 'Where are your wounds?' and if I say, 'I haven't any,' he will say, 'Was there nothing to fight for?' I couldn't face that question."

Can you?

60

THE DIRTY DOZEN

MATTHEW 9:36—10:8

"Entertaining as a blowtorch." So says the *New York Times* thumbnail review of the movie *The Dirty Dozen*, starring Lee Marvin. The plot focuses on a really tough mission given to twelve men during World War II. (Supposedly, the movie is based on a true incident.) The men were to free some American prisoners held by the Nazis, but there was only a ten percent chance that this mission would succeed. No one of the twelve men was expected to return alive.

Lee Marvin, who played the officer in charge, knew that the army would not risk good men in such a suicidal venture. So he went to an American prison where "bad" soldiers were held, to recruit men who had messed up in horrible ways. They were thieves, murderers, con men who brought their vicious lives to the army and were eventually thrown into jail.

Their thieving, lying, and murderous skills were, in fact, just what Lee Marvin needed and what, in the end, made the mission success- ful. They were put in the right kind of situation, given the right encouragement, and presented with a goal in life beyond their own self-centered pride and greed. And so ironically, these losers, this "dirty dozen," became heroes.

Today's gospel is also about a dozen people—not exactly dirty, but no great shakes either—chosen to do a task. To put it mildly, they were hardly qualified to accomplish their mission, which was to bear witness to the greatest story ever told. We know some of the backgrounds of each of these men.

Take Matthew, for example. He was a tax collector. Fishing, which was the occupation of some of the others, was an honorable profession; tax collecting was not. This was primarily because Matthew, a Jew, was collecting money for the Gentiles who occupied the area. Such tax collectors gouged the people, giving some of the tax money to the Romans and skimming the rest for themselves. They were barred from the synagogue and treated as the moral equivalent of robbers and murderers. Spiritually, Matthew was a sick man. He helped the enemy, cheated his neighbors, and embarrassed his family. He was a candidate for Jesus' dirty dozen, if ever there was one.

Peter, of course, appears to be a loser all the way around. He follows Jesus, all the while never knowing what he will eat, where he will sleep, or who might come after them in harm. He struggles to understand Jesus' parables but fails to. He is first to proclaim Jesus as the Messiah and yet is told, "Get behind me, Satan." When Jesus is arrested, he bravely draws his sword to defend him, but is rebuked. He brags that he, above all the others, will never deny Jesus—yet he does precisely that, three times. He falls asleep while Jesus is agonizing. He flees when Jesus is captured. He is absent when Jesus dies. He's another prime candidate for Jesus' dirty dozen.

And so it goes. Greedy James and John want places of honor at Jesus' right and left hand. But when Jesus really reigns from his place of honor on Calvary, James and John are nowhere to be seen. Their places are taken by others considered more worthy: two thieves. Thomas doubts, Jude the zealot stews, Judas betrays, and they all run away, every last one of them, in Jesus' time of need.

Lee Marvin, Jesus Christ—where were their heads when they picked their dirty dozen? What were they thinking of? Lee Marvin selected losers both because their loss would not be felt and because they had the dubious talents he needed. Jesus had other reasons. He selected losers, first of all, because their loss *would* be felt by God. Secondly, these losers had the talents Jesus needed, which was none, so that they would never think it was their enterprise instead of his. All they had to do was the best they could and let Jesus' spirit be their strength.

Finally, Jesus selected these people as an object lesson to us: no one, after seeing the apostolic dirty dozen, could claim that he or she was not worthy of the call. No one could claim exemption from being a disciple, no matter what their background. No one was beyond the pale, even someone like the conniving thief who became a last-minute disciple on Calvary.

Take Cassie Bernall, a seventeen-year-old girl. She was, as you may recall, a student at Columbine High School in Littleton, Colorado, who for a time played around with drugs and was interested in witch-craft. Her parents were worried enough about her that they removed her from the public school and put her in a Christian school. Cassie hated it, but when a friend invited her to a Christian camp, she went, and her life changed. She then did an unusual thing: she asked her parents to put her back into public school, where she could talk with classmates who were willing to listen about her belief in Christ.

On April 20, 1999, in the Columbine library, a teen-aged gunman singled her out and asked, "Do you believe in God?" A friend who saw this later said that Cassie paused, knowing what the answer would probably mean, before she said, "Yes, I believe in God." He said, "Why?" didn't wait for an answer, and shot her. This unlikely candidate became a martyr to the faith.

After her death, her brother found these words which Cassie had written: "Now I have given up on everything else—I have found it to be the only way to really know Christ and to experience the mighty power that brought him back to life again, and to find out what it really means to suffer and to die with him. So, whatever it takes, I will be one who lives in the fresh newness of life of those who are alive from the dead."

Before her death, Cassie had been involved with other members of her youth group in visits to an inner-city Denver storefront church which ministered to prostitutes and drug addicts. Adolescence is a terrible time, and in some of what she told friends it is clear that Cassie knew it was scary. But a drug-flirting, witchcraft-interested, dirty-dozened teenager answering the call to Jesus Christ is scary, too, and it cost this unlikely candidate her life. She was no more worthy than the original twelve, but she was called and she answered.

How about you? You are asked to join quisling Matthew, Peter the denyer, words-more-than-deeds James and John, doubting Thomas,

and the rest of Jesus' dirty dozen. In that crowd, what excuse can you
have? All that you are asked to do is to give the same answer Cassie
Bernall gave when asked, "Do you believe in God?"

I don't think that anybody is going to ask you that question
straight out, of course. But what they observe of you—your language,
your honesty, your courage in not going along with the crowd—will
give the answer loud and clear as to whether you really believe in
God, whether you have answered the call to discipleship, and
whether, in spite of your faults and sins, you belong to the apostolic
dirty dozen. You teenagers here, maybe instead of wearing unusual
clothing to be different, you might wear a "dirty dozen" tag on your
wrist to remind yourself and others that you belong to God, and to
remind you of the answer you must give if someone asks you, with or
without words, "Do you believe in God?"

Someone wrote a little dialogue that fits here as an ending to my
words. It goes like this:

And the Lord said, "Go."
And I said, "Who, me?"
And he said, "Yes, you."
And I said, "But I'm not ready yet,
And there is company coming
And I can't leave my family.
You know that there is no one to take my place."
And he said, "You're stalling."

And the Lord said, "Go."
I said, "But I don't want to."
And he said, "I didn't ask if you wanted to."
And I said, "Listen,
I'm not the kind of person
To get involved in arguments.
Besides, my family won't like it.
And what will the neighbors think?"
And he said, "Baloney."

And yet a third time, the Lord said, "Go."
And I said, "Do I have to?"

And he said, "Do you love me?"
And I said, "Look, I'm scared.
People are going to hate me
And cut me into little pieces.
And I can't take it all by myself."
And he said,
"Where do you think I'll be?"

And the Lord said, "Go."
And I sighed,
"Here I am...send me."

NOTES, SOURCES AND CREDITS

As I indicated in the Introduction, I often find it helpful to draw on the insights of others. These people provide inspiration, and for that I am grateful. Sometimes I will use their very words. Most often, the words of other people spark a further thought and I develop a homily from there.

Some of the stories which I use in this book will not have a source noted. Usually this means they are stories which have been around for a long time, recounted in various forms and by various people, and are thus considered in common use. If there are any omissions in these credits for stories used in this book, it is not intentional. Every effort has been made to give proper credit to sources.

Here, then, follow a few credits and sources that should be noted.

1. "Memory, Mystery, & Majesty." The opening paragraphs are from that great preacher, Fred Craddock, from "The Surprise and Joy of Advent" found in *Living Pulpit*, December 1997. The poem "But You Didn't" is by Stan Gebhardt, and can be found in *Chicken Soup for the Soul*, Vol. 2 (Health Communications, Inc.).

2. "God the Thief." The concept comes from William Willimon and I have developed it on my own.

3. "No Room." The Santa Fe story is from Marvin A. McMickee in *Living Pulpit*, Advent/December 1997. The ending of this homily has to be changed, of course, to reflect the current political situation. Other sources: *Living Pulpit*, Advent/December 1997; Father Walter Burghardt; the Children's Defense Fund.

4. "Rejoice." The story "Lady, Are You Rich?" by Marian Dooley, is taken from *Chicken Soup for the Soul*, Vol. 3. The story of the young man with bone cancer is from *Kitchen Table Wisdom*, by Rachel Naomi Reven, MD (Riverhead Books, a division of Penguin Putnam, Inc., 1996).

5. "Second Thoughts." The passage from Al Staggs is from *Christian Ethics Today*, June 1988.

6. "Emmanuel." Anne Donovan's article, "The Painful Effort to Believe," can be found in *America* magazine, September 19, 1998.

10. "Three Resolutions." The opening story is from *The Americanization of Edward Bok: Bits & Pieces* (Amereon, Ltd.).

11. "God Shows No Partiality." "Margaret Patrick, Meet Ruth Eisenberg," by Margaret Patrick, is from the April 1988 issue of *Guideposts*. (Copyright ©1998 by Guideposts, Carmel, NY 10512. Reprinted with permission.)

12. "The Scandal of the Cross." The idea and imagery of the electric chair comes from Mark Link in his book *Illustrated Sunday Homilies* (Resources for Christian Living, 1987).

13. "No and Yes for Lent." The Kathleen Norris excerpt is from her book, *Amazing Grace: A Vocabulary of Faith* (Penguin Putnam, Inc., 1998).

14. "Mark Becomes a Christian." The material in this homily is taken from my book, *A New Look at the Sacraments* (Twenty-Third Publications, 1983). This homily is very popular, as most people like a little catch-up on the history and meaning of church practice.

15. "Risky Business." The Artful Eddie story is from Max Lucado's book *And the Angels Were Silent* (Copyright ©1992 by Max Lucado. Used by permission of Multnomah Publishers, Inc.).

19. "Ordinary Folk." The Tom Long story is modified from William H. Willimon, *Pulpit Resource*, April/May, 1999. The story about the old man with the chair is from Brennan Manning, *Lion and Lamb* (Chosen Books, a division of Baker Book House, 1986).

20. "The Ragman." This story is from the gifted pen of Walter Wangerin, Jr. and is found in *Ragman and Other Cries of Faith* (HarperCollins Publishers, Inc., 1984).

21. "Knowing Who You Are." The Howard Stern quotes were taken from "The Shock of Recognition," by Diana Rabinowitz, in the *Wall Street Journal*, April, 26, 1999.

22. "Mary's Fifteen Minutes of Fame." The story of Ellen is by Dale Francis. I have read the Christina story in several different versions. This one is retold by Max Lucado in his book *No Wonder They Call Him Savior* (Copyright ©1986 by Max Lucado. Used by permission of Multnomah Publishers, Inc.)

23. & 24. "Signs of a Healthy Parish" and "The Janitor's Hands."

Change the city names, the name of the church, and other specific information to reflect your own parish and experience while still keeping the dynamic of these homilies.

25. "No Compromises." The story of the freedom riders is by Thomas G. Long, from *Whispering the Lyrics* (CSS Publishing Co., 1995. Used by permission.). The poem, "When You Thought I Wasn't Looking," author unknown, is from *Chicken Soup for the Soul*, Vol. 4 (Health Communications, Inc.).

27. "Gather, Affirm, and Challenge." The story of Henry and the peas is from "On the Cutting Edge," by Cori Connors, from the March 1997 issue of *Guideposts*. (Copyright ©1997 by Guideposts, Carmel, NY 10512. Reprinted with permission.)

28. "Seeing As Saints." The Sister Cleophas story is from Melannie Svoboda's book *Traits of a Healthy Spirituality* (Twenty-Third Publications, 1996). The story of Joey Russell's Titanic postcard was recorded in *People* magazine, May 4, 1998.

30. "Stand By Me." I have drawn material for this homily from Tim O'Connell's fine little book, *Tend Your Own Garden* (Thomas More Press, 1999).

32. "A Time to Remember." The Robert Maynard story is from *Dynamic Preaching*, February 1990, Vol. 5, No. 2 (Seven Worlds Corp., Knoxville, TN); originally published in the *New York Daily News*. The high school girl's story is modified from Kathleen Peebles, http:/www.mountdragon. com/memorial.essay/html.

33. "Freedom, Hugs, and Napkins." This homily is based on ideas from the book *Tuesdays with Morrie*, by Mitch Albom (Copyright © 1997 by Mitch Albom. Used by permission of Doubleday, a division of Random House, Inc.)

34. "A Little Room of Your Own." My recounting of the incident in the airport has been modified from a story by Max Lucado, in his book *And the Angels Were Silent* (Copyright ©1992 by Max Lucado. Used by permission of Multnomah Publishers, Inc.).

35. "A Woman for All Times." Although this homily is grounded in the feast of the Assumption, it can be modified to fit any Marian feast.

36. "In the Details." This is a creative composite of previous homilies on the subject.

37. "Who Is My Neighbor?" The development of this homily is derived from the homiletic magazine *Dynamic Preaching*, July 1998. The story of Peter Godwin is from *Mukiwa: A White Boy in Africa* (Atlantic Monthly Press, 1996). The story of Ralph Burke is by Dorothy Willman, and originally appeared in the *Claremore Daily Program* (Oklahoma). The survey is from the book *Influence: The Psychology of Persuasion*, by Dr. Robert Cialdini (William Morrow, 1993).

38. "A Sin of Omission." The Flo Whetley story is from Roger Crawford's book, *How High Can You Bounce* (Copyright ©1998 by Roger Crawford. Used by permission of Bantam Books, a division of Random House, Inc.).

39. "Stalking God." As indicated in the text, "The Bear" is by William Faulkner, but I acknowledge my indebtedness to Robert Barron, SJ, for the summary of this story in his book, *And Now I See...* (Copyright ©1998. Crossroad Publishing Co. Used by permission.).

40. "The Best Wine Saved." The story "Two Big Feet" is by Mary Kasting from the November 1997 issue of *Guideposts*. (Copyright ©1997 by Guideposts, Carmel, NY 10512. Reprinted with permission.)

42. The story about the rape of a thirteen-year-old girl is from an article by Valerie Schultz, "They're Just Movies: Lighten Up!" in *America*, May 8, 1999.

43. "Take Up the Cross." The story of the nun and what follows is considerably modified from material in *The Holy Longing*, by Ronald Rolheiser (Doubleday, 1999). The story of Sweat is taken from William H. Willimon, *Pulpit Resources*, July/September, 1999.

44. "Burying Ol' Blue Eyes." This homily generated much attention and many requests for copies.

45. "On this Shaky Rock." The story "The Mystery of the Hatbox Baby" is by Sharon Elliott, from the December 1993 issue of *Guideposts*. (Copyright ©1993 by Guideposts, Carmel, NY 10512. Reprinted with permission.)

47. "Abraham and the Pleading." The idea for this homily and its development came from Fr. Joe Nolan.

51. "The Narrow Door." The passage from Paula D'Arcy can be found

in her book *Gift of the Red Bird* (Copyright ©1996. Crossroad Publishing Co. Used by permission.). The story of Meadowlark is from *Living Stories of the Cherokee*, edited by Barbara R. Duncan. (Copyright ©1998 by the University of North Carolina Press. Used by permission.)

53. "Touched By an Angel." The statistics cited in this homily are from an article titled "A Faith Loosely Held: The institutional allegiance of young Catholics," by William Dinges, Dean R. Hoge, et al., which appeared in the July 17, 1998 issue of *Commonweal* magazine.

54. "Sloth." The passage by Jonathan Kozol can be found in his book *Amazing Grace: The Lives of Children and the Conscience of a Nation* (Crown Publishers, Inc., 1995). The story of the signers of the Declaration of Independence is from "The Price They Paid," *Psychology For Living*, July 1991 (Narramore Christian Foundation, Arcadia, CA).

56. "True Treasure." This homily can be adjusted to mark the death of any celebrity. It can also be used as a commentary on celebrity in general.

58. "All We Have Is Enough." The idea for the second half of this homily and some of the included material comes from the *St. Paul Pulpit*, by Rev. David E. Leininger (www.unidial.com/Stpaul/hungry.html). The Ann Landers quote is taken from the *Bible Illustrator for Windows*.

59. "The Troubles I've Seen." The story about Robert Mansfield is from the book *Ah, But Your Land Is Beautiful*, by Alan Paton (Simon & Schuster Trade, 1996).

60. "The Dirty Dozen." The concept and opening paragraph are modified from William H. Willimon in his homily for June 13, 1999, in *Pulpit Resource*.

Index of Scripture

Also by William Bausch

A World of Stories for Preachers and Teachers*
and all who love stories that move and challenge

Over 350 tales that aim to nudge, provoke, and stimulate the reader and listener, to resonate with the human condition, as did the stories of Jesus. This book should be in the hands of every preacher, storyteller, teacher, and reader.

0-89622-919-X, 534 pp, $29.95

Storytelling the Word
Homilies & How to Write Them

Helps homilists develop their ability to weave story and scriptural word together. Provides speaking techniques, over 100 stories, and 42 actual story-homilies to help homilists reach the visually-oriented listener of today.

0-89622-687-5, 304 pp, $14.95

Timely Homilies
The Wit and Wisdom of an Ordinary Pastor

With warmth, insight, and vitality, Fr. Bausch demonstrates his driving commitment to helping people live God's Word. These moving homilies are rich in stories and experiences.

0-89622-426-0, 176 pp, $9.95

Storytelling
Imagination and Faith

A treasured wellspring of stories from the masters of antiquity to anonymous authors of more recent days, both religious and secular. Bausch celebrates the power of stories for passing on truths and myths from one generation to the next.

0-89622-199-7, 232 pp, $9.95